FRAME RELAY NETWORKS

SIGNATURE SERIES

Frame Relay Networks
Specifications and Implementations

Uyless Black
Signature Edition

McGraw-Hill
New York ▪ San Francisco ▪ Washington, D.C.
Auckland ▪ Bogotá ▪ Caracas ▪ Lisbon ▪ London
Madrid ▪ Mexico City ▪ Milan ▪ Montreal ▪ New Delhi
San Juan ▪ Singapore ▪ Sydney ▪ Tokyo ▪ Toronto

Library of Congress Cataloging-in-Publication Data

Black, Uyless D.
    Frame relay networks : specifications and implementations / Uyless
Black.—Signature ed.
      p.   cm.
    Includes index.
    ISBN 0-07-006890-9
    1. Frame relay (Data transmission) I. Title.
TK5105.38.B56   1998
004.6'6—dc21   98-33582
                                             CIP

McGraw-Hill

*A Division of The **McGraw-Hill** Companies*

ISBN 0-07-006890-9

The sponsoring editor for this book was Steven Elliot, the editing supervisor was Curt Berkowitz, and the production supervisor was Claire Stanley. It was set in Vendome ICG by Priscilla Beer of McGraw-Hill's Professional Book Group composition unit in cooperation with Spring Point Publishing Services.

Printed and bound by R. R. Donnelley & Sons Company.

McGraw-Hill books are available at special quantity discounts to use as premiums and sales promotions, or for use in corporate training programs. For more information, please write to the Director of Special Sales, McGraw-Hill, 11 West 19th Street, New York, NY 10011. Or contact your local bookstore.

 This book is printed on recycled, acid-free paper containing a minimum of 50% recycled, de-inked fiber.

This book is dedicated to
Paul Kositzka
a fine accountant, and a fine friend

CONTENTS

vii

Contents

Contents

PREFACE

The book you are reading is the signature edition of *Frame Relay Networks*. Since the first edition, Frame Relay has evolved from a niche position in the marketplace to become one of the most successful data communications technologies of the last two decades. Its success rests on its simplicity, efficiency, and attractive operating costs.

This edition reflects several major changes that have taken place in the past two years with the Frame Relay technology. The changes are organized into the following major subjects:

- Voice over Frame Relay (VoFR)
- Internetworking ATM and Frame Relay
- Fragmentation of Frame Relay frames
- Support of multiple communications links between nodes
- Role of Frame Relay in internets and the Internet Protocol (IP)

I have retained the tutorial material in this edition, since I discovered that many of the readers are not familiar with the basic operations of Frame Relay. Also, since many of the Frame Relay features are derived from the OSI Model, ISDN, and X.25, the book contains tutorials on these technologies and shows how Frame Relay uses them (or does not use them).

This book is written for an intermediate-to-advanced audience. It is designed to serve as a tutorial on Frame Relay and as an abbreviated reference guide to the Frame Relay specifications. It is written with the understanding that you are familiar with data communications concepts.

I hope you will find this book helpful in your professional work (and I do hope you are not reading it as part of your social life).

Acknowledgments

I have relied heavily on two sources in the research and writing of *Frame Relay Networks*. First, I work with a number of vendors who build Frame

Relay switches, and I have learned much from these companies. I thank them for sharing their views and experiences with me.

Second, a considerable amount of material in this book provides summaries of several of the specifications published by the *Frame Relay Forum*. I thank the *Forum* for this information. At the time of this writing, *Frame Relay Forum* can be reached at:

Frame Relay Forum
39355 California Street, Suite 307
Fremont, CA 94538
TEL: 510.608.5920
FAX: 510.608.5917
E-Mail: *frf@frforum.com*
http://www/frforum.com./

Contact: Japan Frame Relay Forum
Nisso 22 Building, 11-10, Azabudai 1-chome Minato-ku,
Tokyo 106, Japan
TEL: +81-3-3583-5811
FAX: +81-3-3583-5812(G3), +81-3-5561-6889(G4)
E-Mail: *fmmca@po.infosphere.or.jp*
http://www.iijnet.or.jp/fmmc/jfrf/index-e.html

Be aware that you should obtain the ITU-T and Frame Relay specifications if you are involved in designing, programming, or implementing a Frame Relay network. My hope is that this book will get you started in the right direction.

—Uyless Black

FRAME RELAY NETWORKS

Introduction to Frame Relay Networks

This chapter explains why Frame Relay has become a widespread technology in the data communications industry. It examines the rationale for the Frame Relay design, and explains the advantages and disadvantages of the Frame Relay approach. A comparison is made of local and wide area networks, and the wide area network "bottleneck" is examined. A comparison is made also of Frame Relay and leased lines, and the Frame Relay virtual circuit concept is introduced. We also examine the Frame Relay marketplace and explain why it has achieved so much success in such a short time.

Predictions of Frame Relay Use

In the first edition of this book, I wrote the following introductory paragraph (in 1993): "At this time, no one really knows how the Frame Relay service will be accepted in the marketplace. However, initial indications are that its attractive pricing, low delay, and high throughput will pave the way for substantial growth of the technology in the next few years. Users who have begun the use of Frame Relay believe they will reduce their leased line costs by 10–25%. When all the pricing and services have stabilized, and if these initial thoughts are valid, then it is quite likely that Frame Relay will be a big success."

While I was accurate in my predictions, I was not alone, and other people saw the potential for Frame Relay as well. However, Frame Relay did not start to grow as fast as I had thought. Until 1994, it was languish-

Figure 1-1

Growth of Frame Relay (*Source: Yankee Group and Frame Relay Forum*).

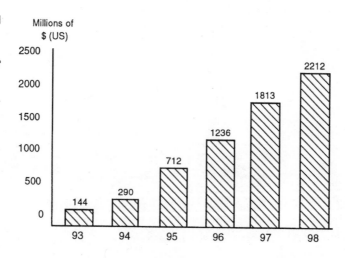

ing, with little interest shown by potential customers. But after companies became more familiar with the technology and the service offerings and prices, its use increased rapidly. Today, Frame Relay is enjoying a huge success, especially in the United States, where the prices are quite attractive in contrast to dedicated lines.

Figure 1-1 shows a study by the Yankee Group and Frame Relay Forum of the growth of Frame Relay and the projected growth in 1998. The dollar amounts are in the millions and track the worldwide revenue for the Frame Relay market.

While pricing has made the technology and its services attractive, Frame Relay also has been designed to solve or ameliorate several problems that have existed (and still exist in many systems) in the data communications industry. This subject is addressed in the next section.

Communications Infrastructure

Dealing with Errors

Modern data transmission systems are experiencing far fewer errors than they did in the 1970s and 1980s. During that period, the communications links and switching facilities were not as reliable as they are today. Excessive noise on the links was not uncommon, nor were link failures. The noise problems often resulted in traffic distortions, with the need for frequent retransmissions.

In those earlier times ("earlier" is certainly a relative term in this fast-changing industry), protocols were developed and implemented to deal with the error-prone transmission circuits. For the uninitiated reader, protocols are conventions that describe how machines communicate with each other. For example, X.25 is a protocol that defines how user computers interact with a packet network switch. Frame Relay is a protocol as well.

These earlier protocols took extensive care of the users' data. Network switches performed editing and error-checking operations on all incoming traffic. In the event that a misformed or erroneous packet was sent to the network switch, it was retransmitted (perhaps more than once) until it arrived error-free. In the event that the retransmissions did not succeed, the packet was discarded, and the user was so informed, often with extensive diagnostic information that explained the nature of the problem.

These measures provided an umbrella of reliability for the end user. The processing overhead in the execution of the software to provide these services was judged to be well worth the costs to obtain them. However, with the increased use of optical fibers and measures to improve the quality of the lines (conditioning), protocols that expend resources dealing with errors have become less important. Indeed, since the error rate on optical fibers is so low, one can argue that applying extensive error checking and diagnostic systems to optical technology is technical overkill. After all, why spend precious resources checking for errors that rarely occur? We have more to say on this subject later (see the section of Chap. 3 entitled "Tradeoffs of Link-to-Link vs. End-to-End Error Recovery").

Communications Capacity

The technology of the 1980s focused on systems that transmitted user traffic in thousands of bits per second (kbps). While they worked well enough then, these systems are inadequate to support applications that need to transmit many bits within a certain period of time, such as color graphics, video, telemetry systems, and database transfers. For example, consider an application that transmits several pages of a bank account document between two computers. This document, if transmitted through a fax machine that does not perform data compression, requires approximately 40–50 million bits to represent the information. The transmission of this information over a 56-kbps line would require over 10 minutes to send this document to another user!

Of course, one can state that this supposition is faulty because fax machines perform data compression operations on the traffic before it is transmitted. For example, a one-page letter, initially scanned by the fax machine, would consist of about 2–4 million bits. Through the use of efficient compression schemes, this document can be sent in a few seconds over a 9.6-kbps communications line.

Yet compression techniques are limited in their ability to reduce the number of bits representing an image, and compression can result in degradation of the *payload* (the term payload refers to the end-user traffic, such as the user's data, voice, video, etc.). Moreover, continued compression reaches a point where the data cannot be compressed further.

It is said by some people in the industry that (eventually) one will not be too concerned about the amount of traffic that needs to be transmitted vis-à-vis the transmission speeds available on the media. The capacity of optical fiber will at last provide the required "bandwidth" for all our needs. For the immediate future, this supposition is still wishful thinking on many communications links. For such a support system to become a reality, optical fiber must be available in workstations and the local loops connecting homes and offices to carrier services. The communications equipment also must have processing capabilities that are several orders of magnitude beyond today's systems. Nonetheless, it is only a matter of time before optical fiber is the preferred medium for these workstations.

Table 1-1 summarizes some of the points made in this section and lists several bit transfer rate requirements and transmission times for three types of images (objects) [ROY94]. The table shows the bit transfer requirements (in bps), the compression ratio, and the peak load requirements to transfer the object (object retrieval). Ongoing object browsing requires even more bandwidth, about two to four orders of magnitude greater than object retrieval. Obviously, these bandwidth requirements impose a burden on many of the present communications systems.

"Intelligence" of Computers

A number of protocols that are in existence today were designed to support relatively "unintelligent" devices, such as nonprogrammable terminals (*unintelligent* in this context is meant to connote a lack of software programmability). In the 1960s and even through part of the 1970s, most

Table 1-1 Transmission Sizes and Speeds	Traffic	Uncompressed Object Size (in Mbps)	Typical Compression Ratio	Peak Requirements (Retrieval) (in Mbps)[*]	
				Uncompressed	Compressed
	ASCII text 8.5×11 page	0.029	2–4	0.015	0.008–0.004
	8.5×11 page 200 pixels per in. 24 bits per pixel	90	10–20	45	4.5–2.3
	Graphics quality	5744	10–20	2872	287–144

[*]Browsing increases bandwidth requirements to 2–4 orders of magnitude over one-time retrieval.

user workstations (terminals) carried little or no software, and they were very slow, typically operating in the range of 50–600 bps. All operations were hard-wired, and these operations were quite limited. Consequently, a network that supported these devices had to assume a number of responsibilities, such as accounting for user traffic, making certain the terminal received reasonable response times, ensuring that the traffic was flow-controlled into and out of the terminal in an orderly fashion, and so forth. In essence, the network assumed almost all responsibilities for the end-user device.

Progress in the computational speed of computers has been extraordinary. For example, one of the first computers, which was called the ENIAC, operated at a speed of 100,000 instructions per second (IPS). This machine, developed in 1946, was considered to be fast enough to handle any business processing problems. In only 30 years since the ENIAC was introduced, the IBM 370/168 (operating in 1975) operated at 2 million IPS (MIPS). Computer technology has progressed even further since that "distant" time. In 1988, IBM's PS2/70 operated at 5 MIPS. Today, small desktop computers easily operate above the 25 MIPS range, and these machines are able to handle tasks that were unthinkable just a few years ago. With the advent of parallel processing, faster central processing units (CPUs), and RISC operations, end-user stations can increasingly absorb more responsibilities and tasks. Chip sets for CPUs are now available that have a processing speed of 1 GIPS (one gigabit of instructions per second).

Moreover, the increasing power and sophistication of software that runs on these machines are giving users a wide variety of applications programs that provide for support functions well beyond that of the raw processing speed of the hardware (Internet browsers, file transfer packages, video applications, etc.).

As a consequence of the progress made in the processing speed and intelligence of computers, many people think that a relatively error-free network should not burden itself with extensive error checking, sequencing, and flow-control operations. Instead, these tasks should be left to end-user computers, implying that the network can operate faster while providing better throughput and response time to the user.

Nonetheless, where one stands on an issue often depends on where one sits. The network administrator, sitting in the network control center, would believe that relegating the important operations of error checking, sequencing, and flow control to the end user makes good sense. It keeps network costs down, it makes the network more efficient, and it makes the network manager's job easier. However, the end user sitting at the customer premises equipment may view this relegation of tasks to the end-user device quite differently. If Frame Relay does not do error checking and flow control, is it incumbent upon the end-user machine to perform these tasks? If so, the end-user machine is then saddled with the additional responsibilities and the resulting overhead.

The question is somewhat irrelevant in today's technology because software is already running in end-user machines to perform error-checking operations. Therefore, in fairness to both parties (networks and network users), end-user software, if operating, should error-check all incoming traffic.

Consequently, since it can be argued that the end-user software makes these error checks as a standard practice, why should the network have to do it also? Current practice entails redundant operations. I have more to say about this matter in several parts of this book.

Frame Relay's Approach to Capacity and Intelligence Problems

The design of Frame Relay networks is focused on ameliorating or eliminating the problems we have just discussed. As we shall see, in many instances Frame Relay does not solve the problems so much as relegate their resolution to the end user by eliminating some network and data link layer operations.

With regard to transmission errors, the premise of Frame Relay is that modern communications systems, which are relatively error-free, do not require the extensive and resource-consuming operations that are required of older networks for the correction of errors. In the event that a rare error occurs, instead of tasking the network and the network components with the correction, Frame Relay assumes that the end-user device will handle the detection and resolution of the error.

What Frame Relay Can and Cannot Do

Frame Relay, in and of itself, can do nothing about increasing the capacity of networks and the communications channels in the networks. Frame Relay simply takes advantage of the availability of newer and higher-capacity transmission facilities. For example, instead of embedding into the Frame Relay architecture a restriction on use of bandwidth (throughput), the implementations of Frame Relay provide a foundation for obtaining the required throughput to support an application.

Bandwidth on Demand. The term *bandwidth on demand* is used today to describe how much capacity the network allocates to a user. This capacity is usually stated in the number of bits per second that can be transmitted, the average number of bits that can be transmitted over a period of time, or some other measure of throughput. A user does not negotiate raw bandwidth. The bandwidth is preallocated through the installation of particular media and transmitting and receiving devices. A practical term would be *capacity on demand*, stated in bits per second (bps). After all, we do not dynamically expand bandwidth. However, capacity on demand is probably not esoteric enough for our industry, so we are stuck with the term bandwidth on demand.

In theory, bandwidth on demand allows a Frame Relay network user to obtain a dynamic allocation of bandwidth capacity. By *dynamic,* I mean that the request can be made any time the user has a need for transmission capacity from the network. The idea is similar to allowing a connection request signal (to the network) to contain the user's bandwidth requirements. Each connection request may request a different bandwidth capacity.

For example, a user might request from the network a bandwidth allocation of 64 kbps for one application and 128 kbps for another application, and both applications could be running over the same physical channel. At a later time, the same applications might request different bandwidths from the network, depending on the nature of the applications' requirements.

Moreover, in certain situations, the Frame Relay bandwidth-on-demand concept allows this agreement to be exceeded, and the Frame Relay network will still attempt to support the service.

These explanations show the potential flexibility of Frame Relay. Actual commercial implementations depend upon the network provider's approach to how these concepts are made available to the customer. As later discussions demonstrate, some networks provide rather limited choices regarding how bandwidth on demand is obtained.

While other technologies, such as X.25, have supported the concept of dynamic bandwidth allocation, they are not as flexible as Frame Relay. For example, X.25's operations involve the ITU-T's notion of *class of service,* which stipulates the types of interfaces (synchronous or asynchronous) to be used with various line speeds (also called the *access rate*). In addition, X.25 provides a feature that allows a user to request a certain throughput, but the throughput rate usually equates to the access rate.

Reliance on the User. As introduced earlier, Frame Relay is based on the supposition that end-user machines are much more intelligent today than they were in the past. Therefore, Frame Relay relies on the end-user machine to be intelligent enough to exercise flow-control measures in order to reduce the flow of traffic, which, when offered to the network, may exceed the network's capacity to handle the traffic. The idea is for Frame Relay to notify the user about actual or potential congestion problems, and for the user to respond accordingly.

We learned earlier that Frame Relay also assumes that a user machine supports the end-to-end acknowledgment of traffic (that is, traffic between two end-user machines). In the past, these services have been the responsibility of the network and (with some exceptions) not the end-user computer.

Frame Relay and Voice Traffic

A number of companies have products that support the transmission of voice traffic over Frame Relay networks. The original intent of Frame Relay was to support data traffic only. It was not designed for constant bit rate (CBR) applications that are associated with many voice communications.

A number of articles in trade journals have stated that voice traffic can be supported in Frame Relay networks. Let us clear up this claim in relation to (a) the architecture of Frame Relay, and (b) the Frame Relay standards. First, Frame Relay is designed to support bursty, asynchronous data applications. Second, Frame Relay has no provision to ensure that frame loss does not exceed a threshold, which would create unacceptable errors during the digital-to-analog conversion process at the receiver. Third, Frame Relay has no provision for the synchronization of clocks between the sending and receiving application, which is needed for synchronous voice traffic.

Nonetheless, products are available that integrate voice (as well as video) and data over Frame Relay networks. The voice traffic is given precedence over data, and a guaranteed bit rate is provided with each synchronous application. But as of this writing, Frame Relay remains primarily a support platform for data applications. The vendors that support voice over Frame Relay must restrict the size of the frame, and provide a method of removing jitter at the receiver.

Notwithstanding these caveats, a great deal of attention is being paid to voice over frame relay (VoFR), and Chap. 14 provides the details for this emerging technology.

Furthermore, the Frame Relay Forum has published a specification that defines the fragmentation of larger frame relay units into smaller ones. This operation will solve the latency problem associated with processing long traffic units (frames) in a switch. This operation is also covered in Chap. 14.

Frame Relay: An Evolutionary Technology

From a technical view, Frame Relay is an evolutionary technology. Its operations rest on much of the existing software and hardware that currently exist in data communications systems. In essence, it eliminates many operations that are supported by the network and requires these operations to be performed by the end-user station.

Frame Relay requires no radical retooling of end-user devices, because many of these devices run protocols (which are part of their standard architecture) that can assume many of the functions that Frame Relay does not support. Frame Relay requires no redesign of the end-user station since there is no new technology introduced with Frame Relay at the end-user station. Rather, the Frame Relay interface is placed (usually) in a router that stands between the user station and the Frame Relay network. The user station is connected to the router through a conventional LAN interface.

Frame Relay: A Dead-End Technology?

Some people view Frame Relay as a dead-end technology, because it is not based on cell relay and does not propose any new switching technology for high-speed relay. Additionally, it is designed to support only data traffic. As we see in later chapters in this book, the industry is moving toward a cell relay–based technology (the switching and relaying of very small units of data that are of a fixed size).

Notwithstanding, Frame Relay has many attractive features (bandwidth on demand, low prices, etc.) that will make it a viable technology *for many years*. In addition, once a technology becomes embedded into products, it is usually guaranteed a long life, regardless of its "technical prowess"—X.25, V.35, and EIA-232-E are just such examples.

Reasons for the Use of Frame Relay

Network World (February 7, 1994) conducted a survey of Frame Relay users. While this study is a few years old, it is still valid today. One of the questions posed to these users was "Why did you select Frame Relay?" Figure 1-2 summarizes the responses to this question. The percentages represent how many respondents answered affirmatively to the reason(s) for choosing Frame Relay. More than one answer was permitted.

As Fig. 1-2 shows, the users of Frame Relay services are primarily those who view the economics of using Frame Relay before other factors.

Figure 1-2
Determining factors for selecting Frame Relay service.

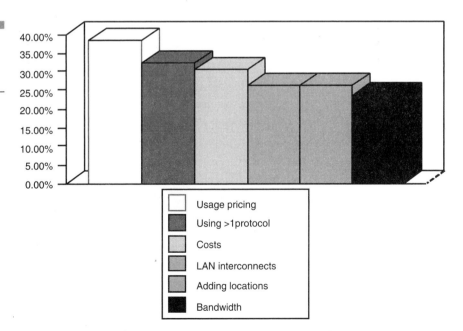

These users like the usage-based aspect of Frame Relay, as well as how it stacks up against leased line costs. Other factors are also considered important. The interconnection of LANs and the ability to add locations in a flexible and fast manner are also key aspects of the Frame Relay service. The ability to run multiple protocols over Frame Relay is not an inherent feature of Frame Relay. Rather, the capability is provided by Internet Request for Comments (RFC) 1490 (obsoletes 1294), which is explained in Chap. 11.

Comparison of Local and Wide Area Networks

Since much of this book is concerned with local and wide area networks, it is a good idea to pause briefly and compare the two types of networks.

Until recently, it has been relatively easy to define wide area networks (WANs) and local area networks (LANs), and to point out their differences. It is not so easy today because the terms *wide area* and *local area* do not have the meaning they once had. For example, a local area network in the 1980s was generally confined to a building or a campus, where the components were no more than a few meters from one another. Today, LANs may span two to three kilometers.

Nevertheless, the prevalent LANs, such as Ethernet, token ring, and the fiber distributed data interface (FDDI), have been designed to be distance-limited. Timers and other operations place a restriction on how far these LANs can be extended.

Moreover, certain characteristics are unique to each of these networks. A WAN is usually furnished by a third party. For example, many WANs are termed *public networks* because the telephone company or a public data network owns and manages the resources and sells their services to users. In contrast, a LAN is usually privately owned. The cables and components are purchased and managed by an enterprise.

LANs and WANs can also be contrasted by their transmission capacity (in bps). Most WANs generally operate in the kbps range, whereas LANs operate in the Mbps range, although this aspect of LANs and WANs is changing as optical fiber is deployed in these networks.

Another principal feature that distinguishes these networks is the error rate. WANs are generally more error prone than LANs due to the wide geographical terrain over which the media must be laid. In contrast, LANs operate in a relatively benign environment, because the data communications components are housed in buildings where humidity, heat, and electricity ranges can be controlled.

The Network "Bottleneck"

In the past few years, LANs and WANs have been interconnected via bridges, routers, gateways, and packet switched networks. These internetworking units are connected into the LANs and WANs through individual leased communications channels.

The use of these lines to connect internetworking units with LANs and WANs is a very expensive process, and reliability problems can occur because individual point-to-point leased lines have no backup capability. In addition, extensive processing of the traffic (edits, error checks) creates unacceptable time delays for certain applications.

A better approach is to develop a LAN/WAN-carrier network that provides efficient switching technologies for backup purposes as well as high-speed circuits. In effect, a WAN should be considered an extension of a LAN.

Circuit switching has been employed for a number of years to provide users with fast switching features and high-capacity transmission facilities. The technology is so named because a "continuous circuit" is provided between the two user devices.

This circuit is virtual in the sense that the bandwidth is divided into time slots and shared by multiple users. Each user device is provided with reservations for time slots that depend on priorities, speeds, and other factors. This technique is called *time division multiplexing* (TDM).

TDM is fast because its services are limited. It does not do much error checking, and does not have any retransmission capabilities. Data are transparent to it. It just provides the slots for the data to "ride" on the channel.

TDM and circuit switching work well enough for applications that need continuous slots on the channel, such as voice and video. However, the slots are not used efficiently for bursty transmissions, because the slots are preassigned on a fixed basis for each user application. Therefore, the circuit switching technology is not well suited to many data communications applications that exhibit bursty transmission characteristics.

Because of the limitations of TDM, many vendors offer modifications to their TDM products, enabling traffic to use the channel in a nonslotted manner. This approach is called *unchannelized T1*. While this approach is effective, each vendor uses a proprietary scheme, and interworking between vendors presents significant problems.

A solution to this problem is to allow multiple users to share a network and the communications lines on an as-needed basis. Statistical time division multiplexing (STDM) technology has been employed for the last 20 years to provide this service. It provides a dynamic approach to the sharing of the bandwidth.

The architecture of the widely used ITU-T X.25 Recommendation employs STDM. Each user is identified by a logical channel number (LCN), and is provided a virtual circuit through the network to the other communicating user (which is also assigned an LCN for purposes of identification). Allocation of the resources is based on user demand and bandwidth availability. The attractive aspect of X.25 is that it allows up to 4095 users to share an individual physical port. It allocates the use of these ports based on STDM techniques.

X.25 was designed in the early 1970s, when transmission speeds were limited and communications network lines were quite error-prone. Consequently, X.25 provides extensive support for error detection and flow-control operations. X.25 has proven to be a valuable resource to support dynamic bandwidth sharing across a standardized network interface between the user machine and the network switch.

The Frame Relay Compromise

A compromise between circuit switching (with its time division multiplexing capabilities) and X.25 (with its statistical multiplexing capabilities) is to combine the best features of the two and eliminate some of the negative aspects of these two approaches. This compromise combines the channel-sharing aspects of X.25 through statistical multiplexing and the high-speed capabilities of time division multiplexing and circuit switching. This is the approach taken by Frame Relay.

Since fixed slots (TDM) are not used in Frame Relay, some means must be available to identify the users of such a system. One useful feature of X.25 is its use of logical channel numbers (LCNs). Each user is assigned an LCN when logging onto the network. In X.25, this service is called a *switched virtual call* (SVC). Alternatively, users may be assigned an LCN called a *permanent virtual circuit* (PVC) before they use the network. Frame Relay uses the same idea, and its identification "tag" is called the *data link connection identifier* (DLCI).

Table 1-2

Summary of X.25, TDM, and Frame Relay

	Fixed Slots	STDM	Port/Line Sharing	Delay	Throughput	Switching
X.25	N	Y	Y	H	L	Y
T1 TDM	Y*	N*	Y†	VL	H	N
Frame Relay	N	Y	Y	L	H	Y

*Unless provisioning is done on a proprietary basis (unchannelized T1).
†But provisioning is slow.

N: No
Y: Yes
L: Low
VL: Very low
H: High

Table 1-2 summarizes the features of X.25, TDM (based on T1 technology, discussed shortly), and Frame Relay. X.25 is attractive for its port sharing, line sharing, and STDM capabilities. Because of its variable slots, it is well suited to bursty environments. It is also well suited to systems such as LANs, which usually use large data units, as well as WANs, which usually use small data units. However, X.25 suffers from relatively low throughput and high delay due to its provision for error control and traffic management, with their resulting processing overhead.

TDM and its use of circuit switching is attractive because it exhibits high throughput and very low delay. These performance factors stem from the fact that TDM uses fixed slots. Such an approach does not work well in bursty environments such as data transfer, but it is well suited to environments that require fixed bandwidths, such as voice processing.

Frame Relay exhibits low delay and high throughput because many of the features found in older data networks are not performed. It is attractive for bursty environments because it enables the line to be shared in a dynamic fashion, using STDM techniques.

A Standardized Interface

In addition to providing the services just discussed, Frame Relay also provides a common and standardized interface between different ven-

Figure 1-3
The Frame Relay
interface.

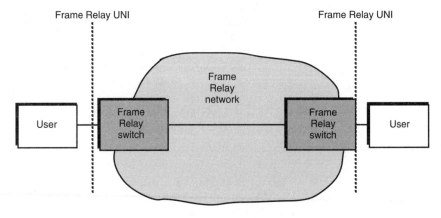

Where: UNI is the user-network interface

dors' equipment at the user-to-network interface (UNI), as depicted in Fig. 1-3. As we just learned, Frame Relay is designed to provide a fast relay service for data applications. The implementation and acceptance of Frame Relay leads to high-speed, standardized network interfaces. The word *standardized* is important. By using Frame Relay, the industry can avoid using proprietary interfaces.

Genesis of Frame Relay

Frame Relay has been in the works for a number of years. Recognizing the drawbacks to a pure TDM and STDM environment, data communications designers began to address the problem in the late 1980s. As depicted in Table 1-3, three standards led the way. ITU-T's I.122 provided the initial framework with the publication of ISDN frame-mode bearer services for additional packet services. Some of the work performed on ITU's Q921 [Link Access Procedure for the D Channel (LAPD)] demonstrated the usefulness of virtual circuit multiplexing for data link layer protocols (layer 2 of the OSI Model). Although generally not recognized, ITU-T's V.120 Recommendation also provided a valuable foundation, because it resulted in a specification defining multiplexing operations across the ISDN S/T interface, and multiplexing is a fundamental aspect of Frame Relay.

Table 1-3

Genesis of Frame
Relay

- Based on:
  I.122: Framework for additional packet mode bearer services
  Q921: LAPD
  V.120: Multiplexing across the ISDN S/T interface

- Today:

	Service Description	Core Aspects	Access Signaling
ITU-T	1.233	Q922, Annex A	Q933
ANSI	T1.606	T1.618	T1.617

The Frame Relay standards organizations are ITU-T and ANSI. The ANSI standards are published as T1.606, T1.618, and T1.617. The ITU-T specifications are published as I.233, Q922 Annex A, and Q933.

The Group of Four

When I.122 became known in the industry, some vendors recognized that it could be used with non-ISDN systems, and could provide for a faster network interface than X.25 because it eliminated much of the overhead associated with that protocol. Since it is much easier to strip functions from an existing technology than to develop a new technology (for example, cell relay), it was decided that adoption of I.122 would provide an effective user-to-network interface (UNI). Furthermore, this approach would suffice until the emerging but unavailable cell relay technology could be developed and implemented.

However, it was recognized by network vendors that this work would proceed too slowly if left to the traditional standards process. Consequently, four vendors formed a group to move the Frame Relay technology forward. These vendors, Digital Equipment Corporation (DEC), Northern Telecom (Nortel), Cisco, and Stratacom, used the ANSI standards for Frame Relay as a reference, and published *Frame Relay Specification with Extensions—Based on Proposed T1S1 Standards* (Document 001-208996) in 1990. This document was intended as an invitation for other vendors to participate in a common effort to develop a Frame Relay interface. Furthermore, this specification extended I.122 and the ANSI standards to meet the needs of these vendors.

The Frame Relay Forum

The initial efforts of this group resulted in the formation of the Frame Relay Forum, which has led the way in the promotion of Frame Relay technology. The Forum has also published several specifications that are discussed in this book.

Other Pertinent Standards and Specifications. Since the publication of the initial documents, several other standards have been issued pertaining to Frame Relay. Table 1-4 lists the original specifications and the new documents.

Initially, Frame Relay was designed to operate over leased line services and to support only permanent virtual circuits (PVCs). In this context, Frame Relay has no call setup procedures. The stations that communicate with each other are so provisioned before transmission actually occurs. ANSI T1.618, T1.617, and ITU-T I.233 describe these procedures.

However, other options are available for Frame Relay services, using a combination of PVCs, switched virtual calls (SVCs), ISDN procedures, and non-ISDN procedures. These services and the standards that are relevant to these various combinations are listed in Table 1-5 [NOLL91]. For virtual call setups, ANSI T1.617, T1.618, and Q933 provide the procedures.

Table 1-4

Frame Relay
Standards*

I.222/I.233	Frame mode bearer services
Q922	ISDN data link layer specification for frame mode bearer services
Q933	ISDN signaling specification for frame mode bearer services
I.370	Congestion management for the ISDN frame relaying bearer service
I.372	Frame mode bearer service network to network interface requirements
I.555	Frame mode bearer service internetworking
ANSI T1.606	Frame relay bearer service architectural framework and service description
ANSI T1.606 Addendum	Congestion management principles
Q922 Annex A	Cores aspects of frame relay
ANSI T1.617	Signaling specification for frame relay bearer service

*Frame Relay Forum specifications are not listed here.

Table 1-5		PVC	SVC
References for Frame Relay and ISDN, PVCs, and SVCs	ISDN	T1.617 Annex D	T1.617, D-channel setup
		T1.618 data transfer	T1.618 data transfer
		I.233	Q933, D-channel setup
		I.233 Annex C	Q933 data transfer
	Non-ISDN	T1.617 Annex D	T1.617, DLCI 0 setup
		T1.618 data transfer	T1.618 data transfer

Frame Relay vs. Leased Lines

An ongoing issue for data communications administrators is choosing between dedicated private lines and private or public switched networks. The cost tradeoffs for these two services vary widely, depending on the types of lines and services purchased. Nonetheless, many enterprises have opted for dedicated circuits, because of their high throughput and low delay. In addition, the network manager has direct control (albeit through the service provider) over the resource.

The T1 and E1 Systems

The T1 system has become one of the most widely used digital systems in North America. E1 has enjoyed similar success in other parts of the world. Originally conceived as a voice transmission technology in the early 1960s, T1 and E1 have evolved to become cost-effective and flexible means of transmitting both voice, video, and data.

T1 is based on time division multiplexing (TDM) 24 users onto one physical circuit. At the inception of T1, it was known that solid copper cable was capable of providing for frequencies above the 100-kHz range. Consequently, the earlier frequency division multiplexed (FDM) telephone system multiplexed 24 users onto one copper wire. Each user was assigned a different 4-kHz frequency band. The composite 24 voice channels totaled 96 kHz, which was also within the capacity of twisted pair wires.

With the advent of analog-to-digital conversion and the cost-effective implementation of pulse code modulation (PCM) techniques, AT&T and the Bell System began to implement digital voice systems in the early 1960s. These systems were designated the T1 carrier, and were constructed initially to connect telephone central offices together.

The T1 system is designed around a 1.544-Mbps rate, which in the 1960s was about the highest rate that could be supported across twisted pair for a distance of approximately one mile. The term *T1* was devised by the telephone company to describe a specific digital transmission scheme. Today, the term *DS1* is also used to describe a T1 carrier system, a data rate, and various framing conventions for the traffic on the channel.[1]

The initial T1 concept has been enhanced, and T1 vendors have continued to increase the data rate and improve the time division multiplexing techniques. Today, many of the T1 systems have moved from copper and microwave media to optical fiber–based systems.

T1 has been successful due to attractive price offerings from the carriers, and a user often finds it advantageous to use T1 links instead of multiple private line services. T1 services also provide some diagnostic capabilities. Perhaps one of its greatest advantages is configuration alternatives. For example, the T1 1.544-Mbps system can be configured to carry voice, data, or video, and the T1 link can be reconfigured based on varying transmission needs during a business period.

However, due to the nature of the evolution of this technology, much of its equipment and software are proprietary, and its structure makes it awkward to switch traffic. Moreover, T1 time division multiplexers do not provide user-to-user endpoint signaling. Therefore, if a user needs connections between multiple endpoints [from the user with local exchange carriers (LEC) as well as interexchange carriers (IXC)], multiple lines must be acquired. As we see shortly in this chapter, Frame Relay requires only one access line to the customer premises equipment (CPE) endpoint.

The most common type of T1 service is the leased line, point-to-point configuration, as shown in Fig. 1-4. Multiplexers are placed at the customer's site or at telephone offices, and are then used to aggregate user traffic (voice, data, fax, video, etc.) into a digital transmission. Several configuration options are available, other than point-to-point lines. As examples, star, multipoint, ring, and mesh networks can be constructed with drop-and-insert multiplexers and digital cross-connect devices.

---

[1]Strictly speaking the term T1 describes the electrical, digital properties of the system and DS1 describes the framing and multiplexing operations.

Figure 1-4
T1/E1 configurations.

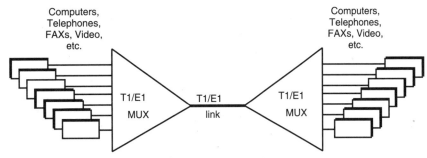

North American and CEPT Multiplexing Hierarchies

Multiplexing schemes have been developed that allow T1s and E1s to be aggregated into higher-capacity bundles. In North America, the T1 scheme is designated Digital Signal Levels (DS). Strictly speaking, T1 refers to the physical wires and regenerators, and DS refers to the framing and multiplexing procedures. In Europe, the Committee of European Postal and Telephone (CEPT) scheme is employed, and is called the E system.

Table 1-6 illustrates these schemes and the aggregate data rates for DS0–DS4 and E0–E4.

Leased Lines and Switched Facilities

Leased Lines.   Notwithstanding the success of T1 and E1, many enterprises favor the use of networks instead of leased lines because of the ability to share the line bandwidth with multiple users through switching facilities. Figure 1-5 illustrates the reason for switched networks over leased lines. Four sites must communicate with one another. To obtain point-to-point services among all four sites with leased lines, an organization must lease services from local exchange carriers (LEC) and interexchange carriers (IXC), and connect the LEC lines to the ports of the computers at the four sites. Thus, the enterprise must expend money for 12 ports, 12 LEC access lines, and 6 connections to IXC circuits. This approach provides a fully meshed connection between all four sites, but it is very costly.

If it is to continue to provide a fully meshed service in a leased-line

Table 1-6

Multiplexing
Hierarchies

North American Hierarchy				
Signal	**Carrier**	**Number of T1s**	**Voice Channels**	**Bps**
DS0			1	64 kbps
DS1	T1	1	24	1.544 Mbps
DS1C	T1C	2	48	3.152 Mbps
DS2	T2	4	96	6.312 Mbps
DS3	T3	28	672	44.736 Mbps
DS4	T4	168	4032	274.176 Mbps

CEPT Hierarchy				
Signal	**Carrier**	**Number of T1s**	**Voice Channels**	**Bps**
0			1	64 kbps
1	E1	1	30	2.048 Mbps
2	E2	4	120	8.448 Mbps
3	E3	16	480	34.368 Mbps
4	E4	64	1920	139.264 Mbps

Figure 1-5
LEC, IXC, and port
connections.

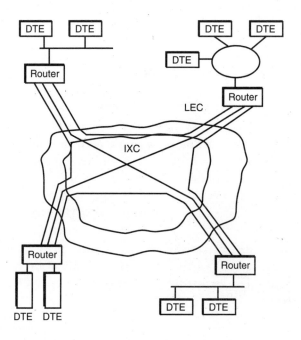

environment, an expanding organization must face the fact that the number of ports, IXC, and LEC lines rises significantly with each additional site connected to the system. For example, the addition of the site in Fig. 1-6 results in an increase of eight additional ports, eight additional local access lines, and four additional interexchange circuits. It is evident that the continued addition of sites will lead to a hopelessly complex and expensive fully meshed network. The number of lines required does not increase linearly with the addition of sites, but in proportion to the square of the number of sites: the full interconnection of N sites requires $N \times (N - 1)/2$ lines. The five-site topology in Fig. 1-6 requires $5 \times (5 - 1)/2$ or 10 lines.

This rather onerous prospect is one of the primary reasons for organizations to use switched facilities rather than leased lines. Thus, packet switching networks have evolved to address the leased line problem. At the same time, their "value-added services" have created delay and throughput problems.

T1 Multiplexers. An alternative to a fully meshed dedicated line network is the deployment of T1 multiplexers (muxes), as seen in Fig. 1-4. In

Figure 1-6
LEC, IXC, and port
connections.

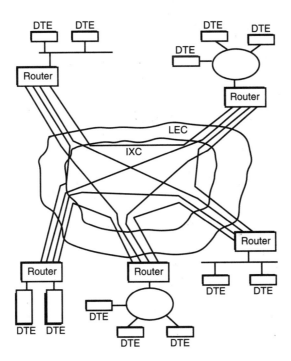

some instances, these muxes can be configured to share lines, but a T1 mux is not a switch, and it still needs multiple LEC access lines in order for the mux to know which input link is associated with outgoing slots on the trunks. That is, the mux must associate an incoming line with an outgoing trunk. Line sharing is cumbersome and requires a ring topology or the use of backhauling techniques, wherein traffic is passed through one mux to another mux, and then passed back to the first mux for demultiplexing.

Most T1 vendors now offer various services for dividing the T1 channel into "smaller pieces." In addition, these vendors have capabilities that allow the customer to use the T1 channel for voice, video, and data. The manner in which this traffic shares the channel differs among vendors. Most vendors allow the dynamic allocation of the slots in the T1 frame, and compress-out periods of silence, sending only talkspurts across the channel.

Unchannelized T1. The absence of set DS0 slots is called *unchannelized T1*. A channelized T1 uses a clocking mechanism that restricts a user to a part of the full capacity of the physical link. For example, a user may be provisioned with a DS0 64-kbps channel, and this is all that is provided, even if the other DS0 channels on the link are not being used. In addition, when the user is given the use of the link, the user can send only at the 64-kbps transfer rate.

In contrast, unchannelized T1 allows the user to take advantage of the full bandwidth of the link; that is, 24 DS0s at 1.544 Mbps. This idea is to exploit the asynchronous nature of the data traffic, and give the user the full bandwidth of the link, if only for a very short time, say a few milliseconds. In this manner, more than 24 asynchronous users can be multiplexed onto the T1 unchannelized link, which results in a more cost-effective use of the communications facilities.

An additional benefit of unchannelized T1 is that the user sends at a very high bit rate, which reduces latency in the transmission process.

Of course, a reasonable question is how does the Frame Relay network manage all this bursty, asynchronous traffic? After all, some means must be available to control the efficient multiplexing of user traffic across the link. This question is answered in Chap. 9, and the curious reader can fast-forward to this Traffic Management chapter.

While all these schemes make better use of the T1 facilities, the technology is still inherently circuit-based, with no switching capabilities, and no headers to identify traffic.

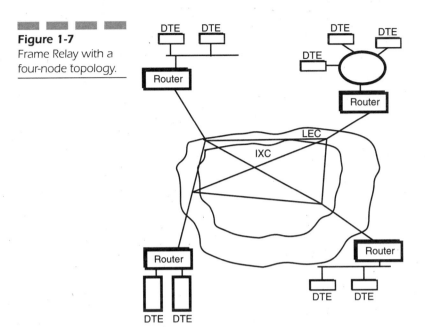

Figure 1-7
Frame Relay with a
four-node topology.

Frame Relay Switched Facilities.   Figure 1-7 shows the use of a
Frame Relay network and its effect on the number of local exchange
carrier private lines and router ports required for a four-node network.
Instead of 12 separate local exchange lines, 4 are required; instead of 12
router ports, only 4 are required. Equally important, the communications links in the network are not reserved to one site. They become virtual circuits, and are shared by multiple users through the use of multiplexing and switching operations.

Of course, it is not Frame Relay per se that provides this attractive feature; these savings can be achieved with any type of switching network
by replacing point-to-point connections. For example, X.25-based networks have been performing this type of service for 25 years.

With the use of switching techniques, the addition of a node is not
quite so onerous as it is in a point-to-point private line network. In Fig.
1-8, the addition of the fifth site and its supporting router results in the
addition of four interexchange carrier private lines, one local exchange
private line, and an additional router port.

It should be emphasized that this simple example could be changed

Figure 1-8
Adding a node in a
Frame Relay network.

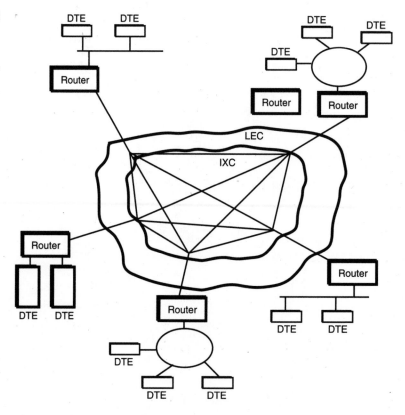

to one in which the topology reduces the number of IXC private lines through the use of additional routers.

Virtual Private Networks (VPNs) with Frame Relay

The use of Frame Relay technology enables an enterprise to implement virtual private networks (VPNs). As shown in Figs. 1-7 and 1-8, the idea of the VPN is to allow multiple users from different organizations to share expensive leased lines. The spare bandwidth on these leased lines is statistically multiplexed by the Frame Relay machine to provide for more efficient utilization of an expensive resource. Consequently, an enterprise can reduce the cost of its communications media, and may also be able to reduce the number of lines that must be leased from interexchange carriers.

Frame Relay Virtual Circuits

Frame Relay borrows many of the virtual circuit concepts of X.25. Two endpoints on a leased line between two Frame Relay nodes are identified with virtual circuit numbers. Like the links on X.25, the virtual circuits are provisioned on an end-to-end basis. Thus, a sending virtual circuit is "premapped" to a receiving virtual circuit. Once again, as we learned earlier, the term *virtual* means that the user has the impression that a dedicated circuit is made available, when in fact multiple users may be using the circuit. These multiple users are uniquely identified by different virtual circuit numbers.

The Frame Relay Virtual Circuit Identifier (DLCI)

While Frame Relay purports to eliminate completely the operations at the network layer, it does not eliminate all network layer operations. Figure 1-9 illustrates one network layer operation that is essential for Frame Relay operations: the identification of virtual connections. Frame Relay uses the data link connection identifier (DLCI) to identify a virtual circuit.

In most networks, the DLCIs are premapped to a destination node, a concept called a *permanent virtual circuit* (PVC). This simplifies the process at the routers, because they only need to consult their routing/mapping table, check the DLCI in the table, and route the traffic to the proper output port based on this identifier. In 1997, some vendors began implementing switched virtual calls (SVCs), which allow the connection to be established on demand. This subject is covered in Chap. 10.

The practice in Frame Relay networks is to assign and manage the DLCIs locally, that is, at each UNI. Local assignment permits the DLCIs to be reused on each physical link in the same machine. The only

Figure 1-9
Data link connection
identifiers (DLCIs).

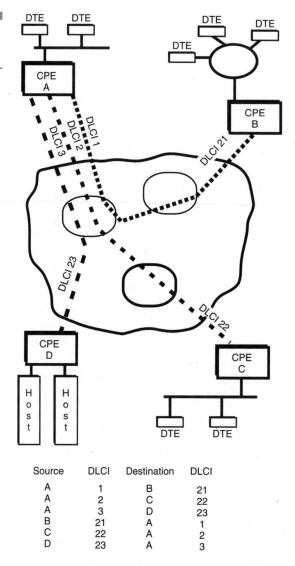

Source	DLCI	Destination	DLCI
A	1	B	21
A	2	C	22
A	3	D	23
B	21	A	1
C	22	A	2
D	23	A	3

requirement is that the DLCIs unambiguously identify the user traffic at both sides of the network—the two UNIs.

Inside the network, the same scheme can be used, although the Frame Relay switches need not maintain a virtual circuit in the network. Connectionless operations can be implemented to allow for dynamic/adaptive routing among the Frame Relay switches. The network must ensure that the frame arrives at the port designated in the DLCI. Therefore, the network may append an internal network header to the frame to direct its transit through the network. At the final destination Frame Relay switch, this header is removed, and the standardized frame is presented across the UNI to the user machine. Vendors vary in their approach to fixed or dynamic routing. Whatever the practice may be, it is transparent to the end user.

Since DLCIs have local significance, a virtual circuit will likely be identified with two different DLCIs at the UNIs. As Fig. 1-9 shows, the three DLCIs of 1, 2, 3, and CPE A are identified at CPEs B, C, and D as DLCIs 21, 22, and 23, respectively.

The bottom of Fig. 1-9 also shows a DLCI "mapping table." It can be seen by examining this table that the virtual circuit is bidirectional, and the DLCIs are related to each other in both directions. For example, if traffic is sent from A to B, DLCI 1 is mapped to DLCI 21. If traffic is sent from B to A, DLCI 21 is mapped to 1.

Because the virtual circuit is bidirectional, different bandwidths can be provided for the two directions. For example, assume an application at location A requests a large file transfer from an application at location B. Since a simple request does not consume much bandwidth, the bandwidth allocation from A to B could be, say, 14.4 kbps. Since the file is being transferred from B to A, the bandwidth in this direction could be, say, 128 kbps.

Guidelines to the Frame Relay Specifications and the Organization of This Book

The Frame Relay specifications can be confusing to the newcomer, not because they are complex, but because they been developed by a number of organizations, such as ANSI, the ITU-T, the Group of Four, and the Frame Relay Forum. Due to the rather fragmented manner in which the Frame Relay specifications developed, some of the standards define similar operations. For example, several documents define how a user device and a Frame Relay node exchange status information with Status and Status Enquiry messages. Additionally, some Frame Relay operations are derived from the ITU-T Q931 Recommendation, which is the original specification for layer 3 of ISDN. Figure 1-10 summarizes the major parts and aspects of the Frame Relay specifications. This

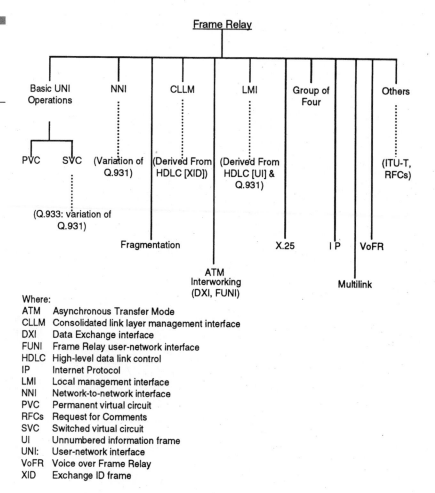

Figure 1-10
Frame Relay specifi-
cations, recommen-
dations, and other
documents.

Where:
ATM   Asynchronous Transfer Mode
CLLM   Consolidated link layer management interface
DXI   Data Exchange interface
FUNI   Frame Relay user-network interface
HDLC   High-level data link control
IP   Internet Protocol
LMI   Local management interface
NNI   Network-to-network interface
PVC   Permanent virtual circuit
RFCs   Request for Comments
SVC   Switched virtual circuit
UI   Unnumbered information frame
UNI: User-network interface
VoFR   Voice over Frame Relay
XID   Exchange ID frame

book will examine each of these areas, and Table 1-7 lists the chapters in
this book that examine these specifications.

SUMMARY

Frame Relay systems are designed to support users who need increased
bandwidth for internetworking their machines. Frame Relay systems are
also designed to support users who need less delay for their traffic. The
technology is so named because most of the operations occur at the

Table 1-7

Guide to Chapters
and Frame Relay
Specifications

Subject	Chapters
CLLM	8
DXI	12
Fragmentation	14
FUNI	12
Group of Four	1, 11
IP and ATM	12
LMI	11
NNI	11
Multilink	14
PVC	6, 7, 8
SVC	10
Voice over Frame Relay	14
X.25 and ATM	12
Others	1, 11

frame layer (layer 2) of the conventional seven-layer model. The basis for Frame Relay is HDLC and HDLC-derived protocols such as LAPD and V.120.

Frame Relay operates with the assumption that the network is quite reliable and fast. It also operates on the premise that end-users' machines have considerable processing power, as well as the software necessary to recover from occasional failures that might occur within the network itself.

Frame Relay uses many of the concepts of X.25—such as statistical time division multiplexing—and includes the concept of the virtual circuit, which is called the data link connection identifier (DLCI).

CHAPTER 2

The OSI and
Internet Protocols

This chapter provides an overview of the Open Systems Interconnection (OSI) Model and the Internet protocols. An analysis is made of the architecture of these protocol stacks and the major protocols that reside in them. The emphasis in this chapter is on the data link, network, and transport layers, because these layers are the point of emphasis for Frame Relay networks. The chapter concludes with an examination of Frame Relay's relationship to the layered OSI model and the Internet protocols.

The reader who is familiar with the subject matter of this chapter should read the last section titled, "Frame Relay's Relationship to a Layered Model."

Layer Operations

Why Layers Are Used

The concepts of layered operations have been in existence for a number of years. They owe their origin to structured programming techniques, which were developed in the 1970s to simplify complex software packages and systems. The idea of layered operations is to partition activities into specific modules, which are called *layers*. Partitioning also occurs within layers. These layers and the entities within the layers are relatively independent of other layers and entities in one machine. Their principal purpose is to communicate with their corresponding (peer) layers in another machine.

These ideas encourage the design of hardware or software systems that have clearly defined interfaces. The systems contain modules that perform one function or several closely related functions. These techniques can also provide for loose coupling, wherein a change to a module in the system does not affect any other component that the changed module does not control.

Layered network protocols allow interaction between functionally paired layers in different locations without affecting other layers. This concept aids in distributing the functions to the layers. In the majority of layered protocols, the protocol data unit (PDU), such as a message or packet that is passed from one layer to another, is usually not altered, although the data unit contents may be examined and used to append additional data (trailers/headers) to the existing unit.

How Layers Are Used

In a layered system, a layer is considered to be a service provider to the layer above it. Frame Relay is based on this premise. This upper layer is considered to be a service user by its lower layer. The service user avails itself of the services of the service provider by sending a transaction to the provider. This transaction informs the provider as to the nature of the service that is to be provided (or at least that is requested).

The end user rests on top (figuratively speaking) of the application layer. Therefore, the user obtains all the services of the layers in the system. This idea is illustrated in Fig. 2-1.

In accordance with the conventions of layered operations, a layer cannot be bypassed. Even if an end user does not wish to use the services of a particular layer, the user must still "pass through" the layer on the way to the next adjacent layer. This pass through may entail the invocation of only a small set of code, but it still translates to some processing overhead. However, not every function in each layer need be invoked. A minimum subset of functions may be all that is necessary to comply with the standard.

The OSI Model refers to layers with the terms N, $N + 1$, and $N-1$. The particular layer that is the focus of attention is designated layer N. Thereafter, the adjacent upper layer above layer N is designated layer $N + 1$

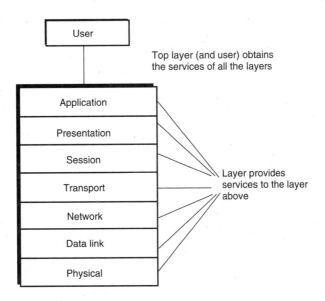

Figure 2-1
Services of the layered model (using OSI as the example).

and the adjacent lower layer below layer N is designated layer N − 1. For example, if the network layer is the focus of attention, then it is designated layer N. The transport layer is designated layer N + 1, and the data link layer is designated layer N − 1.

In this manner, designers can use generic terms in describing the OSI layers. Moreover, the transactions between the layers can be developed in a more generic sense as well.

Each layer contains entities that exchange data and provide functions (horizontal communications) with peer entities at other computers. For example, in Fig. 2-2, layer N in machine A communicates logically with layer N in machine B, and the N + 1 layers in the two machines follow the same procedure. Entities in adjacent layers in the same computer interact through the common upper and lower boundaries (vertical communications), via function calls or operating system library calls, to define the operations between the layers.

Typically, each layer at a transmitting station (except the lowest in some systems) adds header information to data. The headers are used to establish peer-to-peer sessions across nodes (horizontal communications).

Figure 2-2

Horizontal and vertical communications.

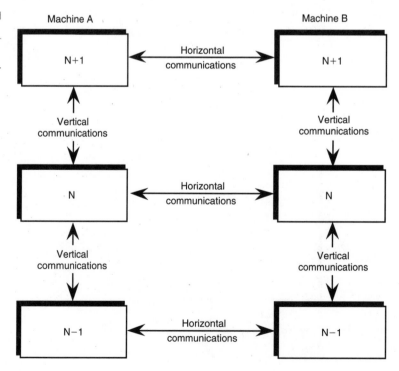

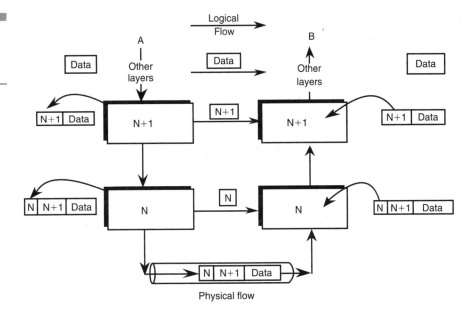

Figure 2-3
Sending data and
headers to another
machine.

At the receiving site, the layer entities use the headers to implement actions created by the peer entity at the transmitting site.

Figure 2-3 shows an example of how machine A sends data to machine B. Data are passed from the upper layers or the user application to layer N + 1. Layer N + 1 adds a header to the data (labeled N + 1 in the figure). Layer N + 1 also performs actions based on the information in the transaction that accompanied the data from the upper layer.

Layer N + 1 passes the data unit and its header to layer N. This layer performs some actions, based on the information in the transaction, and adds its header N to the incoming traffic. This traffic is passed across the communications line (or through a network) to the receiving machine B.

At B, the process is reversed. The headers that were created at machine A are used by the peer layers at machine B to determine what actions are to be taken at the peer layer. As the data and existing headers (known as traffic or transactions) are sent up the layers, the respective layer removes its header, performs the defined actions, and passes the traffic on up to the next layer.

The user application at machine B is presented only with user data, which was created by the sending user application (machine A). These user applications are unaware of the many operations in each layer that were invoked to support the end-user data transfer.

The headers created and used at peer layers are not to be altered by any nonpeer layer. As a general rule, the headers from one layer are treated as "transparent data" by any other layer.

There are some necessary exceptions to this rule. As examples, data may be altered by a nonpeer layer for the purposes of compression, encryption, or other forms of syntax alteration. This type of operation is permissible, if the data are restored to the original syntax when presented to the receiving peer layer.

As an exception to the exception, the presentation layer may alter the syntax of the data permanently, because the receiving application layer has requested the data in a different syntax (such as ASCII instead of a bit string).

Examples of Each Layer's Operations

The Physical Layer.   The lowest layer in the model is called the *physical layer* (see Fig. 2-4). The physical layer is responsible for activating, maintaining, and deactivating a physical circuit between data terminal equipment (DTE) and data circuit-terminating equipment (DCE) and the communicating DCEs. A DTE is an end-user device, such as a workstation, computer, and the like. A DCE is a device that connects the DTE into the communications link (such as a modem, multiplexer, etc.).

This layer defines the type of physical signals (electrical, optical, etc.), as well as the type of media (wires, coaxial cable, satellite, etc.). Physical level protocols are also called physical level interfaces. Either term is acceptable.

The physical layer's most common operations deal with the creation and reception of physical signals. For example, conventions may exist to represent a binary one with a plus voltage and a binary zero with a minus voltage (although many systems are just the opposite).

The physical connectors are also described in the layer. These connectors are published by a number of standards groups. For example, the ISO 2110 connector and the RJ-45 telephone-type connector are used widely in physical level interfaces. Operations at the physical level also describe the speed (typically) in bits per second (bps). If analog lines are used, the rules for modulation must be agreed upon as well.

For digital systems, standardized coding rules are essential. For exam-

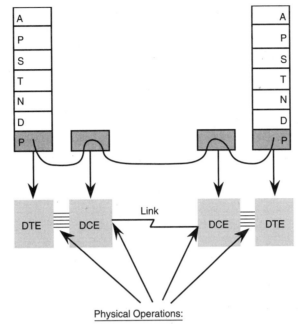

Figure 2-4
The physical layer
operations.

ple, return to zero (RZ) and nonreturn to zero (NRZ) codes are described at this level. For proper synchronization, clocking functions must also be stipulated. The physical layer is also responsible for this important function.

Figure 2-4 lists some of the more common services offered at the physical layer. In addition, the arrows depict where the physical layer operations reside in a typical data communications system.

The Data Link Layer. The *data link layer* is responsible for the transfer of data across one communications link (see Fig. 2-5). It delimits the flow of bits from the physical layer. It also provides for the identity of the bits. It usually (but not always) ensures that the traffic arrives safely at the receiving DTE. It often provides for flow control to ensure that the DTE does not become overburdened with too much data at any one time.

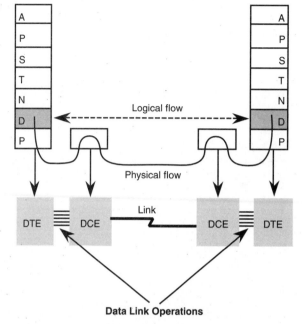

Figure 2-5
The data link layer
operations.

Data Link Operations

Traffic accountability: e.g. ACK, NAK
Detecting traffic: e.g. Sync, start bit, flag
Flow control: e.g. RR (receive ready)
Controlling traffic: e.g. Polls
Squencing: e.g. Send nr & receive nr
Resending: e.g. Resend timer

One of its most important functions is to provide for the detection of transmission errors, and many data links provide mechanisms to recover from lost, duplicated, or erroneous data. If this operation is supported, traffic is accounted for by the exchange of positive acknowledgments (ACKs) or negative acknowledgments (NAKs) between the sending and receiving stations.

Special signals are used by the data link layer to determine when traffic ends and when it begins. These signals are known as preambles, sync bytes, flags, or simply a start or stop bit.

Many data links are responsible for sending the receive ready (RR) and receive not ready (RNR) signals for flow control. Another method of controlling traffic is the issuance of a polling signal. A *poll* is a solicitation for data from another machine.

The data link layer may use sequence numbers. These numbers sequence the traffic into and out of the machines and the machines' buffers. The numbers are checked to ensure that all traffic on the link has been received in the proper order. They are also used by the receiving station to send back an acknowledgment to the transmitting station.

Some data link layers also have the ability to resend in the event the responding machine does not respond. This operation is controlled with the resend timer (often labeled the T1 timer).

Figure 2-5 lists some of the more common services offered at the data link layer. In addition, the dashed arrows depict where the data link layer operations reside in a typical data communications system.

Frame Relay relies on several of the data link layer operations. These options are discussed in more detail in Chap. 3.

The Network Layer. The *network layer* specifies the network/user interface of the user into a network, as well as the interface between two DTEs across a network (see Fig. 2-6). It enables users to negotiate options with the network and one another. For example, the negotiation of

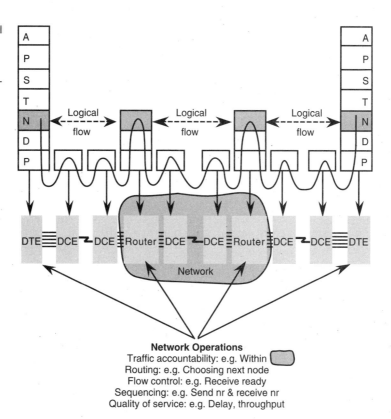

Figure 2-6
The network layer operations.

Network Operations
Traffic accountability: e.g. Within
Routing: e.g. Choosing next node
Flow control: e.g. Receive ready
Sequencing: e.g. Send nr & receive nr
Quality of service: e.g. Delay, throughput

throughput, delay, and acceptable error rates are common transactions.

The network layer defines switching/routing procedures within a network. It also includes the routing conventions to transfer traffic between networks (internetworking). The network layer also has sequence numbers and flow control capabilities, but these operations are used at the user-to-network interface for controlling traffic into and out of the network, and not just between the links (as they are in the data link layer).

Some networks assume responsibility for the integrity of the traffic while the traffic is in the network. Other networks pass that responsibility to the end user. Almost all communications networks allow the user to select and/or negotiate a quality of service (QOS) with the network.

Figure 2-6 lists some of the more common services offered at the network layer. In addition, the dashed arrows depict where the network layer operations reside in a typical data communications system.

Frame Relay uses a few of the functions of the conventional network layer, and these functions are examined in more detail in Chap. 5.

The Transport Layer. The *transport layer* provides the interface between the data communications network and the upper three layers (generally part of the user's system; see Fig. 2-7). This layer gives the user options in obtaining certain levels of quality of service (and cost) from the network itself (i.e., the network layer). It is designed to keep the user isolated from some of the physical and functional aspects of the network.

The transport layer provides for the end-to-end accountability of user traffic across more than one data link. It also is responsible for end-to-end integrity of users' data in internetworking operations. Therefore, it is a vital layer for sending traffic to users attached to different networks.

Apart from timers, the transport layer also has sending and receiving numbers. This feature may seem redundant when these timers and sequence numbers also exist at the network and data link layers. Indeed, they may be redundant. However, in some situations these timers and sequence numbers are quite important. For example, in internetworking situations where networks are connected together, these timers and sequence numbers are used to ensure the integrity of the traffic through multiple networks, a service not provided at the lower layers. For example, the data link layer provides services only for an individual link, and the network layer is tasked with providing service at the user-to-network interface. In contrast, the transport layer provides services (if necessary) across multiple networks.

The transport layer also provides for flow control between two trans-

Figure 2-7
The transport layer
operations.

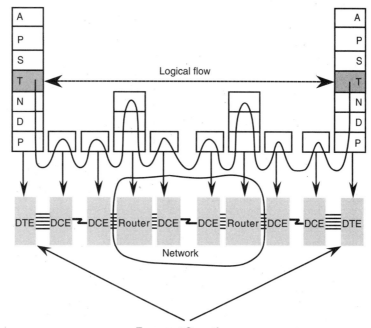

Transport Operations:
Traffic accountability between DTEs: e.g. Send and receive nrs
Recovery from network errors: e.g. Timers
Flow control between DTEs: e.g. Credits
Network transparency: SDU concept

port entities through the use of credit values exchanged by these entities. The credit values provide guidance on how much traffic the transmitting transport layer can send to the receiver.

As a general statement, the transport layer tries to remain transparent to the network layer. Its traffic is passed transparently through the network, which is in conformance with OSI's service data unit (SDU) concept.

Figure 2-7 lists some of the more common services offered at the transport layer. In addition, the dashed arrows depict where the transport layer operations reside in a typical data communications system.

The Session Layer.   The *session layer* serves as a user interface to the transport layer, and is responsible for managing an end-user application program's exchange of data with another end-user application (see Fig. 2-8).

The layer provides for an organized means to exchange data between user applications, such as simultaneous transmission, alternate transmis-

Figure 2-8
The session layer
operations.

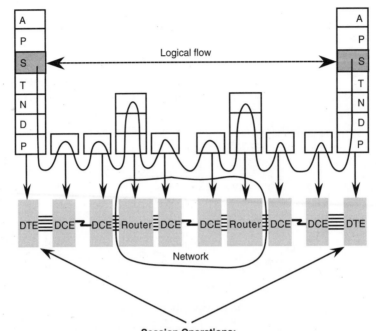

Figure 2-8
The session layer
operations.

Session Operations:
Management of Applications' sessions: e.g. Connection set up
Provision for checkpoints: e.g. Major 7 minor syncs
Provision for resynchronization: e.g. Resync
Graceful close sevices: e.g. Negotiatied release

sion, checkpoint procedures, and resynchronization of user data flow between user applications. The users can select the type of synchronization and control needed from the layer.

The session layer's principal service involves the establishment of a connection between two end-user applications. Its checkpoint procedures are provided with either a major checkpoint or a minor checkpoint, sometimes called *sync points*. A major checkpoint requires that all traffic stop flowing (upon its issuance) until the checkpoint is acknowledged. On the other hand, traffic can continue to flow when a minor checkpoint is issued.

The resynchronization procedure is performed with a resync service, which enables users to "go back to an established point and begin again."

Perhaps one of the most important features of a session layer (at least in the OSI Model) is the provision for a graceful close. This means that the two session services must negotiate the release, and ensure that all traffic has been "rounded up" before the disconnect occurs.

Figure 2-8 lists some of the more common services offered at the session layer. In addition, the dashed arrows depict where the session layer operations reside in a typical data communications system.

The Presentation Layer.   The *presentation layer* provides services dealing with the syntax of data; that is, the representation of data (see Fig. 2-9). It is not concerned with the meaning or semantics of the data. Its principal role is to accept data types (character, integer) from the application layer and then negotiate with its peer layer at the receiving site (in this case machine B) as to the syntax representation (such as ASCII). The layer consists of many tables of syntax (teletype, ASCII, Videotex, etc.).

This layer also contains a language called Abstract Syntax Negotiation One (ASN.1), which is used to describe the structure and syntax to be used for the representation of data.

The presentation layer also contains protocols that are used to describe the basic encoding rules (BER) for the transfer of data between computers.

As discussed in the previous paragraphs, the two major services of the

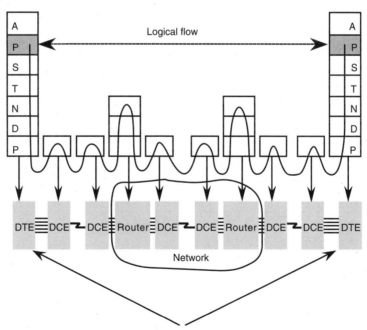

Figure 2-9
The presentation layer operations.

Presentation Operations:
Description of files, PDUs, objects: e.g. ASN.1
Syntax for data transfer: e.g. BER (transfer syntax)

presentation layer are object description with ASN.1 and transfer syntax establishment and negotiation with BER.

Figure 2-9 lists the common services offered at the presentation layer. In addition, the dashed arrows depict where the presentation layer operations reside in a typical data communications system.

The Applications Layer. The *applications layer* is concerned with the support of the end-user application process (see Fig. 2-10). It serves as the end-user interface in a layered model.

The application layer contains service elements to support application processes such as file transfer, job management, financial data exchange,

Figure 2-10
The application layer operations.

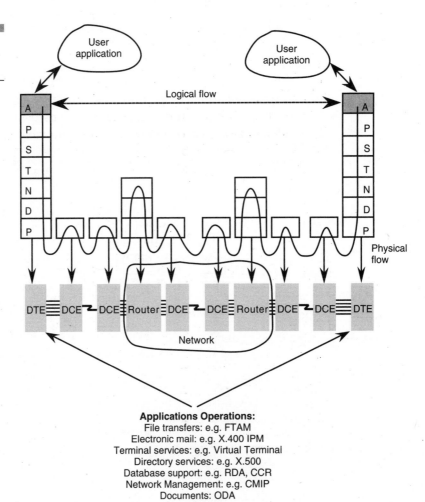

Applications Operations:
File transfers: e.g. FTAM
Electronic mail: e.g. X.400 IPM
Terminal services: e.g. Virtual Terminal
Directory services: e.g. X.500
Database support: e.g. RDA, CCR
Network Management: e.g. CMIP
Documents: ODA

programming languages, electronic mail, directory services, and database management.

The principal operations at the applications layer are quite varied. However, almost all OSI-based applications support at least two services: (1) file transfer using the file transfer and management service (FTAM), and (2) message handling systems with the X.400 interpersonal messaging system (IPM). Some organizations have implemented other facets of the OSI application layer—typically terminal services, directory services, database support, network management, and document services have been implemented in some systems.

Figure 2-10 lists some of the more common services offered at the application layer. In addition, the arrows depict where the application layer operations reside in a typical data communications system.

The OSI-Based Protocols

The Open Systems Interconnection (OSI) Model was developed by several standards organizations and is now a widely used model for the design and implementation of computer networks, notably the ITU-T and the ISO. The OSI Model has been under development for about 15 years, and is now finding its way into a number of networks and vendor products. This model will serve as a convenient tool to explain some of the operations of Frame Relay and other protocols. This section concentrates on the network and transport layers; later chapters examine the data link layer.

As illustrated in Fig. 2-11, the OSI Model is organized into seven layers. Each layer contains several to many protocols, which are invoked according to the specific needs of the user.

Figure 2-11
Some principal OSI-based protocols.

Application	X.400, FTAM, CMIP, ROSE, ACSE, etc.
Presentation	X.226, X.216, ASN.1, BER
Session	X.225, X.215
Transport	TP classes 0-4, Connectionless TP
Network	X.25, CLNP, X.75, ISDN, etc.
Data link	HDLC, LAPB, LAPD, ISDN, etc.
Physical	EIA-232-D, V.24, V.28, ISDN, etc.

OSI has met with opposition since its inception. The reasons are primarily that it never had a sponsor, as did the U.S. Government's funding of the Internet protocols; some of its protocols are not very well designed; and it is simply misunderstood by almost everyone in the industry, including some people who write books about OSI.

If one were to examine the Internet suite of protocols, approximately 25 are used in almost all installations. Some 15 to 20 others are used in other systems and operations. Therefore, about 40 to 45 Internet-sponsored protocols make up the Internet protocol stack.

If one were to compare the Internet stack of protocols to the OSI stack of protocols, it would be revealed that OSI has very few protocols. (I am using the ITU-T OSI standards in this discussion, because they are easily identified in the X.200 recommendations and the original OSI Recommendations as published in the 1984 Red Book.) The reason for this seeming discrepancy is that with a few exceptions, OSI does not define and specify protocols. Rather, it defines and specifies a model from which to build protocols. In fact, if the X.200 service definitions (primitives) standards are excluded, I count only eight protocols that were part of the OSI Model when it first came under fire in the 1980s, and they all reside in layers 4–7 of the OSI Model. No protocols are defined for the communications layers—the bearer services at layers 1–3.

Some people in our industry (I am sure the reader is not one of them) state that X.400 is an OSI protocol, as is FTAM, and X.500, and so on. Their suppositions are simply incorrect. Some of these ITU-T and ISO standards make reference to OSI, but that is the point of this discussion. They make reference to a model upon which they are based.

In the past, when I have made this fact known to various people, they have stated that I am indeed correct, and that my claim of the design of X.400, FTAM, X.500, and so forth, resting on the OSI Model is a clear demonstration of the unworthiness of OSI, because these protocols are overly complex and inefficient.

If that is the case, then we must also accept that OSI is the model from which the following systems and protocols have been designed: Frame Relay, the IEEE LANs (802.3, 802.4, 802.5, 802.2, 802.6, etc.), ATM, parts of CPDP, FDDI, GSM, ISDN, SONET, SS#7, etc.

The OSI critic cannot discount X.500, FTAM, and so on, without discounting the systems listed in the previous paragraph, simply because the critic cannot have it both ways. So, let us get on with life, and stop the sophomoric debate about OSI. It has great utility if it is adopted as a model.

Not every protocol in a layer need be invoked, and the OSI model provides a means for two users to negotiate the specific protocols desired for the session between them.

The Network Layer

As with a conventional layered model discussed earlier, the network layer specifies the interface between the user and a network, as well as the interface between two DTEs through a network. Remember, it allows users to negotiate options with the network and each other. For example, the negotiation of throughput, delay (response time), and reverse charges are common negotiations.

Common network layer protocols at this layer are X.25 (a network interface standard) and the connectionless network protocol (CLNP), which provides internetworking operations. CLNP is an OSI-based standard that was designed based on the widely used Internet Protocol (IP). IP is not part of the OSI Model. X.25 is described in more detail in later chapters, because of the perception that Frame Relay is a competitor to X.25.

While this layer does include switching/routing and route discovery operations, many networks use proprietary solutions to these tasks. Only recently has the industry begun a migration to standardized switching/routing and router discovery protocols.

The Transport Layer

We learned earlier in this chapter that the transport layer provides the interface between the data communications network and the upper three layers, and gives the user options in obtaining certain levels of quality (and cost) from the network. We have learned that it provides for end-to-end accountability across more than one data link. It also is responsible for end-to-end integrity of users' data in internetworking operations.

It is a vital layer if a user sends traffic to another user on a different network, and is especially important in a Frame Relay network, in which data might be discarded by Frame Relay without any corrective action.

The OSI transport layer requires the user to specify a quality of service (QOS) to be provided by the underlying network types. Consequently, the transport layer must know the types of service offered by

Table 2-1

Types of Networks

- A *type A network* provides acceptable residual error rates and acceptable rates of signaled failures (acceptable quality). Packets are assumed not to be lost. The transport layer need not provide recovery or resequencing services. In other words, it is an ideal network.

- A *type B network* provides for acceptable residual error rates, but an unacceptable rate for signaled failures (unacceptable signaled errors). The transport layer must be able to recover from errors.

- A *type C network* connection provides a residual error rate not acceptable to the user (unreliable) or an unacceptable method of signaling failures. The transport layer must recover from failures and resequence packets. A type C network could include some local area networks, mobile networks, and datagram networks.

the network(s) below it. Table 2-1 summarizes the types of networks defined by the OSI Model.

Upon receiving the user's request for a network connection and a quality of service associated with the connection, the transport layer selects a class of protocol to match the user's quality of service parameters in relation to the supporting network(s). Even though a variety of networks exist (connection-oriented, connectionless, etc.), the transport layer ensures that a consistent level of service is provided to the end user.

The QOS parameters are passed by the transport user to the transport layer, which uses them to pass parameters to the network layer in order to invoke the requested services. It is certainly conceivable that the underlying network or the remote user cannot or will not accept the QOS values. If this is the case, the services can be negotiated down to a lower quality level, or the connection request can be rejected.

The idea in defining network types is to recognize that different qualities of networks exist, yet provide the user with a consistent level of service regardless of network type. For example, a type C network might be one in which the transmissions take place without end-to-end acknowledgments, such as a Frame Relay network. On the other hand, a type B network would likely be one using X.25 functions and capabilities, and occasionally issuing network resets.

The existence of a type A network means the transport layer has an easy job. However, most of the complexity of this layer stems from the fact that many networks exhibit the characteristics of type B or type C networks.

The OSI transport layer supports a user with two types of services. One set of services is based on the class of protocol desired by the requesting user (the requester) and negotiated with the responding user (the responder) and the transport entity. The second set of services involves a number of quality-of-service (QOS) parameters that are passed

Table 2-2

OSI Transport Layer
Protocol Classes

- Class 0 Characteristics
  For type A networks
  Simple arrangement
  Underlying network support is sufficient

- Class 1 Characteristics
  For type B networks
  Designed to recover from network reset/disconnect
  Supports retention until acknowledgment of TPU's Element of Procedure

- Class 2 Characteristics
  For type A networks
  Supports connection multiplexing
  Underlying network support is sufficient

- Class 3 Characteristics
  For type B networks
  Class 2 + recovery from network reset/disconnect
  Supports retention until acknowledgment of TPU's Element of Procedure

- Class 4 Characteristics
  For type C networks
  Class 3 + recovery from datagram type networks

by the service user to the transport layer. Table 2-2 summarizes the protocol classes and Table 2-3 summarizes the QOS parameters.

The transport layer is responsible for selecting an appropriate protocol to support the quality-of-service parameters established by the user. Since the transport layer knows the characteristics of a network (types A, B, or C), the layer can choose five classes of protocol procedures to support the QOS requested by the user.

The transport layer quality-of-service parameters are created at the application layer and passed down to the transport layer. As far as possible,

Table 2-3

OSI Transport Layer
Quality-of-Service
(QOS) Parameters

- TC establishment delay
- TC establishment failure probability
- Throughput
- Transit delay
- Residual delay
- Residual error rate
- Transfer failure probability
- TC release delay
- TC release failure probability
- TC protection
- TC priority
- Resilience of TC

Note: TC is transport connection.

the parameters are intended to allow the user to define a level of service that is independent of the characteristics of the underlying network(s).

While the OSI transport layer (especially class 4) provides for a wealth of functions, as demonstrated by the quality-of-service parameters, there is no provision in the Frame Relay standards for how to handle the OSI QOS features. Once again, the point is that Frame Relay is a minimal service network. To burden the Frame Relay network with interpreting and acting upon these QOS features would entail a considerable amount of delay, as well as considerable overhead.

The Internet Protocols

In the early 1970s, several groups around the world began to address the problem of network and application compatibility. At that time the term *internetworking*, which means the interconnecting of computers and/or networks, was coined. The concepts of internetworking were pioneered by the ITU-T, the ISO, and (especially) the original designers of ARPANET. [ARPA stands for Advanced Research Projects Agency, a U.S. Department of Defense (DoD) organization.] In fairness to the pioneers of internetworking concepts (and layered protocols, discussed previously), the ARPA protocols were well in existence before the ISO and the ITU-T took an interest in this important subject.

The procurement for ARPANET took place in 1968. The machines selected for this procurement were Honeywell 316 interface message processors (IMPs). The initial effort was contracted through Bolt, Beranek & Newman (BBN), and the ARPANET nodes were initially installed at UCLA, University of California at San Bernardino, Stanford Research Institute (SRI), and the University of Utah. The well-known "Request for Comments" (RFCs) came about from this early work.

These initial efforts were organized through the ARPANET Network Working Group. It was disbanded in 1971 and the Defense Advanced Project Research Agency (DARPA) assumed the work of the earlier organization. DARPA's work in the early 1970s led to the development of an earlier protocol, the network control program, and later the *Transmission Control Protocol* and the *Internet Protocol* (TCP/IP).

Two years later, the first significant parts of the Internet were placed in operation. At about this time, DARPA started converting some of its computers to the TCP/IP suite of protocols. By 1983, DARPA stated that all computers connected to ARPANET were required to use TCP/IP.

Perhaps one of the most significant developments in TCP/IP was DARPA's decision to implement TCP/IP around the UNIX operating system. Of equal importance, the University of California at Berkeley was selected to distribute the TCP/IP code. Because the TCP/IP code was nonproprietary, it spread rapidly among universities, private companies, and research centers. Indeed, it has become the standard suite of data communications protocols for UNIX-based computers.

At that time, other networks were coming into existence, based on funding from the government and other research agencies, and using TCP/IP protocols. The NSFnet was established as a high-capacity network by the National Science Foundation. Its goal is to provide a communications backbone for scientific and research centers, initially in the United States and now in other parts of the world. Its high-capacity lines are designed to support supercomputer transmissions. The supercomputer centers perform backbones to which lower-speed networks are attached. Today, NSFnet has evolved from 56-kbps carrier lines to T1 speeds of 1.544 Mbps, and MCI has installed optical fiber connections over the NSF backbone network.

The Internet Layers

Many implementations of Frame Relay also use several of the Internet protocols. Subsequent chapters explain these systems. For the present, we examine the Internet layers and concentrate on those protocols that are often used with Frame Relay.

As illustrated in Fig. 2-12, the lower layers (data link and physical layers) are not defined in the Internet standards. The Internet authorities

Figure 2-12
The principal Internet protocols.

Application	FTP, SMTP, Telnet, SNMP, etc.
Presentation	Limited use
Session	Not defined
Transport	TCP, UDP
Network	IP
Data link	Not defined (with some exceptions)
Physical	Not defined

have wisely chosen not to reinvent the wheel, but instead rely on the present physical level and data link standards (with a few exceptions) to support the Internet protocols.

The Internet Protocol (IP)

The *Internet Protocol* (IP) operates in the network layer of a conventional layered model. It permits the exchange of traffic between two host computers without any prior call setup. (However, these two computers usually share a common connection-oriented transport protocol.) IP is responsible for the routing of traffic, but it is not responsible for the integrity of the data while performing its operations. That is to say, IP does not provide any sequencing, flow control, or acknowledgment services. Therefore, it is possible for datagrams to be lost between two end-user stations. For example, the IP gateway enforces a maximum queue length size, and if this queue length is violated, buffers will overflow. In this situation, the additional datagrams are discarded in the network. For this reason, a higher-level transport layer protocol (such as TCP) is essential to recover from these problems.

IP hides the underlying subnetwork from the end user. In this context, it creates a virtual network for that end user. This aspect of IP is quite attractive, because it allows different types of networks to attach to an IP gateway. As a result, IP is reasonably simple to install, and because of its connectionless design it is quite robust.

Since IP is an unreliable, best-effort datagram-type protocol, it has no reliability mechanisms. As just mentioned, it provides no error recovery for the underlying subnetworks. It has no flow-control mechanisms. The user data (datagrams) can be lost, duplicated, or even arrive out of order. It is not the job of IP to deal with most of these problems. Most of the problems are passed to the next higher layer, TCP.

IP supports fragmentation operations. The term *fragmentation* refers to an operation whereby a protocol data unit (PDU) is divided or segmented into smaller units. This feature can be quite useful, because not all networks use the same size PDU. For example, X.25-based wide area networks (WANs) typically employ a PDU (called a packet in X.25) with a data field of 128 octets.

IP also offers a number of other optional services, such as route recording, which records the IP addresses of all nodes that processed the datagram. The time-to-live (TTL) operation is used to measure the time a datagram has been in the Internet. Each node in the Internet is required to check this field and discard it if the TTL value equals 0. A node is also required to decrement this field in each datagram it processes. In actual implementations, the TTL field is a number-of-hops value.

The Internet Transport Layer with Transmission Control Protocol (TCP) and the User Datagram Protocol (UDP)

The Internet transport layer supports two transport layer protocols: the *Transmission Control Protocol* (TCP) and the *User Datagram Protocol* (UDP). TCP is a connection-oriented protocol that provides several data integrity functions. In contrast, UDP is a connectionless protocol that does not perform data management.

TCP. The Internet Protocol (IP) is not designed to recover from certain problems, nor does it guarantee the delivery of traffic. IP is designed to discard datagrams that are outdated or have exceeded the number of permissible transit hops in an internet.

Certain user applications require assurance that all datagrams have been delivered safely to the destination. Furthermore, the transmitting user may need to know that the traffic has been delivered at the receiving host. The mechanisms to achieve these important services reside in TCP (UDP is connectionless, and does not provide these services).

TCP must be able to satisfy a wide range of applications requirements, and equally important, it must be able to adapt to a dynamic environment within an internet. It must establish and manage sessions (logical associations) between its local users and these users' remote communicating partners. This means that TCP must maintain an awareness of a user's activities in order to support that user's data transfer through the Internet.

Since IP is a simple connectionless network protocol, tasks involving reliability, flow control, sequencing, opens, and closes are given to TCP. Although TCP and IP are tied together so closely that they are used in the same context (TCP/IP), TCP can also support other protocols. For example, another connectionless protocol, such as the ISO 8473 (Connectionless Network Protocol, or CLNP), can operate with TCP (with adjustments to the interface between the modules). In addition, the application protocols, such as the File Transfer Protocol (FTP) and the Simple Mail Transfer Protocol (SMTP), rely on many of the services of TCP.

TCP is a connection-oriented protocol. This term refers to the fact that TCP maintains status and state information about each user data stream flowing into and out of the TCP module. The term used in this context also means TCP is responsible for the end-to-end transfer of data across one network or multiple networks to a receiving user application (or the next upper layer protocol).

TCP is responsible for the reliable transfer of each of the characters passed to it from an upper layer (characters are also called *bytes* or *octets*). Consequently, it uses sequence numbers and positive acknowledgments.

A sequence number is assigned to each octet transmitted. The receiving TCP module uses a checksum routine to check the data for damage that might have occurred during the transmission process. If the data are acceptable, TCP returns a positive acknowledgment (ACK) to the sending TCP module. If the data are damaged, the receiving TCP discards the data and uses a sequence number to inform the sending TCP about the problem. Like many other connection-oriented protocols, TCP uses timers to ensure that the lapse of time is not excessive before remedial measures are taken for either the transmission of acknowledgments from the receiving site and/or the retransmission of data at the transmitting site.

TCP also checks for duplicate data. In the event the sending TCP retransmits the data, the receiving TCP discards the redundant data. Redundant data might be introduced into an internet when the receiving TCP entity does not acknowledge traffic in a timely manner, in which case the sending TCP entity retransmits the data.

In addition to using sequence numbers for acknowledgment, TCP uses them to resequence the segments if they arrive at the final destination out of order. Because TCP rests upon a connectionless system, it is quite possible for duplicate datagrams to be created in an internet. TCP also eliminates duplicate segments.

TCP uses an inclusive acknowledgment scheme. The acknowledgment number acknowledges all octets up to and including the acknowledgment number less one. This approach provides an easy and efficient method of acknowledging traffic, but it does have a disadvantage. For example, suppose that ten segments have been transmitted, yet due to routing operations, these segments arrive out of order. TCP is obliged to acknowledge only the highest contiguous byte number that has been received without error. It is not allowed to acknowledge the highest arrived byte number until all intermediate bytes have arrived. Therefore, like any other connection-oriented protocol, the transmitting TCP entity can eventually time out and retransmit the traffic not yet acknowledged. These retransmissions can introduce a considerable amount of overhead in a network.

The receiver's TCP module is also able to control the flow of the sender's data, which is a very useful tool to prevent buffer overrun and a possible saturation of the receiving machine. The concept used with TCP is somewhat unusual among communications protocols. It is based on issuing a "window" (or credit) value to the transmitter. The transmitter is allowed to transmit a specified number of bytes within this window, after which the window is closed and the transmitter must stop sending data.

TCP also has a very useful facility for multiplexing multiple user sessions within a single host computer onto the upper layer protocols (ULPs). This is accomplished through some rather simple naming conventions for ports and sockets in the TCP and IP modules.

TCP provides full duplex transmission between two TCP entities. This permits simultaneous two-way transmission without having to wait for a turnaround signal, which is required in a half-duplex situation. TCP provides a graceful close to a virtual circuit (the logical connection between two users). A graceful close ensures that all traffic has been acknowledged before the virtual circuit is removed.

UDP. The *User Datagram Protocol* (UDP) is classified as a connectionless protocol. It is sometimes used in place of TCP in situations where the full services of TCP are not needed. For example, the Trivial File Transfer Protocol (TFTP) and the Remote Procedure Call (RPC) use UDP.

UDP serves as a simple application interface to the IP. Since it has neither reliability, flow control, nor error-recovery measures, it serves principally as a multiplexer/demultiplexer for the receiving and sending of IP traffic.

Like TCP, UDP makes use of the port concept to direct the datagrams to the proper upper layer applications. The UDP datagram contains a destination port number and a source port number. The destination number is used by the UDP module to deliver the traffic to the proper recipient.

The TCP/IP Protocol Stack

Figure 2-13 depicts an architectural model of TCP/IP and several of the major related protocols. The choices in the stacking of the layers of this model vary, depending on the needs of network users and the

Figure 2-13
Frame Relay and the
TCP/IP protocol stack.

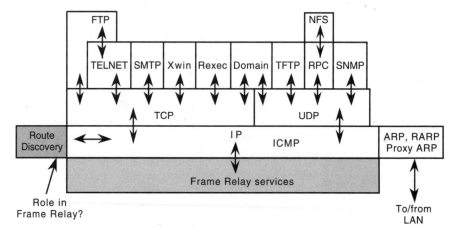

decisions made by network designers. IP is the key protocol at the network layer. Several other protocols are used in conjunction with IP, serving as route discovery and address mapping protocols. The protocols that rest over TCP (and UDP) are examples of the application layer protocols.

The lower two layers represent the data link and physical layers. These layers are implemented with a wide choice of standards and protocols, and Frame Relay operates at the data link layer.

This figure shows how the TCP/IP suite is stacked on Frame Relay. The striped area in the figure represents Frame Relay core operations and physical operations. Communications between Frame Relay and the user typically occur with the Internet Protocol (IP) or an IP-type protocol, such as XNS or IPX.

The issue of route discovery and how the host machine participates in route discovery is considerably different in a Frame Relay network than it is in a typical network. In the former, the intervening Frame Relay network determines routes. In the latter, the IP routers determine the routes. Another point that bears further investigation is how the vendor "terminates" IP at the host machine and at the router, vis-à-vis the Frame Relay network. Subsequent chapters explore this issue.

Also (to complete the explanation of this figure), the mapping protocols (ARP, RARP, Proxy ARP) have no relationship to the Frame Relay layers, because they are invoked only after the Frame Relay network has delivered the traffic to the destination router, which in turn has delivered the traffic to the destination LAN.

Frame Relay's Relationship to a Layered Model

Frame Relay is designed to eliminate and/or combine certain operations residing in layers 3 and 2 of a data communications seven-layer model. It implements the operational aspects of statistical multiplexing found in the X.25 protocol, and the efficiency of circuit switching found in TDM protocols. The net effects of this approach are enhanced throughput, reduced delay, and the saving of CPU cycles within the network because some services are eliminated.

It should be emphasized that Frame Relay provides for better delay performance than X.25, but it cannot match TDM performance, because TDM does little processing of the traffic.

In addition, Frame Relay (and X.25) support variable lengths of data units, which makes for a flexible arrangement when internetworking different types of networks (LANs and WANs). However, variable data units translate into variable delay. Consequently, Frame Relay does not work well in systems that are delay-sensitive (digitized voice, compressed video).

Table 2-4 summarizes the relationship of Frame Relay to conventional layered protocols.

Figure 2-14 shows another way of viewing Frame Relay operations. On the left is a depiction of a typical data communications protocol stack, which encompasses the physical, data link, and network layers.

Table 2-4 Aspects of Frame Relay	Eliminates these aspects of level 3 operations: ■ Sequencing ■ ACKs and NAKs ■ Most management packets (diagnostic packets) Eliminates these aspects of level 2 operations: ■ Sequencing ■ Flow control management ■ ACKs and NAKs ■ Most management frames (supervisory frames) Uses some aspects of STDM This means that Frame Relay: ■ Works well in bursty transmission environments ■ Not intended (initially) for delay-sensitive traffic Continues to perform error checking but does *not* request retransmission of errored traffic

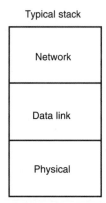

Figure 2-14
Comparison of typical stacks and the Frame Relay stacks.

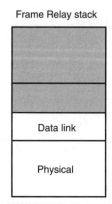

These layers perform conventional operations. For example, the physical layer is responsible for terminating traffic, providing connections, and physical signaling. The data link layer is responsible for error checking and retransmission of corrupted traffic that may appear on the communications link. The network layer is responsible for managing the traffic within the network, establishing virtual connections, and negotiating quality of services between the network and the users.

In contrast, the Frame Relay stack eliminates most of the network layer and several aspects of the data link layer. It is no wonder, then, that Frame Relay is fast; it does very little.

SUMMARY

Like the OSI and Internet models, Frame Relay uses the concepts of layered protocols. It uses only a small part of the conventional network layer and limited features of the data link layer. The stripping away of these functions provides for minimal (yet fast and efficient) service, which requires that additional operations be performed at the upper layers typically located in the user computer.

What a Frame Relay System Does and Doesn't Do

This chapter continues the discussion of the last part of Chap. 2. I describe what operations Frame Relay systems perform and, equally important, what they do not perform. This chapter also examines conventional operations of the data link layer and how Frame Relay utilizes some of these operations.

Distinction Between a Frame, Packet, Datagram, and Other Data Units

The reader might reasonably ask, "Why is Frame Relay called Frame Relay?" The answer to this question relates to the fact that the term *frame* is used to describe the data link layer (layer 2) protocol data unit (PDU). The term *PDU* is used in the OSI Model to describe a complete unit of data at each layer, including the header used at that layer. Therefore, as depicted in Fig. 3-1, the OSI Model describes application protocol data units (APDU), presentation data units (PPDU), session protocol data units

Figure 3-1
Frames and other protocol data units (PDUs).

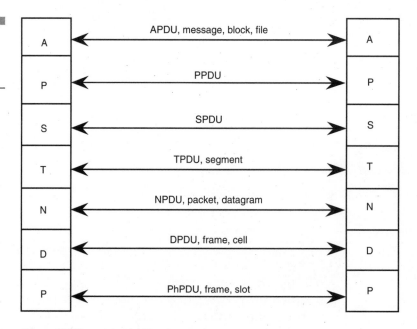

APDU, message, block, file
PPDU
SPDU
TPDU, segment
NPDU, packet, datagram
DPDU, frame, cell
PhPDU, frame, slot

Where: PDU is a protocol data unit

(SPDU), transport protocol data units (TPDU), network protocol data units (NPDU), data link protocol data units (DPDU), and physical protocol data units (PhPDU). Figure 3-1 also shows the relationship of the PDUs and some more commonly used terms associated with certain PDUs.

As illustrated in Fig. 3-1, frames are transmitted logically between data link layers in two different machines. As discussed in the previous chapter, these PDUs are sent down the layers of the transmitting machine and up the layers of the receiving machine. Therefore, the arrows in this figure denote logical communications whereby the headers of each of the PDUs are exchanged between layers.

The terms *packet* and *datagram* are often associated with the network layer PDUs. These terms are subject to different interpretations, but this illustration shows a widely accepted convention. With few exceptions, a packet is associated with a connection-oriented network layer, and a datagram is associated with a connectionless network layer.

The term *segment* is associated with the transport layer and TCP. The OSI model uses the conventional term *TPDU* for the PDU at this layer. Other terms that are commonly used in the industry—but are subject to many interpretations—are message, block, file, record, and so forth. Generally, these terms are associated with application layer PDUs, although a number of people use the term *message* for a PDU at the network layer.

It will become evident as we proceed through this book that several aspects of the network layer have been "folded" into the data link layer, and many of the network layer functions have been eliminated. In Frame Relay, the frame header contains fields associated with both the data link and network layers.

Operations of a Conventional Data Link Protocol

The basic data link operation is quite simple: it delivers the traffic safely between two machines, from the sending machine to the receiving machine. It is unaware of the nature of the user's data. It has no understanding of the user fields (or headers of the upper layers) in the data. Consequently, the application's data is simply an information field (I field) to data link control.

Upon receiving data from the upper layer, the data link layer adds various control fields and data link addresses. It then creates an error check field. This error check field is relayed with the I field and the link control headers and trailers to the receiving machine. A copy of this traffic is retained at the sending device.

The receiving machine performs an error check on the protocol data unit (PDU), which we learned earlier is called a frame. If the error check passes, it then examines the link control headers and trailers to determine what actions are to occur at the receiving device.

Frame Relay link operations are much simpler than the conventional data link control operations. Essentially, the Frame Relay link performs two major operations (and other minor ones, described later): it uses flags to check for the presence of the frame on the link, and it performs an FCS check. If the FCS check reveals an error, the frame is discarded and the link layer takes no remedial action. A comparison of a conventional data link control protocol and Frame Relay is provided in Table 3-1.

Operations on One Link

As depicted in Fig. 3-2, in conventional data link operations, the transmitting data link entity returns a positive acknowledgment (ACK) to the sending machine if the traffic is acceptable. The ACK is returned in a frame that consists of link headers and trailers. When the originating computer receives the acknowledgment, it can delete the copy of the traffic it was holding in its buffer.

Generally speaking, the sending data link protocol does not pass any further acknowledgment to the end-user application. Consequently, the application must "trust" data link control to deliver the traffic safely across the communications link.

Table 3-1

Link Control and
Frame Relay

Basic operations of a conventional data link control protocol
- Delineating the frame from noise and other spurious signals
- Accounting for all traffic on the link
- Performing a frame check sequence (FCS)
- Sequencing of the traffic on the link
- Providing flow control operations between two machines

Basic operations of frame relay data link control
- Delineating the frame from noise and other spurious signals
- Performing a frame check sequence (FCS)

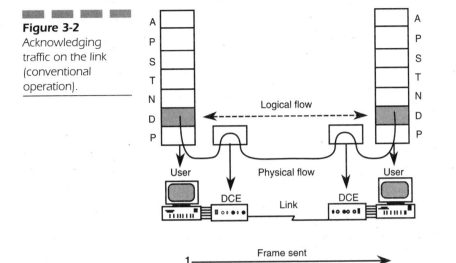

Figure 3-2
Acknowledging traffic on the link (conventional operation).

At the receiving side, after the error check has been performed, the data link control headers and trailers have been examined, and appropriate actions taken, the end-user data is passed through the upper layers to the receiving application.

Link Layer Flow Control

Devices on a data link may be able to govern the amount of traffic they receive from one another. This concept is known as *flow control*. It is usually quite important, because machines have a finite amount of memory from which buffer space can be allocated. In Fig. 3-2, event 3 could have included, in addition to the frame acknowledgment, an indication that the receiving machine wishes to continue to receive traffic, or conversely does not wish to receive traffic. These notifications are performed with a receive ready (RR) frame and receive not ready (RNR) frame, respectively.

An *acknowledgment number*, usually denoted by N(R), serves to notify the transmitter that the frame represented by this number has been received, and that the transmitter is therefore allowed to send yet another frame. A more common practice is to allow the transmitter to send a number of frames. The receiver then acknowledges these frames by sending one acknowledgment frame. The sequence number in this frame inclusively acknowledges all the traffic the transmitter has sent.

The concept of receiving traffic and responding with an acknowledgment number (thereby allowing the transmitting station to open its transmit "window") is known as a *window turn*. The term *window* in a data link protocol is used to describe conceptual buffers. You can think of a transmit window as a number of frames that can be sent without flow control restrictions. In turn, the receive window is represented by a buffer. Therefore, when the receive window is closed, the buffer is full, and when a window is open, buffer space is still available to receive traffic.

Consequently, a conventional data link protocol manages the buffers between the transmitter and receiver by opening and closing windows. Obviously, these windows are conceptual only. As I just mentioned, they are represented by counters and variables in software or hardware.

Operations on More Than One Link

In a wide area network, data link operations must be performed on each link. This includes not only the links between the user and the network, but also all links within the network (see Fig. 3-3).

In the event that the receiving data link control entity detects an error in the transmitted traffic, it usually sends a negative acknowledgment (NAK) back to the transmitting machine. The traffic is discarded at the receiving machine (obviously, it is not a good idea to send corrupted data to the end-user application). At the originating site, the sending machine receives the NAK and accesses its buffer to obtain a copy of the data in question. It then retransmits this traffic to the receiving station.

If all goes well with the retransmission and the error check reveals that the traffic is not distorted, the receiving machine returns an ACK to the sender. It then passes the data to the next upper layer, which is the network layer in a typical system. The network layer makes a routing decision and the data is given to the next data link entity; the process is then repeated.

The concepts of flow control and windows pertain to operations on each link. That is, each link maintains its own send and receive windows and its own flow control arrangements between the stations on that link. For example, in Fig. 3-3, three links rest between the two end-user

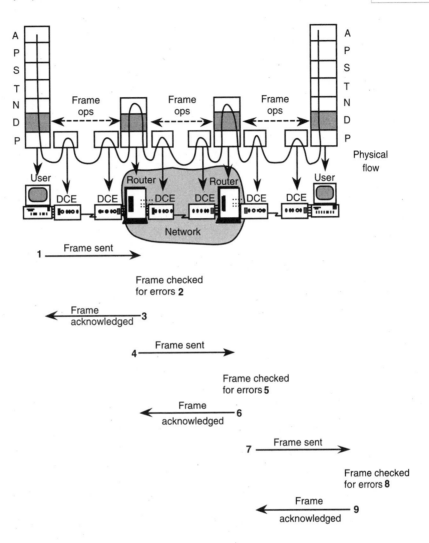

Figure 3-3
Frame operations on each link in the end-to-end connection (conventional operation).

devices. Each link is completely independent of the other links. As traffic is routed and relayed among multiple links, the frame header is stripped away and reassembled on each link. With this approach, a different data link protocol can run on each link.

Contents of a Conventional Data Link Frame

The data link frame varies, depending on the vendor's preference and the type of link being used. However, almost all data link controls use

Figure 3-4

A conventional data link frame.

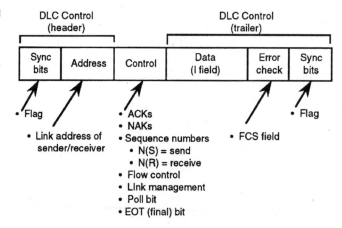

similar frame formats, based on the High Level Data Link Control (HDLC) standard published by the ISO.

As shown in Fig. 3-4, the data link control frame generally consists of synchronization bits (often called *sync bits* or *flags*) at the beginning and end of the frame. The purpose of these fields is to alert the receiver to the arrival of a frame and to identify the end of the transmission.

The frame header also contains a link layer address or addresses. These fields identify the sending station and the receiving station.

The frame usually contains at least one control field. It is coded in a number of ways to provide for NAKs, ACKs, and to support sequence numbers [generally referred to as N(S) for a send sequence number and N(R) for a receive sequence number]. The N(R) field is used to acknowledge data, and its receipt at the transmitting station enables this station to open its transmit window up to the value that is in the N(R) field. As we learned earlier, this operation is called making a window turn.

The control field is also used for various link layer management operations to provide flow control for the traffic between the stations. These operations are the receive ready (RR) and the receive not ready (RNR), discussed earlier. It also contains functions described shortly, called the poll bit and the final [or end of transmission (EOT)] bit. Finally, an error check field [the frame check sequence (FCS)] is used for the detection of corrupted traffic and possible retransmissions.

Operations of the Data Link Layer with Frame Relay

Operations on One Link

Frame Relay continues to do an error check on the frame at the user-to-network interface (UNI). The conventional cyclic redundancy check (CRC) operation is employed using the frame check sequence (FCS) field. However, if this check reveals that the frame was corrupted during transmission across the communications channel, the frame is not only discarded but a negative acknowledgment (NAK) is returned to the sender. Figure 3-5 shows these operations. Note that the user machine is a router, which is a typical configuration. You may wish to review Fig. 1-3 in Chap. 1 for a review of the Frame Relay configuration.

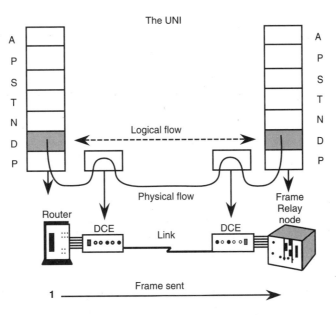

Figure 3-5
The Frame Relay approach.

Figure 3-6
Frame Relay UNI
operations.

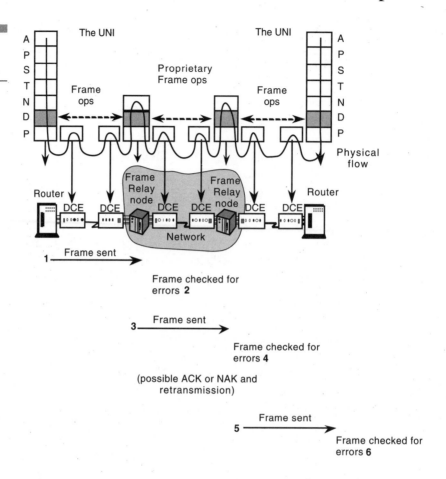

Operations on More Than One Link
and the UNI
==

Figure 3-6 shows how Frame Relay operates at each UNI. The operation requires the router and the network node to perform the FCS check. Both machines have the option of managing congestion through the use of the Frame Relay congestion notification bits. Moreover, it may discard traffic because of congestion problems, or because of a bad FCS check. The operations inside the network are not defined by Frame Relay. The network provider might provide ACKs, NAKs, and retransmissions, or it might not. You should check with your Frame Relay service provider about this matter; the section in this chapter entitled "Tradeoffs of Link-by-Link vs. End-to-End Error Recovery" discusses the issues in more detail.

Figure 3-7
The Frame Relay
frame.

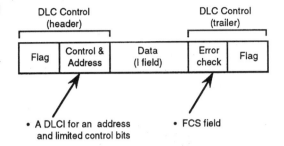

Contents of a Frame Relay Frame

The Frame Relay frame is based on the HDLC and LAPD frames (see Fig. 3-7). It uses the beginning and ending flags, the FCS, and the I field. However, it does not have a separate control field and address field. These two fields are combined into one. Frame Relay does not use the HDLC control field format, other than the command/response (C/R) bit, the address extension bit, and an address field. The address field does not identify station addresses in the Frame Relay operation; it identifies a virtual circuit with the DLCI.

Tradeoffs of Link-by-Link vs. End-to-End Error Recovery

Since Frame Relay does not acknowledge traffic, the processing at the nodes is simpler and faster. How much faster is a function of each node's processing speed and the amount of traffic it is processing. Nevertheless, subsequent discussions reveal that node processing speed is not so significant a factor as the overall delay of the frame's transmission through the network (link speed is the main factor).

The main reason for not performing ACKs, NAKs, and retransmissions is illustrated in Fig. 3-8. In a conventional system, the information (I field) of the frame is held at the machine while the machine performs the FCS calculation. It cannot be forwarded until the machine completes this check, and returns either an ACK or a NAK to the transmitting machine. The end result is that the machine must wait until all bits

Figure 3-8
FCS operations.

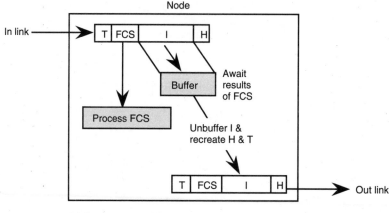

(a) Conventional FCS operation.

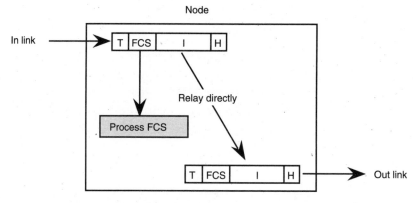

(b) Frame Relay FCS operation.

have arrived from the incoming link before it can start the error check, and before it can start sending these bits on to the outgoing link.

In contrast, since Frame Relay does not send ACKs or NAKs, it need not await the arrival of all the bits in the frame. It can begin forwarding the bits as soon as it has interpreted a field in the header that reveals the outgoing link.

Thus, in this example, the internal network does not rely on a store-and-forward process, but rather a semidirect relay through the switch. In this manner, Frame Relay can reduce the transit delay at each node in the network. This concept is called *cut-through switching*. It reduces latency considerably, but the approach does not allow a retransmission of an errored frame.

Keep in mind, however, that Frame Relay does not define the operations inside the network, and some individual implementations provide full error checking on each link inside the network. The reasons for this approach are described in the next section of this chapter.

Link-by-Link Error Recovery

Figure 3-9 shows examples of link-by-link error recovery operations. The top part of the figure shows two user machines (A and F) connected to Frame Relay switches B and E, which are connected to switches C and D. Five links are connected to these machines, numbered 1–5 in the figure. The dashed lines represent other lines, but are not relevant to this dis-

Figure 3-9

Link-by-link error recovery.

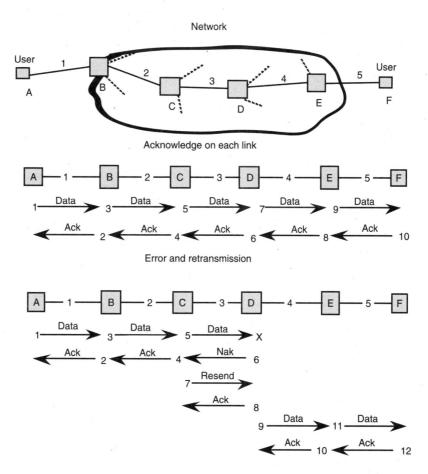

cussion. Each receiving machine performs an error check as described in Fig. 3-8, and returns an ACK to the sending machine. If an error is detected, as seen in the bottom part of the figure (the x symbolizes this error), a NAK is returned to the sending machine, which resends the traffic.

End-to-End Error Recovery

Figure 3-10 illustrates the operations in an end-to-end recovery. In this example, error recovery is performed at the transport layer (layer 4). Once again, an error is detected by the data link layer at switch D, which takes no other action except to discard the damaged frame (or frames). The dotted lines in the bottom figure signify that the traffic is not sent on to the other links and is not received by user B.

Figure 3-10
End-to-end error recovery.

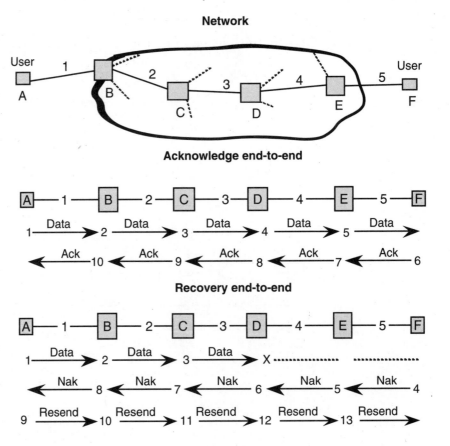

Recovery from this error can occur in a number of ways. If other frames are being sent to user F, the transport layer will note that traffic is arriving out of sequence, since the discarded transport PDUs (TPDUs) are not received by F. Therefore, a layer 4 NAK is sent from user F to user A, which has stored copies of the TPDUs in a transport layer buffer. The transport layer at A will resend the traffic to F, as shown in the bottom part of Fig. 3-10.

Another approach is for the transport layer at F to do nothing but send back a TPDU indicating that it is still expecting the traffic for which it is has missing sequence numbers. Eventually, a timer at A will expire, and the transport layer will resend the missing traffic.

Pros and Cons of Each.   As a rule of thumb, link-to-link error recovery is more effective on error-prone links, and end-to-end error recovery is more effective on relatively error-free links. For example, in Fig. 3-9, the error recovery is made in a timely manner at the link layer between the two machines on the link. No other traffic is introduced into the network.

In contrast, in Fig. 3-10, the transport layer NAK and resend operations introduce additional traffic into the network. Each link must carry the layer 4 NAK, and the retransmitted TPDU(s). This additional overhead is not a big problem if the incidence of errors is low, but frequent errors will require many layer 4 retransmissions, which will invariably lead to a heavier load on the links and machines operating between the two users.

Most vendors still employ link-to-link error recovery in their products. Even though it introduces more overhead, this overhead is not very great, and layer 2 error recovery operations are very fast. One exception to this practice is found in networks running the asynchronous transfer mode (ATM) protocol, which performs error checking at each link, but does not perform any ACK/NAK or retransmission services. ATM assumes the link is relatively error free.

Layer 2 Requirements Cited by ITU-T Q.921 and ANSI T1.602

The ITU-T Q.921 and ANSI T1.602 core functions are organized around five very elementary procedures (see Table 3-2). Most of them pertain to

Table 3-2

"Core" Functions of
Frame Relay

- Frame delimiting, alignment, and flag transparency
- Virtual circuit multiplexing and demultiplexing
- Octet alignment of the traffic
- Checking for maximum and minimum frame sizes
- Detection of transmission, format, and operational errors

layer 2 operations. First, a Frame Relay system must provide services to delimit and align a frame, and to provide transparency of the flags with zero bit stuffing and unstuffing. Second, the Frame Relay system must support virtual circuit multiplexing and demultiplexing through the use of the DLCI field in the frame. Third, the system must inspect the frame to make certain it aligns itself an integral number of octets prior to the zero-bit insertion and following the unstuffing of the zero bit. Fourth, the system must inspect the frame to ensure that it does not exceed the maximum and minimum frame sizes. Fifth, the system must be able to detect transmission errors through the use of the FCS, as well as formatting problems and other operational errors.

A Typical Frame Relay Configuration

With the preceding discussion in mind, let us redraw Fig. 3-6 slightly, yielding a more practical depiction of a Frame Relay configuration (Fig. 3-11). In most installations, Frame Relay does not operate in the end-user workstation/host. Rather, Frame Relay is loaded into a router. This approach keeps the user stations isolated from Frame Relay, which also means the users' equipment and software do not have to be revamped when Frame Relay is installed.

If a station is attached to a local area network (LAN), the router terminates the LAN protocol, and encapsulates headers and payload of the upper layers into a Frame Relay frame, which includes all layers from layer 3 to layer 7 (N, T, S, P, A) in Fig. 3-11.

This information is transported through the Frame Relay network to the final destination. There it is passed to a router, which strips off the Frame Relay headers and trailers, places the traffic into a LAN frame, and delivers the traffic to the destination end station.

Figure 3-11
Typical Frame Relay
configuration.

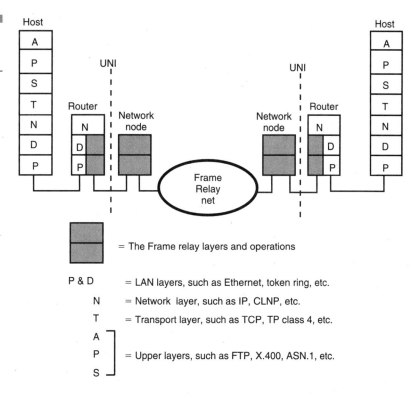

= The Frame relay layers and operations

P & D   = LAN layers, such as Ethernet, token ring, etc.

N   = Network layer, such as IP, CLNP, etc.

T   = Transport layer, such as TCP, TP class 4, etc.

A
P   = Upper layers, such as FTP, X.400, ASN.1, etc.
S

SUMMARY

The data link layer is the focus of operations for Frame Relay. Thus, the name Frame Relay is used because the data link PDUs are called frames. Frame Relay is a "stripped down" implementation of the data link layer, and provides only the services required for traffic to be transmitted and received on a data link. The operations are based on HDLC and LAPD.

Basics of ISDN

This chapter introduces the reader to the Integrated Services Digital Network (ISDN). The layers of ISDN are examined with particular emphasis on layers 2 and 3, since these layers are part of many Frame Relay operations. Examples of operations on these layers are examined, and the final part of the chapter describes the relationship of Frame Relay to ISDN. The reader may wish to pay particular attention to the discussions on LAPD and Q931, since these protocols are used by Frame Relay (with some modifications).

Rationale for ISDN

The communications facilities to support user applications are numerous and diverse. The communications systems are supported by analog dial-up telephone lines (POTS: plain old telephone service). These dial-up lines may support voice and/or data, which require different types of interfaces. In addition, many companies have dedicated leased lines, either analog or digital, or perhaps a combination of both. Added to these systems are the older Telex services. To make matters more complex, many organizations subscribe to public packet network carrier services, or may have their own private packet network. Finally, some organizations have installed their own private circuit switched systems.

This mélange of systems creates many types of access problems. Different access protocols are used for the voice and data carriers. In many instances, different physical connectors are used for the devices, and different protocols are required. Moreover, different types of lines are needed to support these services.

The goal of ISDN is to reduce the number of interfaces, access protocols, and connectors. Equally important, these components are standardized, and vendor-specific solutions are eliminated.

In essence, ISDN gives digital connectivity to the end user. ISDN extends digital technology over the subscriber loop to the end-user terminal by using common telephone wiring, common protocols, and standard interfaces. Ideally, numerous and diverse interfaces are reduced (or eliminated) by adopting a limited set of common conventions.

Thus, an integrated services digital network (ISDN) provides end-to-end digital connectivity to support a wide range of services. In essence, all images (voice, data, television, facsimile, etc.) are transmitted with digital technology.

The ISDN approach is to provide an end user with full support through the seven layers of the OSI model. However, ISDN does not define all these layers. ISDN is divided into two kinds of services: *bearer services*, which are responsible for supporting the lowest three layers of the seven-layer standard, and *teleservices* (for example, telephone, Teletex, Videotex message handling), which are responsible for providing support through all seven layers of the model, generally making use of the underlying lower-layer capabilities of bearer services. The services are referred to as low-layer and high-layer functions, respectively. ISDN operates at the lower three layers of OSI.

The ISDN Layers

The ISDN functions are allocated according to the layering principles of the OSI and ITU-T standards. Various entities of the layers are used to provide full end-to-end capability. These layered capabilities may be supplied by postal, telephone, and telegraph ministries (PTTs), telephone companies, or other suppliers.

The ISDN layers are depicted in Fig. 4-1, with the appropriate ISDN standards identified for each layer. Many of the I Series documents cited in Fig. 4-1 do not contain any information on the operations of the lay-

Figure 4-1
The layers of ISDN.

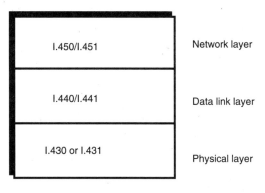

I.450/I.451	Network layer
I.440/I.441	Data link layer
I.430 or I.431	Physical layer

I.430 = Basic Rate
I.431 = Primary Rate
I.440 = LAPD
I.441 = LAPD
I.450 = Message layer
I.451 = Message layer

Note: Similar standards are published in the ITU-T
Q series (the I Series defer to the Q series)

ers. Rather, the documents refer to the ITU-T Q Series recommendations. The reader should obtain the Q Series for a description of the details of the layers. For example, the network layer documents titled I.450/I.451 actually reference Q931.

The ISDN Terminal

The ISDN user device depicted in Fig. 4-2*a* is identified by the ISDN term *TE1* (terminal equipment, type 1). The TE1 connects to the ISDN

Figure 4-2
ISDN configurations.

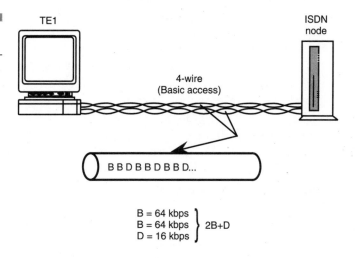

(a) TE1 configuration.

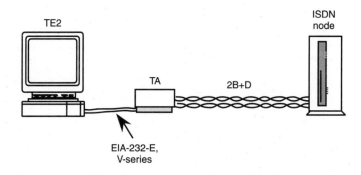

(b) TE2 configuration.

through a twisted-pair four-wire digital link. This link uses time division multiplexing (TDM) to provide three channels, designated B, B, and D (or 2 B + D). The B channels operate at a speed of 64 kbps; the D channel operates at 16 kbps. Thus, the user access rate is 64 kbps + 64 kbps + 16 kbps = 144 kbps. The 2 B + D is designated the basic rate interface. ISDN also allows up to eight TE1s to share one 2 B + D channel (an ISDN bus).

Figure 4-2*b* illustrates another ISDN option. In this scenario, the user DTE is called a *TE2* device. This is the current equipment in use today; examples are workstations, personal computers, and so forth. The TE2 connects to the terminal adapter (TA), which is a device that allows non-ISDN terminals to operate over ISDN lines. The user side of the TA typically uses a conventional physical level interface such as EIA-232, EIA-422, or one of the V-series Recommendations. It is packaged as an external modem, or as a board that plugs into an expansion slot in the TE2 devices.

Other Configurations, Basic Access, and Primary Access

The TA and TE2 devices are connected through the basic access to either an ISDN NT1 or NT2 device (*NT* stands for network termination). Figure 4-3 shows one of the options. The NT1 is a customer premises device that connects the four-wire subscriber wiring to the conventional two-wire local loop. ISDN allows up to eight terminal devices to be addressed by an NT1. The NT1 is responsible for physical layer functions, such as signaling synchronization and timing. It provides the user with a standardized interface.

The NT2 is a more intelligent piece of customer premises equipment. It is typically found in digital PBXs, multiplexers, and the like. The NT2 device is capable of performing concentration services. It multiplexes 23

Figure 4-3
ISDN network termination (NT).

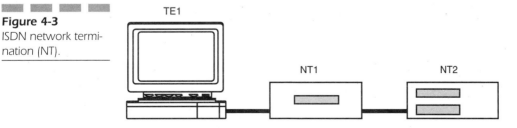

B + D channels onto the line at a combined rate of 1.544 Mbps, or 30 B + D channels for a combined rate of 2.048 Mbps. This function is called the *ISDN primary rate access*. The 1.544-Mbps rate is designated T1 in North America and Japan; the 2.048-Mbps rate is designated E1 in Europe.

ISDN also supports other channels. The H0 channel supports six B channels at 384 kbps; the H11 channel supports 24 B channels at 1536 kbps; the H12 channel supports 30 B channels at 1920 kbps.

The NT1 and NT2 devices can be combined into a single device called NT12. This device handles the physical, data link, and network layer functions.

Layer 2 of ISDN

LAPD (Link Access Procedure, D Channel) is the data link control protocol (Fig. 4-4). LAPD allows devices to communicate with one another across the ISDN D Channel. It is specifically designed for the link across the ISDN user-to-network interface.

LAPD has a frame format very similar to that of HDLC and LAPB. LAPD provides for two octets for the address field. Each ISDN basic access can support up to eight stations. The address field is used to identify the specific terminal on the channel. The *service access point* (SAP) identifies a layer entity operating in the terminal above the LAPD layer. The address field contains the address field extension bits, a

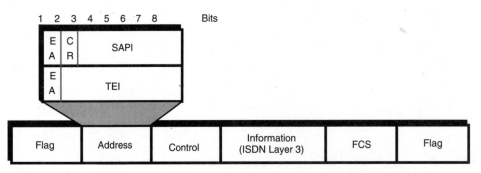

Note: Frame relay uses this format, with major changes to the address and control fields.

Figure 4-4   The LAPD frame.

command/response indication bit, a *service access point identifier* (SAPI), and a *terminal endpoint identifier* (TEI).

The purpose of the address field extension is to provide more bits for an address. The presence of a 1 in the first bit of an address field octet signifies that it is the final octet of the address field. Consequently, a two-octet address would have a field address extension value of 0 in the first octet and 1 in the second. The address field extension bit allows the use of both the SAPI in the first octet and the TEI in the second octet, if desired.

The command/response (C/R) field bit identifies the frame as either a command or a response. The user side sends commands with the C/R bit set to 0. It responds with the C/R bit set to 1. The network does the opposite—it sends commands with C/R set to 1 and responses with C/R set to 0.

The service access point identifier (SAPI) identifies the point where the data link layer services are provided to the layer above LAPD. The terminal endpoint identifier (TEI) identifies a specific connection within the SAP. It can identify either a single terminal (TE) or multiple terminals. The TEI is assigned by a separate assignment procedure. Collectively, the TEI and SAPI are called the *data link connection identifier* (DLCI), which identifies each data link connection on the D channel. Table 4-1 lists and describes the SAPI and TEI fields.

Table 4-1

LAPD Address Values

SAPI	
Value	**Related Entity**
0	Call control procedures
16	Packet procedures
32–47	Reserved for national use
63	Management procedures
Others	Reserved

TEI	
Value	**User Type**
0–63	Nonautomatic assignment
64—126	Automatic assignment

Layer 3 of ISDN (Q.931)

The ISDN layer 3 specifications (ITU-T recommendations I.450/I.451 and Q.930/Q.931) use many of the OSI concepts. They encompass circuit switch connections, packet switch connections, and user-to-user connections, and specify the procedures to establish, manage, and clear a network connection at the ISDN user-to-network interface.

The more widely used messages are summarized in Table 4-2 and a brief description of these messages follows. The table also shows which

Table 4-2

ISDN Layer 3
Messages

Call Establishment Messages	Call Disestablishment Messages
ALERTING*	DETACH
CALL PROCEEDING*	DETACHACKNOWLEDGE
CONNECT*	DISCONNECT*
CONNECTACKNOWLEDGE*	RELEASE*
SETUP*	RELEASECOMPLETE*
SETUPACKNOWLEDGE	
PROGRESS*	

Call Information Phase Messages	Miscellaneous Messages
RESUME	CANCEL
RESUME ACKNOWLEDGE	CANCEL ACKNOWLEDGE
RESUME REJECT	CANCEL REJECT
SUSPEND	CONGESTION CONTROL
SUSPEND ACKNOWLEDGE	FACILITY
SUSPEND REJECT	FACILITY ACKNOWLEDGE
USER INFORMATION	FACILITY REJECT
	INFORMATION
	REGISTER
	REGISTER ACKNOWLEDGE
	REGISTER REJECT
	STATUS*
	STATUS ENQUIRY*

*These messages are used for Frame Relay Digital Subscriber Signaling System Number 1 (DSS1).

Q931 messages are used with the Frame Relay Digital Signaling System Number 1 (DSS1). This specification is published by the ITU-T (Q933) and ANSI (T1.617) to define the operations for the establishment of a connection. A more detailed explanation of how they are used with Frame Relay is provided in Chap. 10.

The SETUP message is sent by the user or the network to the establishment procedures. The message contains several parameters to define the circuit connection, and it must contain the following three:

- *Protocol discriminator:* Distinguishes between user-to-network call control messages and others, such as other layer 3 protocols (Frame Relay and ATM, for example).
- *Call reference:* Identifies the ISDN call at the local user-to-network interface. It does not have end-to-end significance. All messages pertaining to one connection contain the same call reference number value.
- *Message type:* Identifies the message function; that is to say, the types shown in Table 4-2.

Other parameters include the specific ISDN channel identification, origination, and destination addresses, an address for a redirected call, the designation for a transit network, and so forth.

The SETUP ACKNOWLEDGE message is sent by the user or the network to indicate that call establishment has been initiated. The parameters for the SETUP ACK message are similar to the SETUP message.

The CALL PROCEEDING message is sent by the network or the user to indicate the call is being processed. The message also indicates that the network has all the information it needs to process the call.

The CONNECT message and the CONNECT ACKNOWLEDGE messages are exchanged between the network and the network user to indicate that the call is accepted by either the network or the user. These messages contain parameters to identify the session, facilities, and services associated with the connection.

To clear a call, the user or the network can send a RELEASE or DISCONNECT message. Typically, the RELEASE COMPLETE is returned, but the network can maintain the call reference for later use, in which case the network sends a DETACH message to the user.

A call can be temporarily suspended. The SUSPEND message is used to create this action. The network can respond to this message with either a SUSPEND ACKNOWLEDGE or a SUSPEND REJECT.

During an ongoing ISDN connection, the user or network can issue CONGESTION CONTROL messages to control the flow of USER INFORMATION messages. The message simply indicates whether or not the receiver is ready to accept messages.

The USER INFORMATION message is sent by the user or the network to transmit information to a (another) user.

If a call is suspended, the RESUME message is sent by the user to request resumption of the call. This message can invoke a RESUME ACKNOWLEDGE or a RESUME REJECT.

The STATUS message is sent by the user or the network to report on the conditions of the call.

REGISTER ACKNOWLEDGE, REGISTER REJECT: Initiates the registration of a REGISTER facility (as well as confirmation and/or rejection).

FACILITY, FACILITY ACKNOWLEDGE, FACILITY REJECT: Initiates access to a network facility (as well as confirmation or rejection).

CANCEL, CANCEL ACKNOWLEDGE, CANCEL REJECT: Indicates a request to discontinue a facility (as well as confirmation or rejection).

The ISDN supports numerous facilities (see Table 4-3), which are managed with the following messages. Most of these facilities are self-explanatory. It is evident that the connections of ISDN and X.25 have been given much thought by the standards groups.

Network Layer Message Format

The ISDN network layer protocol uses messages to communicate between the user device and the network. Frame Relay DSS 1 also uses this message for its operations. The format for these messages is shown in Fig. 4-5. The message consists of the following fields (these fields were explained with the SETUP message):

- Protocol discriminator (required)
- Call reference (required)
- Message type (required)
- Mandatory information elements (as required)
- Additional information elements (as required)

The ISDN also enables other message formats to accommodate equip-

Table 4-3

ISDN Layer 3
Facilities

Delivery of origin address barred
Connected address required
Supply charging information after end of call
Reverse charging requested
Connect outgoing calls when free
Reverse charging acceptance (allowed)
Call redirection/diversion notification
Call completion after busy request
Call completion after busy indication
Origination address required on outgoing calls
Origination address required on incoming calls
Destination address required on incoming calls
Connect incoming calls when free (waiting allowed)
X.25 extended packet sequence numbering (Modulo 128)
X.25 flow control parameter negotiation allowed
X.25 throughput class negotiation allowed
X.25 packet retransmission (allowed)
X.25 fast select (outgoing) (allowed)
X.25 fast select acceptance allowed
X.25 multilink procedure
X.25 Local charging prevention
X.25 extended frame sequence numbering

Figure 4-5
The ISDN layer 3
message format.

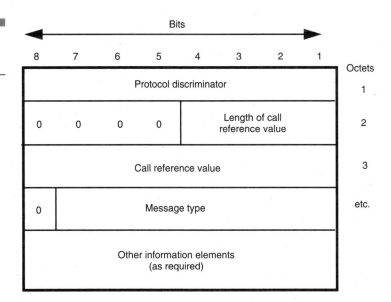

Note: This message format is used by frame relay DDS1.

ment needs and different information elements. This feature provides considerable flexibility in choosing other options and ISDN services.

Example of an ISDN Call

Figure 4-6 illustrates a typical procedure for an ISDN call. Note the use of the ISDN messages that were discussed earlier. For the sake of simplicity, the physical and data link layer operations are not shown in this figure, and the local side of a connection is illustrated.

When the telephone is picked up (goes off-hook), the TE1 device issues a SETUP message to the ISDN network. As we learned earlier, this

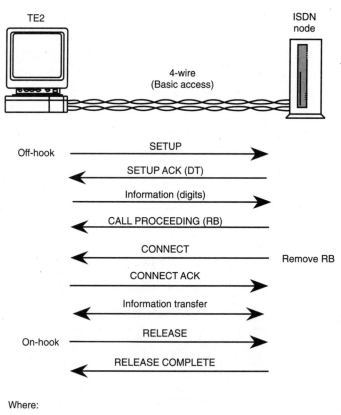

Figure 4-6
The ISDN layer operations (local side).

message initiates the call setup procedures. It contains a protocol discriminator, call reference identifier, plus the message type and other optional identifiers that depend on the actual implementation. The ISDN node replies with a SETUP ACK, which is used by the TE1 to provide dial tone to the telephone. The user then enters the telephone number (the dialed digits), which are sent to the ISDN node.

A CALL PROCEEDING message is returned from the ISDN node to the originating device; it is used by the TE1 to transmit a ring-back to the user telephone. Once the connection has been made, the network sends a connect message to the originating device, which removes the ring-back signal.

Once these procedures have occurred on both sides of the ISDN interface, the users are allowed to send traffic through the B or D channels. The session is disconnected with the RELEASE and RELEASE COMPLETE messages illustrated at the bottom of the figure. These actions tear down a B channel.

Relationship Between Frame Relay and ISDN

The ANSI T1.617 and ITU-T Q.933 recommendations define procedures for the use of Frame Relay operations at an ISDN user-to-network interface. These standards define the procedures at an I, S, T, or U reference point for B channel, H channel, and D channel operations. The operations are also applicable to basic rate and primary rate interfaces.

Frame Relay operations can utilize semipermanent access connections or demand access connections (that is to say, access on an as-needed basis). These operations are in accordance with conventional ISDN interfaces.

The Frame Relay connection control operations are performed (whenever possible) by the Q and I standards published by the ITU-T. As examples, the ISDN user call states are implemented, as are some of the Q.931 messages (described earlier in this chapter).

Since the ISDN-based layer 3 Frame Relay operations are described in the Q.933 and T.617 specification, we will defer more detailed discussions to Chap. 9, which is devoted to these standards and the Frame Relay signaling procedures.

SUMMARY

The ISDN architecture is a fundamental and important aspect of Frame Relay services between the user side and the network interface. Many of the Frame Relay operations at the link layer are derived from ISDN's link access procedure for the D channel (LAPD), and the ISDN network layer functions published in Q931 are used to set up calls and negotiate various Frame Relay parameters.

Basics of X.25

This chapter provides an overview of X.25. The major operations of X.25 are discussed, as is the rationale for the design decisions made by the X.25 developers. X.25 packets and X.25 facilities are described as well. The chapter concludes by providing a comparison of X.25 and Frame Relay operations.

Why X.25 Was Developed

In the late 1960s and early 1970s, many data communications networks were created by companies, government agencies, and other organizations. The design and programming of these networks were performed by each organization to fulfill specific business needs. During this time, an organization had no reason to adhere to any common convention for its data communications protocols, since the organization's private network provided services only to itself. Consequently, these networks used specialized protocols that were tailored to the organization's requirements.

During this period, several companies and telephone administrations in the United States, Canada, and Europe implemented a number of public data networks. These systems were conceived to provide a service for data traffic that paralleled the telephone system's service for voice traffic. They are known today by several other names: *public packet networks* (PPN), *public packet switched networks* (PPSN), and *packet switched data networks* (PSDN).

X.25 was conceived with the goal of establishing a limited set of interface conventions to a data communications packet network. It was developed primarily due to the impetus and direction of several telecommunications organizations, especially the European telecommunications administrations. Consequently, the specification is written more from the perspective of the network than from the user device, and earlier implementations of X.25 were sometimes ill-defined as to the required actions of the user device.

Assumptions Made by the X.25 Designers

X.25 is an old protocol. It was developed in the early 1970s and published by the ITU-T in 1974. Consequently, the assumptions made by the designers of X.25 were based on the correct perceptions (at that time) that user devices were quite limited in their intelligence, and communications systems were unreliable. From these two valid assumptions, X.25 was designed to provide service to relatively unintelligent user devices by providing rather extensive editing, flow control, and error-checking services.

X.25 was also designed as a connection-oriented system, in which calls were mapped up between the users and the network in a fashion somewhat similar to a telephone call. This means that X.25 is a connection-oriented protocol. Therefore, the concepts of *switched virtual calls* (SVCs) and *permanent virtual circuits* (PVCs) are fundamental to the architecture of X.25. The idea of the connectionless datagram, while implemented in an earlier version of X.25, does not exist in current X.25-based networks.

Assumptions Made by the Frame Relay Designers

The design assumptions that led to X.25 are important to understand, because Frame Relay networks make exactly the opposite assumptions. They assume that end-user devices are quite intelligent and can perform rather extensive editing, flow control, and data integrity services. They also assume that networks are much more reliable than they were a few years ago, and that errors are few. Therefore, it makes little sense to expend resources on error resolution operations.

The X.25 Layers

The X.25 Recommendation is divided into three layers (see Fig. 5-1). It consists of entities that reside in the lower three layers of the OSI Model. The *physical layer* provides the physical signaling and connections between the user DTE and the DCE. At this layer, standards such as X.21, X.21bis, EIA-232-E, and V.35 are used. This layer is also called *X.25, layer 1*. The physical layer, while focusing on a few standards (such as the ITU-T V Series modems), can be implemented with a variety of techniques, such as Ethernet interfaces, T1 carriers, and so forth.

The *data link layer* is responsible for the management of the flow of

Figure 5-1
The X.25 layers.

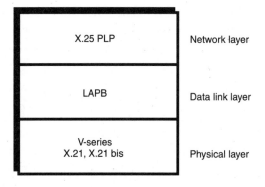

X.25 PLP	Network layer
LAPB	Data link layer
V-series X.21, X.21 bis	Physical layer

PLP = Packet layer procedures
LAPB = Link access procedure, balanced

data between the user equipment, called *data terminal equipment* (DTE), and the network equipment, called *data circuit terminating equipment* (DCE). It performs error checking and retransmits data if they are distorted during transfer on the link. It is responsible for the error-free transmission of the X.25 packet across the link. This layer uses the LAPB protocol (link access procedure, balanced). It is also called the *frame layer* (because it creates and uses the LAPB frame), as well as *X.25, layer 2*.

The *network layer* is responsible for creating the X.25 packet and managing the connection with the network through the exchange of packets with the DCE. It relies on the data link layer to transport the packet safely between the DTE and the DCE. It is also called the *packet level* and *X.25, layer 3*. The packet is encapsulated into the frame for transmission to/from the DTE and DCE.

X.25 Data Link Layer Operations

The primary purpose of the X.25 data link layer is to transport the packet error-free across the communications link between the user device and the packet exchange. The data link layer is also responsible for controlling the flow of traffic on the link, and informing the X.25 network layer about unusual link problems such as excessive errors or a link failure. While these services are limited, they are quite important, and X.25 cannot function without them.

The X.25 data link layer performs the services described in Chap. 3

(see "Operations of a Conventional Data Link Protocol"). The uninitiated reader should refer to that section.

Today, the vast majority of offerings support the X.25 data link layer with link access procedure, balanced (LAPB). Earlier versions use link access procedure (LAP). Some organizations still use the older binary synchronous (Bisync) protocols for the data link layer.

X.25 Network Layer Operations

X.25 network nodes and DTEs employ *statistical time division multiplexing (STDM)* techniques to transfer the users' traffic into and out of the network. The user DTE and the network nodes are jointly responsible for multiplexing user sessions onto a single communications line. In other words, instead of dedicating one line to each user, the DTE and network nodes interleave many users' bursty traffic across an X.25 interface (the interface is between the DTE and network nodes). The user perceives that a line is dedicated to that user's application, but the user is actually sharing it with other users.

The multiplexing of more than one user onto a physical communications line is one aspect of an important feature of X.25, called the *virtual circuit* (see Fig. 5-2). In this context, *virtual* means that a user perceives

Figure 5-2
X.25 architecture.

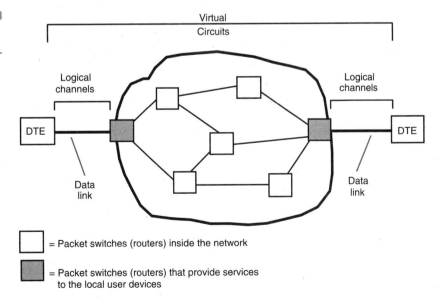

Virtual
Circuits

Logical channels

Logical channels

DTE

DTE

Data link

Data link

☐ = Packet switches (routers) inside the network

▨ = Packet switches (routers) that provide services to the local user devices

the availability of a dedicated, physical resource, when in practice the resource is being shared. X.25 uses the term *logical channel* to describe another aspect of this concept. The terms virtual and logical are often used erroneously to convey the same meaning. It is preferable to define these two terms more concisely:

- *Virtual circuit* is the end-to-end connection relationship (through a network) between two user devices (DTEs). Since intermediate packet switches are used to route the data through the network, the virtual circuit usually consists of multiple physical circuits. It is the responsibility of the network to maintain the end-to-end connection of the users.

- *Logical channel* is the local connection relationship between the user DTE and the network—that is, the connection between the user device and the packet exchange. The logical channel has significance only at the DTE and DCE interface on each side of the network. Therefore, a logical channel exists on each side of the network cloud. It is the task of the network to map the two logical channels to a virtual circuit.

Permanent Virtual Circuits

A *permanent virtual circuit* (PVC) is analogous to a leased line in a telephone network (see Fig. 5-3). The transmitting computer is assured of obtaining a session (connection) with the receiving computer through

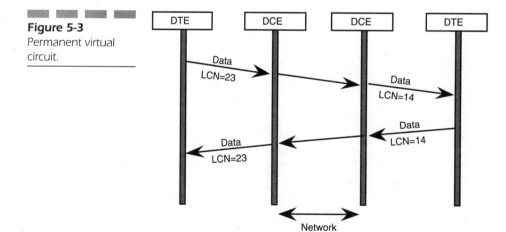

Figure 5-3
Permanent virtual circuit.

Basics of X.25

the packet network. X.25 requires that a PVC be established before the session begins. Consequently, an agreement must be reached by the two users and the packet network carrier before a permanent virtual connection will be allocated. Among other things, this includes the reservation of a *logical channel number* (LCN) for the PVC user.

Thereafter, when a device sends a packet into the packet network, the LCN in the packet identifies that the requesting machine has a PVC to the receiving machine. Consequently, services are provided by the network without further session negotiation. PVCs require no call setup or clearing procedures, and the logical channel is continually in a data transfer state.

Switched Virtual Calls

An X.25 *switched virtual call* (SVC) resembles some of the procedures associated with telephone dial-up lines, because call setup and breakdown procedures are employed (see Fig. 5-4). The calling machine (an X.25 DTE)

Figure 5-4
Switched virtual call.

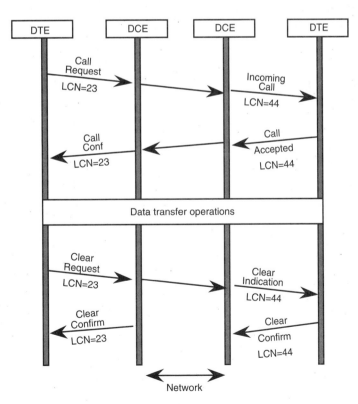

issues a special X.25 packet called a Call Request packet to the network with an LCN and the address of the called DTE. The network uses the address to route the Call Request packet to the remote switch that is to support the call at the remote end. This DCE then sends an Incoming Call packet to the proper DTE.

Logical channel numbering is done on each side of the network, and the LCN at the local DTE/DCE (LCN = 23) is most likely a value different from the LCN at the remote DTE/DCE (LCN = 44). The specific DTE-to-DTE session is identified at all times with the same pair of LCNs. Inside the network, the intermediate packet-switching nodes may also perform their own LCN numbering, but X.25 does not require LCN identification within a network. Remember, the activities within the network are beyond the scope of the X.25 recommendation.

If the receiving DTE chooses to acknowledge and accept the call request, it transmits a Call Accepted packet to the network. The network then transports this packet to the requesting DTE in the form of a Call Connected packet. The channel enters a data transfer state after the call establishment. This action creates an end-to-end virtual circuit.

To terminate the session, a Clear Request packet is sent by either the DTE or the network. It is received as a Clear Indication packet and confirmed with the Clear Confirm packet. After the call is cleared, the LCNs are made available for another session. If the DTEs establish another virtual call session with each other, they must repeat the procedures just discussed.

X.25 Packets

This section introduces the X.25 packet and the fields within the packet. Using Fig. 5-5 as a reference, the standard convention in the X.25 document is to show the octets (bytes) in the packet on a vertical plane, with the first octet stacked on top of the second octet, and so on. The eight bits of each octet are aligned in a horizontal plane with the low-order bits placed to the right side of the page.

Every X.25 packet must contain a three-octet header. The header consists of the *general format identifier* (GFI), the *logical channel fields,* and the *packet type identifier.*

The GFI is used to identify the range of values to be used for the

Figure 5-5
The X.25 packet format (for connection management packets).

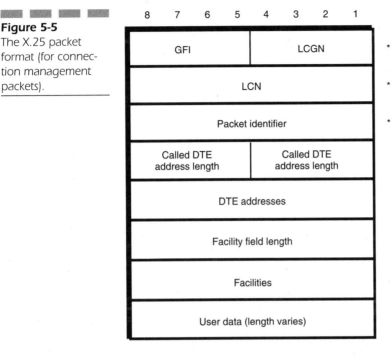

8	7	6	5	4	3	2	1	
GFI				LCGN				*
LCN								*
Packet identifier								*
Called DTE address length				Called DTE address length				
DTE addresses								
Facility field length								
Facilities								
User data (length varies)								

Note: * = one octet each, other fields of variable length. For connection management packets.

sequence numbers in the packets; the type of address to be used during the session setup, if the user wishes end-to-end acknowledgments of the packets; and some other operations.

The two logical channel fields are the logical channel group number (LCGN) in bits 1–4 of the first octet and the LCN in the second octet. The LCN combined with the logical channel group number provides the complete logical channel identification of 12 bits, which gives a total possibility of 4095 logical channels (256×16 less the 0 channel). The 0 LCN is reserved for DCE control use. Networks use these two fields in various ways. Some networks use the two together; other networks treat them as separate fields.

The third octet of the packet header is the packet type identifier field. It is used to identify the type of packet and provide other control functions for a data packet. The X.25 packets are used for a variety of functions. Some of the packets are used to set up a virtual circuit, as in

Fig. 5-4. Others are used for flow control operations, such as the Receive Ready (RR) packet and the Receive Not Ready (RNR) packet. Others are used to recover from problems, such as the Reset, Restart, and Diagnostic packets.

Why Sequence at the Packet and Frame Levels?

Sending and receiving numbers are used to coordinate and acknowledge transmissions of the packets between the DTE and DCE. The receiving DTE or DCE must know which packet receiving sequence number to send back to the transmitting device to properly acknowledge the specific packet.

X.25 sequencing is similar to the operations found in LAPB sequencing. LAPB and X.25 provide for independent (R) and (S) sequencing. However, the difference between the data link and network sequencing is significant. The data link layer sequence numbers are used to account for *all* the logical channels' traffic on the communications link, and to manage the flow control on the link. However, the network level sequence numbers are used to manage the traffic of *each* logical channel session on the line.

The supposition of Frame Relay is that these operations are both redundant and unnecessary. Therefore, Frame Relay provides no sequencing in any of its operations. As we have stated before, sequencing is left to the end-user application, typically in the transport layer.

X.25 States, Error Handling, and the Frame Relay Approach

Since X.25 is a connection-oriented protocol, it must maintain considerable information about the ongoing connections. It must also maintain information about data transfer operations. It contains many rules on how connections are managed through the state tables, and the actions that must be taken by the DCE or DTE upon the receipt of specific packets while in certain states.

The point is that X.25 has extensive editing and diagnostic tools, all resulting in a very feature-rich service—with resultant delay and overhead. These operations create computational overhead. As we shall see, Frame Relay eliminates almost all of these operations.

The Frame Relay Approach to States and Errors

Frame Relay also uses states, which are based on the ISDN Q931 Recommendation. A number of vendors do not implement Q931 with Frame Relay, however. Furthermore, Frame Relay has very few error checking and diagnostic features. Thus, the Frame Relay approach yields a relatively featureless service that is considerably faster than X.25.

X.25 Facilities and the Frame Relay Approach

X.25 has some very useful features called *facilities*. They are described in X.25 and in X.2. Table 5-1 lists the X.25 facilities that were published in the 1988 Blue Book. They are largely self-explanatory. As the reader might expect, Frame Relay networks do not offer facility services.

Comparison of X.25 Operations to Frame Relay Operations

This section provides a more detailed comparison of Frame Relay and X.25 operations at the data link and network layers.

First a brief discourse is provided on the physical layer. X.25 has been criticized because its physical layer is slow. It stipulates slow-speed physical interfaces such as V.28 and EIA-232-E. In contrast, Frame Relay typically employs a high-speed physical interface between the user device and the network switch, such as DS1, E1, or subrates thereof. Nothing precludes using a faster physical level operation on an X.25 interface. This approach would entail placing X.25's layer 2 (LAPB) and layer 3 (packet layer procedures) on top of a technology such as DS1 and E1. Therefore, the claim by some people that X.25 is inherently slow at the physical layer is due to the fact that many products are packaged with

Table 5-1

Facilities for Packet
Switched Service

Facility Name
Extended frame sequence numbering
Multilink procedure
Online facility registration
Extended packet sequence numbering (Modulo 128)
D-bit modification
Packet retransmission
Incoming calls barred
Outgoing calls barred
One-way logical channel outgoing
One-way logical channel incoming
Nonstandard default packet sizes 16, 32, 64, 256, 512, 1024, 2048
Nonstandard default window sizes
Default throughput classes assignment
Flow control parameter negotiation
Throughput class negotiation
Closed user group
Closed user group with outgoing access
Closed user group with incoming access
Incoming calls barred within a closed user group
Outgoing calls barred within a closed user group
Bilateral closed user group
Bilateral closed user group with outgoing access
Fast select acceptance
Reverse charging acceptance
Local charging prevention
Network user identification subscription
NUI override
Charging information
RPOA subscription
Hunt group
Call redirection
A bit (TOA/NPI)
Direct call

the X.25-compliant physical layer, but higher-speed interfaces can certainly be obtained.

The Data Link Layer

Table 5-2 shows the major operations of X.25's link layer, LAPB, and the Frame Relay data link services. It is readily evident that LAPB provides a much more extensive service than Frame Relay. Of course, this concept is central to the philosophy of Frame Relay: eliminate much of the overhead and operations at the data link layer.

The Network Layer

Table 5-3 shows the major operations of X.25's network layer and the Frame Relay "network layer" services (one could argue that Frame Relay does not have a network layer). It is readily evident that X.25 provides a much more extensive service than Frame Relay. As with the data link

Table 5-2

Link Layer Features of X.25 and Frame Relay

Feature	X.25 LAPB	Frame Relay
Flag management	X	X
Bit stuffing	X	X
FCS operations	X	X
Discard errors	X	X
Resend errored frames	X	
Sequencing	X	
Retransmission timers	X	
Retry operations	X	
P/F bit operations	X	
Address translation	X	X
Flow control (link layer)	X	
Aborts	X	X
Commands/Responses	X	
Frame muxing/demuxing	X	X

Feature	X.25 LAPB	Frame Relay
PVCs	X	X
SVCs	X	X
Fast selects	X	
Flow control (explicit)	X	
Sequencing	X	
Logical channel ids	X	X
A bit	X	
M bit	X	
D bit	X	
Q bit	X	
Discard eligibility		X
State management	X	
Segmenting	X	
Blocking	X	
Diagnostics	X	L
Facilities (QOS)	X	L
Congestion notification		X
LCN resets	X	
Port restarts	X	
Rejects	X	

Note: L = Limited

layer, this concept is central to the philosophy of Frame Relay relative to the network layer: eliminate much of the overhead and operations at the network layer.

Joint Use of X.25 and Frame Relay?

The reader might wonder how all these X.25 services can be obtained in a Frame Relay network. The answer is that they cannot be obtained in a pure Frame Relay network. If services such as diagnostics, extensive editing, and facilities are desired by a user, then the user should use X.25. Technically speaking, nothing precludes the joint use of X.25 and Frame Relay. However, as a practical matter, Frame Relay was designed to eliminate some of the overhead and cumbersome features of X.25, so running X.25 and Frame Relay together is somewhat akin to reinventing the wheel and then adding yet another wheel.

However, since X.25 contains facilities, and these facilities are often used with applications for direct customer support (for example, a call redirect to another user), it may not be feasible to substitute Frame Relay for X.25. An effective approach in some situations is to run X.25 as part of a user application (layer 3 only), and use Frame Relay as the UNI and transport facility. This means X.25 is tunneled through the Frame Relay network. Chapter 12 provides more information on X.25 and Frame Relay joint operations.

SUMMARY

X.25 is designed to support relatively unintelligent devices through error-prone networks. It has extensive features such as facilities, flow control, and acknowledgments. Its physical layer is based on slow interfaces. Its data link layer is based on LAPB, and its network layer is based on rather cumbersome, but feature-rich packet layer procedures. The Frame Relay approach is to eliminate almost all of these features for the sake of efficiency and speed.

Basic Operations
of Frame Relay

This chapter provides a tutorial on the major functions of Frame Relay networks. The initial part of the chapter describes how Frame Relay manages connections and user data. Issues such as congestion control and congestion notification are discussed. The chapter picks up the earlier discussions on connection identifiers and explains how Frame Relay users are identified to the network through logical connections called *data link connection identifiers* (DLCIs).

Frame Relay: Connection Services and Data Management

Before discussing how Frame Relay manages connections and user data, the reader should be aware that data networks and data communications systems use different techniques for establishing user sessions and managing user traffic. This section provides a brief overview of these important features. Later on, we relate these features to Frame Relay operations.

Connection Services

Protocols are classified as either *connection-oriented* or *connectionless*. The principal characteristics of connection-oriented and connectionless operations are summarized in Table 6-1 and explained in this section.

Connection-Oriented Protocols.   A pure, nonhybrid connection-oriented protocol sets up a connection between the communicating parties before the transfer of data. Usually, some type of relationship is maintained between the data units being transferred through the connection, such as labels that identify the end-to-end connection. These labels

Table 6-1

Connection-Oriented and Connectionless Networks (A Pure Model)

Connection-oriented networks
- Connection mapped through network(s) (may be premapped)
- State tables and other control blocks are maintained
- Abbreviated identifiers (labels) are used after connection setup

Connectionless networks
- Connection mapping does not occur
- State tables and other control blocks are not used
- Full addressing required in each data unit

are usually called *logical channels* or *virtual circuits*; Frame Relay uses the term *data link connection identifiers* (DLCIs).

If the service is between two users and a network, the connection-oriented service requires a three-way agreement between the two end users and the service provider—for instance, the network. This agreement can be made before a session takes place; that is, the connection and services are "premapped"—established (provisioned) before any data transfer takes place. This approach is called a *permanent virtual circuit* (PVC), and is used by Frame Relay.

Many networks allow the communicating parties to negotiate certain options and quality-of-service (QOS) functions before each session. This approach does not use PVCs, but a procedure known as a *switched virtual call* (SVC). During connection establishment, all parties store information about one another, such as addresses and required QOS features. Frame Relay also supports SVC operations.

Once data transfer begins with either a PVC or SVC, the *protocol data units* (PDUs) need not carry much overhead *protocol control information* (PCI, or *headers*). All that is needed is an abbreviated identifier (such as a Frame Relay DLCI) to allow the Frame Relay users' traffic to be identified.

Since certain session characteristics can be negotiated with an SVC, the communicating parties need not have prior knowledge of all of one another's characteristics. If a requested service cannot be provided, some systems allow any of the parties to negotiate the service to a lower level or reject the connection request.

Connectionless Protocols.   The principal characteristics of connectionless systems (also called connectionless-mode) are as follows. First, no logical connection is established between the users and the network. This means that no PVCs or SVCs are created.

Second, the connectionless service manages user *protocol data units* (PDUs) as independent and separate entities. No relationship is maintained between successive data transfers, and few records are kept of the ongoing user-to-user communications process through the network(s).

Generally, the communicating entities must have a prior agreement on how to communicate, and the QOS features must be prearranged. Alternatively, QOS can be provided for each PDU that is transmitted. If so, each PDU must contain fields that identify the types and levels of service.

By its very nature, connectionless service can achieve a high degree of independence from specific protocols within a subnetwork, considerable independence of the subnetworks from one another, and a high degree of independence of the subnetwork(s) from the user-specific protocols.

A connectionless network is more robust than its connection-oriented counterpart, because each PDU is handled as an independent entity. Therefore, PDUs can take different routes to avoid failed nodes or congestion at a point in the network(s). However, connectionless networks do consume more overhead (relative to the length of the headers; proportional to the amount of user data in the PDU) than their connection-oriented counterparts.

A logical connection (i.e., the virtual circuit) can certainly be "nailed up" across more than one physical route in a network, and in the event a primary route fails, the switch can relay the PDU to a secondary route. Therefore, in practice, alternative routing can be obtained for connectionless operations, PVC operations, or SVC operations.

Data Integrity Management Services

The issue of connectionless or connection-oriented services must be separated from that of data integrity management services, because some protocols support one and not the other. Many protocols provide a rich variety of features for the management of user data. As examples, protocols can provide *positive acknowledgments* (ACKs) of traffic through the use of sequence numbers to ensure both that all traffic arrives safely at the receiver, and that it arrives in the proper order. In the latter case, many protocols will resequence the traffic. Data management services often also invoke flow control procedures to prevent devices from sending more traffic than a network or a user device can accommodate.

Negative acknowledgments (NAKs) can also be provided by the protocol, thereby notifying the originator of the traffic that it must resend the traffic or take some type of remedial action.

A protocol that is connection-oriented does not necessarily mean that it also provides data management services. For example, one of the IEEE standards, called *logical link control* (LLC) type 3, is connectionless, yet it provides acknowledgment services.

Is Frame Relay Connection-Oriented or Connectionless?

Even though Frame Relay is connection-oriented, it has very limited data management services. As we have seen in earlier chapters and emphasize more in the remainder of this book, Frame Relay provides no ACKs, no NAKs, and no resequencing operations. Therefore, we can conclude that Frame Relay exhibits connection-oriented behavior in regard to connection management, but that it does not provide many features for the caretaking of user traffic. This function is left to the end-user device, in software that typically resides at the transport layer in a conventional layered model.

Congestion Control

Networks must deal with the problem of *congestion,* a problem that is typically handled in conventional systems at the network layer. Many networks enforce transmission rules, which include agreements on how much traffic can be sent to the network before the traffic flow is regulated (flow-controlled). *Flow control* is an essential ingredient to prevent congestion in a network. Congestion is a problem that is avoided by network administrators (at almost any cost), because it results in severe degradation of the network both in throughput and response time.

Network throughput may increase linearly with the load being offered, but only up to a point. Referring to Fig. 6-1, as the traffic (offered

Figure 6-1
Potential network
congestion problems.

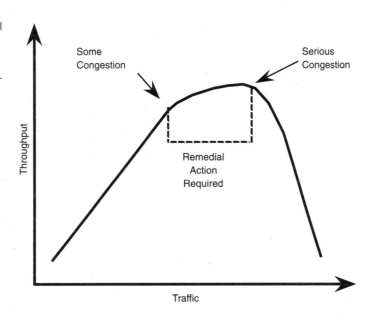

load) in the network reaches a certain point, mild congestion begins to occur, with a resulting drop in throughput. If this drop in performance proceeded in a linear fashion, it would not be much of a problem. However, a point may be reached at which the network traffic load reaches a level that results in a sudden drop in throughput, due to serious congestion and the resultant buildup of the network nodes' queues.

Therefore, even relatively simple networks such as Frame Relay must provide some type of mechanism to inform routers, switches, and other elements in the network when congestion is occurring. They often also provide a flow-control mechanism that can be applied to user devices.

Managing Congestion with Sliding Window Procedures

Many communications protocols use the concept of transmit and receive windows to aid in congestion management operations. A window is established between the communicating partners to provide for reservation of resources at both stations. These "windows" represent the reservation of buffer space at the receiver for the transmitter. In most systems, the window provides both buffer space and sequencing rules. During the initiation of a session (handshake) between the parties, the window is established. For example, if stations A and B are to communicate with each other, station A reserves a receive window for B, and B reserves a receive window for A (see Fig. 6-2).

The windowing concept is necessary to full-duplex protocols because they entail a continuous flow of PDUs into the receiving site without any intermittent stop-and-wait acknowledgments. Consequently, the receiver must have sufficient buffer space to handle the incoming traffic.

A useful feature of the sliding window scheme is the ability of the receiving station to restrict the flow of data from the transmitting station by withholding acknowledgments. This action prevents the transmitter from "opening its windows" and reusing its send sequence number values until the same send sequence numbers have been acknowledged. A sending station can be completely "throttled" if it receives no ACKs from the receiver.

As an example, let us assume a protocol uses numbers in the range of 0–255 for its counters and sequence numbers in the PDU. Once the state variables are incremented through 255, the numbers are reused, beginning with 0. Because the numbers are reused, the stations must not be

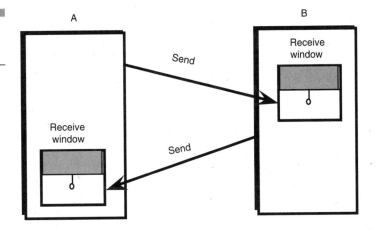

Figure 6-2
Sliding window concepts.

- "Windows" are implemented as reserved buffers, sequence number ranges, and other resources.
- Each station has a negotiated or pre-established window
- A station's sending operations have nothing to do with its receive window.
- Windows "slide" up-and-down as traffic is received and acknowledged.

allowed to send a PDU with a sequence number that has not yet been acknowledged. For example, the station must wait for PDU number 100 to be acknowledged before it uses the value 100 again.

The use of sliding windows provides a relatively simple yet effective method for managing traffic. Since Frame Relay does not have any sequence numbers, it cannot perform any congestion management with sliding window operations. This important task is relegated to an end-user protocol, usually residing in the transport layer of a layered model.

We have much more to say about the subject of congestion management and window in Chap. 9. For the present, the subsequent sections introduce some of the principal congestion management features of Frame Relay.

Major Frame Relay Operations

We now introduce, in a general manner, the major Frame Relay operations. Thereafter, subsequent chapters delve into these operations in more detail. An effective way to get started with the explanation is to examine the contents of a Frame Relay PDU (the Frame Relay frame).

The Frame Relay Frame

The *Frame Relay frame* resembles many other protocols that use the HDLC frame format (see Fig. 6-3). It contains the beginning and ending flag fields which are used to delimit and recognize the frame on the communications link. It does not contain a separate address field; the address field and the control field are combined, and designated in Frame Relay as the *header.* The information field contains user data. The *frame check sequence* (FCS), like other link layer protocols, is used to determine whether the frame has been damaged during transmission on the communications link.

The Frame Relay header consists of six fields. They are listed here and explained in more detail shortly:

- DLCI: The data link connection identifier
- C/R: The command response bit
- EA: The address extension bits
- FECN: The forward explicit congestion notification bit
- BECN: The backward explicit congestion notification bit
- DE: The discard eligibility bit

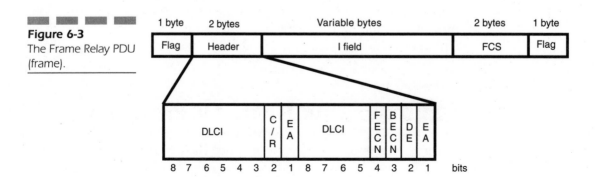

Figure 6-3
The Frame Relay PDU (frame).

The DLCI

The *DLCI* identifies the Frame Relay virtual connection, which is also called a *logical port*. It can identify a user-to-network (UNI) or network-to-network (NNI) virtual connection. The DLCI identifies both directions of the virtual connection. That is, it identifies both the entity to which information is delivered and the entity from which information is received.

The DLCI can vary in size, and can contain two, three, or four octets. This approach allows the use of more DLCI numbers. The extended DLCI fields are explained in Chap. 8.

The FECN and BECN Bits

Two mechanisms are employed to notify users, routers, and/or Frame Relay switches about congestion, and to take corrective action. Both capabilities are achieved by the *backward explicit congestion notification* (BECN) bit and the *forward explicit congestion notification* (FECN) bit (see Fig. 6-4).

Figure 6-4
The congestion notification bits.

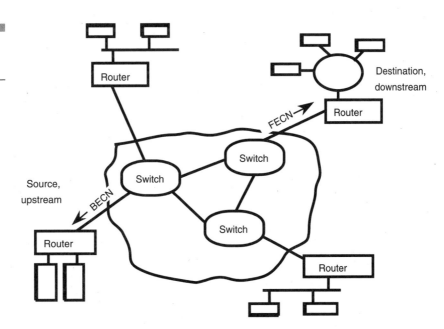

Let us assume that a Frame Relay switch is starting to experience congestion problems due to its buffers (queues) becoming full and/or experiencing a problem with memory management. The switch may inform both the upstream and downstream nodes of the problem by the use of the BECN and FECN bits, respectively. The BECN bit is turned on (set to 1) in the frame and is sent upstream to notify the source of the traffic that congestion exists at a switch in the connection. This notification permits the source machine to flow-control its traffic until the congestion problem is resolved.

In addition, the FECN bit can be set to 1, placed in a frame, and sent to the downstream node to inform it that congestion is occurring upstream. One might question why the FECN is used to notify downstream devices that congestion is occurring upstream. After all, the upstream device is the one creating the traffic problem. The answer varies, depending on the remedial action the downstream (destination) machine might wish to take. For example, the FECN bit might be passed to an upper layer protocol (such as the transport layer), which would enable it either to slow down its acknowledgments to the upstream transport layer (which in some protocols would close the transmit window at the upstream transport layer), or to establish its own restrictive flow control measure with the source machine (which is also allowed in some protocols).

A seemingly obvious solution to the problem is for the source machine to flow-control itself in order to ameliorate the network congestion problem. This might appear to work, but it bears further investigation, and we do just that in Chap. 9.

The DE Bit

Since congestion can be a major problem in any demand-driven network (in which traffic arrives in a somewhat unpredictable or bursty manner), Frame Relay simply discards traffic to avoid congestion problems. In some instances, it is desirable to discern among the user's traffic exactly which data units should be discarded.

Frame Relay uses the *discard eligibility* (DE) bit in its approach. How the DE bit is acted upon is an implementation-specific decision. However, in most instances the DE bit is set to 1 to indicate to the network that in the event of problems the frame with this bit is "more eligible" to be discarded than others in which the bit is set to 0.

While an end user is allowed to manipulate the DE bit, another approach is for the network to use this bit to aid in determining what to do with the traffic. One approach is the technique called the *committed information rate* (CIR). An end user estimates the amount of traffic that it will be sending during a normal period of time. The network measures this traffic during a time interval in relation to a contract between the user and the network, and if it is less than the CIR value, the network will not alter the DE bit. If the rate exceeds the CIR value during the specified period of time, or exceeds an agreed-upon excess burst rate, the network will tag the frame by setting the DE bit to 1. The network will allow the traffic to go through unless it is congested. If the network is congested, this excess traffic will be discarded.

DLCI Interpretations

Frame Relay traffic is exchanged between network users by mapping a connection from an incoming line to an associated connection onto an outgoing line. The end user (such as a router) is responsible for building the Frame Relay frame, placing a DLCI value in the frame header, and delivering the frame across the local UNI to the Frame Relay switch. Given this information, the Frame Relay network must relay this traffic to the end-user machine at the remote UNI. The mapping and routing are accomplished through tables, variously called *label switching tables, routing tables, mapping tables,* or *cross-connect tables.* Two approaches can be employed to relay the traffic through the network between the local and remote UNIs. The first approach (illustrated in Fig. 6-5) uses DLCIs within the network. The second approach (illustrated in Fig. 6-6) uses an internal network header within the network.

Using DLCIs Inside the Network

In Fig. 6-5, Frame Relay switch A (SW A) accepts frames from incoming physical port A containing DLCI 1 and DLCI 2 in the frame headers. It accesses its cross-connect table and finds that the frame containing DLCI 1 should be switched to physical port B and DLCI 1 changed (mapped) to DLCI 21. The frame containing DLCI 2 is to be switched to physical port C and the DLCI 2 mapped to DLCI 45. These frames are relayed to switches B and C (SW B and SW C). Cross-connect tables at these switches are used to perform operations similar to those in switch A, with the

Figure 6-5
DCLI mappings.

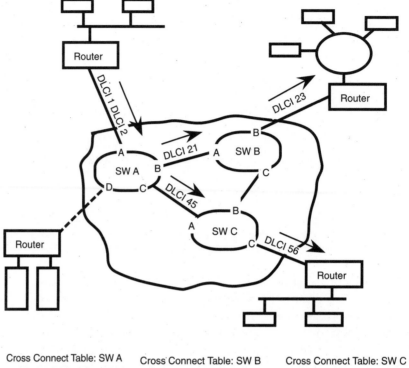

Cross Connect Table: SW A				Cross Connect Table: SW B				Cross Connect Table: SW C			
In Port	DLCI	Out Port	DLCI	In Port	DLCI	Out Port	DLCI	In Port	DLCI	Out Port	DLCI
A	1	B	21	A	21	B	23	A	45	C	56
A	2	C	45								

two frames delivered across the remote UNIs to the end-user machines, which in this example are routers.

Using Internal Network Headers Inside the Network

The Frame Relay standards establish procedures for the mapping of DLCIs between machines at the UNI and NNI. How operations occur within a network can certainly follow the Frame Relay guidelines. However, some vendors and network providers use a proprietary scheme for header operations inside a network if the network switches are manufactured by the same vendor. This approach is taken because the switches

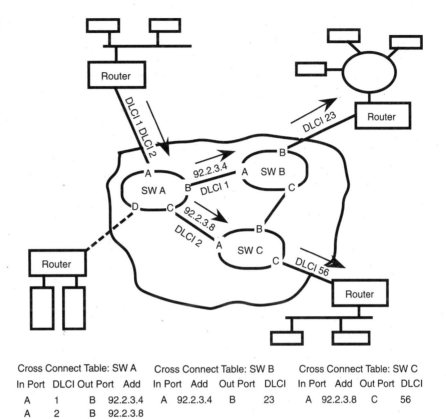

Figure 6-6
Using internal
network headers.

Cross Connect Table: SW A				Cross Connect Table: SW B				Cross Connect Table: SW C			
In Port	DLCI	Out Port	Add	In Port	Add	Out Port	DLCI	In Port	Add	Out Port	DLCI
A	1	B	92.2.3.4	A	92.2.3.4	B	23	A	92.2.3.8	C	56
A	2	B	92.2.3.8								

are already configured with the proprietary protocols and can be connected together quite easily. The internal network headers usually support connectionless operations, allowing for dynamic, adaptive routing within the network. Once again, see Fig. 6-6.

Significance of DLCIs

Local Significance. The DLCIs can be managed in such a way that the numbers can be reused by a network. This approach is known as *local significance,* and enables more virtual circuits to be created in a Frame Relay network, because the DLCI values can be reused at each physical interface (physical port) at each UNI. However, in order for this capability to be used, care must be taken that the DLCI number has only local significance and is not known to other routers.

Global Significance. A number of additional options are part of the Frame Relay standard. The *global addressing* option allows a DLCI to be assigned in such a way that a number has universal significance. This means that this number "points" to the same destination regardless of the source router.

The idea behind global addressing is to simplify addressing administration, but it should be recognized that with the two-octet frame header, it allows for 1024 DLCIs in the entire network because the DLCIs cannot be reused at another port. Actually, the standard only makes available 992 DLCIs, because 32 DLCIs are reserved for internal network management.

The use of global DLCIs on PVCs requires that DLCIs be preassigned and used only once throughout the network. Each Frame Relay switch has tables that provide instructions on how to route the traffic between the switches and to the end-user devices.

Multicasting

The Frame Relay specification also provides for an optional feature called *multicasting.* This is a "semibroadcast" technology in which a user can receive or send traffic from or to multiple users. The operation relies on virtual circuits, so connections must be set up before the multicast traffic can be transmitted.

The user need send only one copy of the frame with the reserved DLCI value in the header. The network is then required to duplicate the frame and deliver copies to a set of users.

The standards for multicasting are ITU-T X.6 and Frame Relay Forum FRF.7. Presently, only PVC-based multicasting is defined. SVC multicasting is under continuing study, as is the operation for dynamic changes during the connections.

Figure 6-7 shows the operations for one-way multicast service. The rules for this service are as follows:

- Traffic is one-way only (as the name implies).
- The destination station (leaf) is treated like any virtual circuit. The multicast server must map the multicast DLCI (Mdlci) from the source station (root) to a conventional DLCI.
- Traffic from the leaves to the root are not supported with two-way multicasting. Separate unicast services are invoked.

Figure 6-7
Frame Relay multicast
(one-way service).

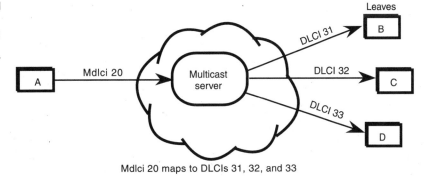

Mdlci 20 maps to DLCIs 31, 32, and 33

(a) One direction only, leaves cannot send to root.

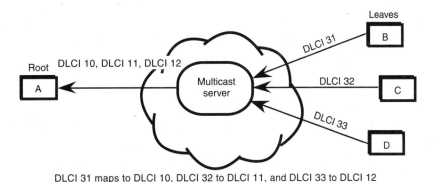

DLCI 31 maps to DLCI 10, DLCI 32 to DLCI 11, and DLCI 33 to DLCI 12

(b) Leaves to root must use conventional unicast operations.

■ Mulitcasting and unicasting are separate services, and the ordering of frames is performed within each service, not between them.

Two-way multicasting is a duplex operation (see Fig. 6-8). Traffic flows in both directions—from the root to the leaves, and from the leaves to the root. The top part of Fig. 6-8 shows this operation. All stations have two-way capability. The root still employs an Mdlci, and the leaves still use their conventional identifiers. The multicast server has a mapping table that translates these DLCIs in both directions.

The bottom part of Fig. 6-8 shows the last option for multicasting, called *N-way multicast service*. It is a duplex, multicast service in that all stations send and receive traffic to one another at any time (subject to

Figure 6-8
Frame Relay multicast
(two-way service).

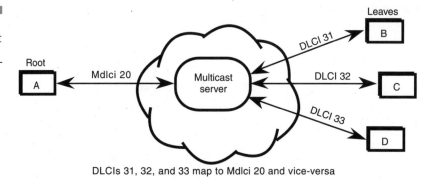

DLCIs 31, 32, and 33 map to Mdlci 20 and vice-versa

(a) Two-way service is a duplex operations: root-to-root and leaves-to-root.

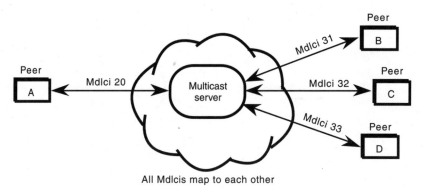

All Mdlcis map to each other

(b) N-way service is a duplex and multiplex operation:
all stations receive all traffic.

traffic management arrangements). In this operation, no root or leaves exist; all stations are considered peers.

Although I have not yet described the *committed information rate* (CIR), the *committed burst rate* (B_c), and the *excess burst rate* (B_e) in much detail, it should be noted that CIR, B_c, and B_e can be employed for all these operations. As a general rule of thumb, the egress port of the connection should have a CIR that is equal to or greater than the sum of the CIRs at the ingress ports of the connections.

However, individual implementations may choose to override this rule, since the users of a multicast service may be constrained (outside of any CIR threshold) as to how they use the bandwidth. CIR, B_c, and B_e are examined in Chap. 9.

SUMMARY

Frame Relay operations use a subset of the data link layer and the network layer operations. Data link connection identifiers (DLCIs) are used for identification of user sessions. With few exceptions, DLCIs are premapped before data transmission occurs. Congestion notification is handled with the BECN and FECN bits, and discarding excessive traffic can be handled through the discard eligibility (DE) bit. Options are available to allow for global or local addressing with DLCIs, as well as multicasting capabilities.

Service Description

This chapter examines the Frame Relay service description specifications published in the ANSI T1.606 and ITU-T I.233 documents. In addition, recent publications by ITU-T that pertain to congestion management and ISDN multiplexing and rate adaptation are also examined.

The discussions pertaining to CIR, B_c, and B_e that are part of ANSI T1.606 and ITU-T I.233 are deferred to Chap. 9.

Frame Relay and the C-, U-, and M-Planes

If the Frame Relay UNI operates with ISDN, service is provided through the ISDN C-plane and U-plane procedures. Virtual calls may be established on an as-needed basis, in which case they are negotiated during call setup procedures through the C-plane procedures. The C-plane is a logical out-of-band signaling channel, implemented through the D channel. C-plane procedures can also be established on a permanent virtual call basis, in which case, the DLCI and associated quality-of-service (QOS) parameters must be defined by administrative-specific operations.

The planes and layers operating at the UNI are shown in Fig. 7-1. These operations are modeled as seven layers in conformance with OSI, although as we learned in Chap. 4, ISDN operates at the lower 3 layers of the OSI model. For the user network interface, three signaling planes are used. As just stated, the *control plane* (C-plane) concerns itself with establishing and terminating connections. The use of C-plane is intended to support a full range of integrated services, such as call control and OAM&P (operations, administration, maintenance and provisioning) operations that pertain to the call setup and clear.

The *user plane* (U-plane) contains the operations, service definitions, and protocols needed for exchanging user data. In an ISDN user-to-network interface, this data relates to applications running on channels D, B, or H. Finally, the *management plane* (the M-plane) is used for management operations between the U- and C-planes.

The Frame Relay service uses the ISDN bearer service (ISDN's layers 1/3). A bearer service through the Frame Relay operations provides bidirectional transfer of user traffic from the S or T interface to the other S or T interface. Routing through a network is provided by using an attached label, which is the DLCI field in the frame header (but as explained in Chap. 6, some implementations append an internal net-

Figure 7-1
The C-, U-, and
M-planes.

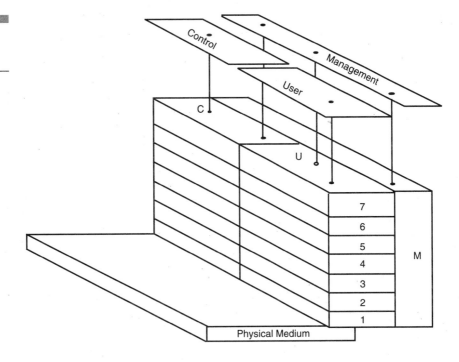

work header to the frame and use this header for routing through the network). While QOS features can be negotiated (on switched systems), negotiations occur in the C-plane only. For permanent virtual circuits, the QOS is predefined and associated with an appropriate DLCI value. The standards require that the order of the Frame Relay service data units (SDUs) be preserved from the local S/T interface to the remote S/T interface. The network detects errors but does not act upon them.

Negative acknowledgments (NAKs) and positive acknowledgments (ACKs) are not used. In effect, the SDUs are sent transparently through the network.

Frame Relay User-to-Network Interface Architecture

The Frame Relay service is modeled on the OSI layered architecture and the ISDN architecture relating to the C-plane and the U-plane. For

Frame Relay, the network does not support the full features of Q922 layer 2 protocol. It supports only the core aspects of Q922 (note once again that Q922 is derived from Q921). Core service offerings can be made on either basic access or primary access interfaces and on ISDN channels B, D, and H. A Frame Relay bearer service is provided only when no user functions are implemented above the core function in the network. In other words, functions above the core functions must be implemented on an end-to-end basis and not on a user-to-network basis.

This architecture is designed to simplify procedures established in other standards, yet allow these other standards to provide for additional services that are negotiated (if needed) in the C-plane before any data transfer occurs.

Figures 7-2 and 7-3 depict the ANSI Frame Relay protocol layered architecture. ANSI bases its Frame Relay platform on the ITU-T Q921/Q922 standards. ANSI document T1.602 is the counterpart to ITU-T's Q921/Q922. ANSI's implementation of the ISDN physical layer is published in ANSI T1.601-1988, *Integrated Services Digital Network—Basic Access Interface for Use on Metallic Loops for Application on the Network Side of the NT* (Layer 1 specification).

The C-plane uses the D channel in accordance with ANSI T1.601-1988. The U-plane can use any channel (i.e., B, D, or H). Typically, additional requirements will be placed on terminals (such as sequencing and flow control) because the core functions do not provide these services.

Left unstated in the standards documents are the user-specified services. Frame Relay, after establishing a connection with either PVC or SVC operations, makes no attempt to take care of the user traffic (other than congestion notification and discard bit functions). Consequently,

Figure 7-2

The ANSI user-to-network configuration.

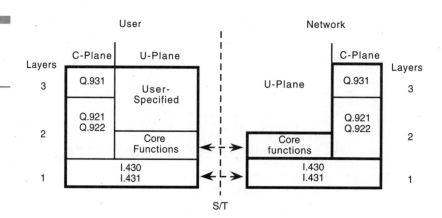

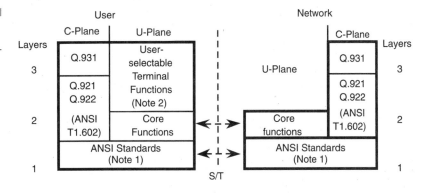

Figure 7-3
The planes.

Note 1:   C-Plane uses D-channel (see Q.921 and ANSIT1-601-1988)
           U-Plane uses D, B or H channel!

Note 2:   Additional requirements (such as congestion control) may be
           placed on terminals

data integrity is the responsibility of the user, so "user specified options" take on a major role. The ITU-T U-plane configuration is shown later in this chapter.

Service Attributes

The ANSI and the ITU-T publish supplemental information on the Frame Relay bearer services, called *service attributes*. This information provides a convenient summary of the major features of the protocol. The service description specifications are organized around three attributes: information transfer attributes, access attributes, and general attributes.

Information Transfer Attributes

The *information transfer attributes* define information, such as the type of transfer mode, what the information transfer rate may be, the type of communication establishment, the nature of the traffic, and how it is sent across the line.

Generally, the ANSI and ITU-T standards are the same with regard to information transfer attributes. Some editorial differences exist. For

Table 7-1

*Information
Transfer Attributes*

▪ Information transfer mode	Frame (packet in T1.606)
▪ Information transfer rate	Less than or equal to maximum user channel bit rate
▪ Transfer capability	Unlimited
▪ Structure	Service data unit (SDU) integrity
▪ Communication establishment	Demand—permanent
▪ Configuration	Point-to-point

example, ITU-T defines its information transfer mode as *frame,* while
ANSI refers to the mode as *packet* (which contradicts the aspect of
"frame" relay). Table 7-1 summarizes the ANSI and ITU-T information
transfer attributes.

Access Attributes

The ANSI and the ITU-T also define the access attributes for the Frame
Relay service. In essence, *access attributes* describe the type of channels
that are used and the particular protocols that are required at each layer,
both for information access and signaling (control access).

Table 7-2 summarizes the ITU-T values for its access attributes. The
ANSI attributes are the same, except for minor editorial differences.

General Attributes

ANSI and ITU-T differ in their definition of *general attributes.* The major
difference is in supplementary services. At the present time, the ITU-T
has a provisional list of supplementary services, while ANSI has supplementary services defined as being under further study. Both organizations have listed QOS as being under further study. Thus, as of this writ-

Table 7-2

Access Attributes

▪ Access channel	D, B, or H
▪ Signaling access protocol, layer 1	I.430 or I.431
▪ Signaling access protocol, layer 2	Q921
▪ Signaling access protocol, layer 3	Q930 Series
▪ Information access protocol, layer 1	I.430 or I.431
▪ Information access protocol, layer 2, core functions	Core functions of Q922
▪ Information access protocol, layer 2, data link control	User specified

Table 7-3

General Attributes

▪ Supplementary services	Note: several are provisional or for further study
▪ Quality of service (QOS)	For further study
▪ Interworking possibilities	For further study
▪ Operational and commercial	For further study

ing, the ITU-T and ANSI efforts do not have much useful information. The ITU-T refers to the I.500 series for interworking possibilities, whereas ANSI describes the interworking possibilities in section 7.2.1 of ANSI T1.606-1990. Table 7-3 summarizes the ANSI and ITU-T general attributes.

Performance Criteria

Annex A of I.233 and section 4 of T1.606 contain several definitions of Frame Relay performance parameters. Several of these parameters, such as throughput and committed information rate, are used by commercial networks in establishing contracts with their customers. These parameters are examined in Chap. 9.

Recommendation I.464 on Multiplexing, Rate Adaptation, and Interfaces for 64-kbps Transfer Capability

The ITU-T Recommendation I.464 is a brief description of how user traffic can be placed on a 64-kbps channel. This recommendation assumes the user traffic does not use ISDN interfaces or data rates. This recommendation guides the reader to previously published ITU-T recommendations that define multiplexing and rate adaptation across the ISDN 64-kbps channel.

In this interface, procedures cited in X.31, X.30, X.110, and X.120 apply. The discussion of these individual procedures and protocols is beyond the scope of this book, but a brief summary is provided in this section. (For more information on these procedures, the reader may wish to study *X Series Recommendations* by Uyless Black, published by McGraw-Hill.)

X.30

X.30 is used to aid in the transition from the X Series interfaces to an all digital system using the ISDN standards (I and Q Series). X.30 describes the connections of X.21 and X.21bis devices to an ISDN. X.30 also describes the connections of X.20-based devices with an ISDN utilizing asynchronous data rates of 600, 1200, 2400, 4800, and 9600 bit/s. The X.20bis connection must use user classes-of-service 1 and 2 as stipulated in Recommendation X.1. The recommendation stipulates the use with both circuit switched and leased line systems.

X.30 covers the rate adaptation scheme between the user device through the user ISDN terminal adapter (TA). It does not cover the requirements for the data transfer speed conversion in the event of internetworking (for example, between ISDNs and circuit switched networks).

X.31

The ITU-T Recommendation X.31 provides two scenarios (cases A and B) for the interface of an X.25 packet mode terminal into an ISDN node. The case A scenario supports a rudimentary and basic service. The ISDN provides transparent handling of the packet calls from the DTE to the packet network. This scenario supports only B channel access. Moreover, if two local DTEs wish to communicate with each other, their packets must be transmitted through the ISDN and through the packet network before the packets can be relayed to the other DTE. This minimum integration scenario uses the B channels for all call management. This is performed using ISDN signaling procedures prior to initiating the X.25 level 2 and level 3 procedures. In essence, the ISDN node passes the X.25 call transparently to the X.25 network.

The case B scenario provides for several additional functions. The ISDN provides a packet handling (PH) function within the node. Actual implementations of case B use two separate facilities for the interconnection. The ISDN switch is provided through a vendor's ISDN NT1 product, and the packet handler function is provided by the vendor's packet switch.

Case B permits two options: access via the B channel, and access via the D channel. With the first option, the X.25 packet and data link layer procedures are conveyed through the B channel. Access through the D channel requires that all active logical channels be established through a D channel connection, and all X.25 packets (including connection setups, connection disconnects, and data packets) must be transmitted over the D channel on the LAPD link.

X.110

Recommendation X.110 establishes several routing principles for circuit switched and packet switched calls on data networks. Its intent is to foster international procedures for internetworking between national networks and international data switching exchanges (IDSEs). Its value is in its definitions and general examples. It does not contain enough detailed information for any meaningful detailed design decisions.

The OSI Architecture and Frame Relay

ITU-T I.233, Annex C

The ITU-T has published Annex C to I.233, which defines the relationship of the relaying bearer service to the OSI network layer service. This bearer service is intended to support the network layer service, in accordance with ITU-T Recommendation X.213.

OSI network service consists of three phases: connection establishment, data transfer, and connection release. Connection establishment and release services are provided by the Q930 series, and the data transfer phase is provided by the Q922 series.

ITU-T requires that several functions be supported above Q922: segmentation/reassembly of PDUs; RESET of a connection; protocol discrimination to identify the protocol running over Q922; expedited data; and qualified data indication (which is a service tailored to a specific implementation).

The actual transfer phase must be provided by a protocol that resides in the end-user systems. This protocol must reside above the data link

Figure 7-4
The CSAP.

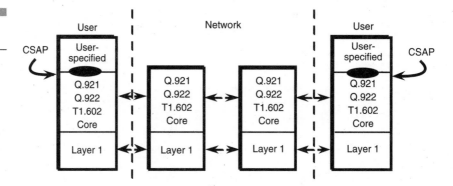

layer—in other words, above Q.922. This end-user protocol can be an existing X.25 protocol, a user-specific protocol, or a connectionless protocol [such as ISO 8473, the connectionless network protocol (CLNP)].

The core service is made available through the *core service access point* (CSAP). The *core service* provides connection-oriented transparent transfer of data between core users. The core service must be independent of any type of underlying physical layer. It is the function of core service to isolate the user from the physical layer, with the exception of certain QOS features that depend on the physical layer (such as basic or primary data rates, etc.).

As depicted in Fig. 7-4, the core service must also ensure transparency of information transfer. This means that the user need not be concerned with the core layer interpreting the content of its data. Conversely, the core layer does not care about the content, syntax, coding, or format of the data it receives. Its only concern in this regard is with the length of the *core service data unit* (CSDU).

The core service must provide several features to the user above it. It must support connections that remain transparent to the end user. Additionally, it must support certain QOS parameters that have been coordinated by the user through the use of the C-plane and perhaps the systems management plane.

It must provide a transparent connection and transfer of CSDUs on behalf of the user through the network. It must also be able to measure certain QOS features to see whether they are consistent with the user's requested QOS. It must be able to provide congestion information to the core service user, and it must also be able to provide some type of information about the release of the connection in the event of problems.

The OSI model requires the use of primitive calls between the core service user and core service provider (see Fig. 7-5). These primitives are

Figure 7-5
The primitives in the
data transfer.

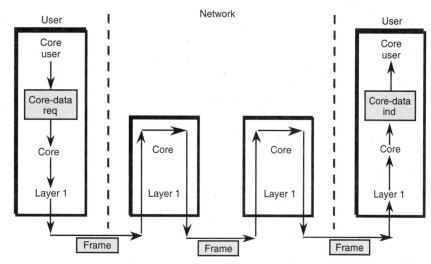

core data request and core data indication primitives, and are mapped in operating-system-specific calls between the two software elements.

The core data request and the indication primitives contain up to five parameters (described shortly).

All primitives are passed as unconfirmed services. This means no confirmation is given to the core service user that the core data has been accepted either by the service provider or by the peer user. No responses are furnished either by the provider or by the other user.

The service primitives contain up to five parameters: core user data, discard eligibility (DE), congestion encountered (CE) backward, congestion encountered (CE) forward, and connection endpoint identifier (CEI) (see Fig. 7-6).

The *core user data* parameter is used to convey data between the end users in the Frame Relay service. This data must be transferred in accordance with OSI's SDU (service data unit) concept, which means it must be transmitted without modification. The *discard eligibility* parameter is sent from the core service user to the service provider. It is used by the provider to select CSDUs, which may be discarded, assuming that the Frame Relay network decides that discarding is required.

The two congestion parameters are sent by the core data service provider to the core data service user to supply information about congestion encountered on the network. The *congestion encountered forward* parameter is used to indicate that the provider has determined that congestion has occurred in transferring data to the receiving user. The *conges-*

Figure 7-6
The parameters in
the primitives.

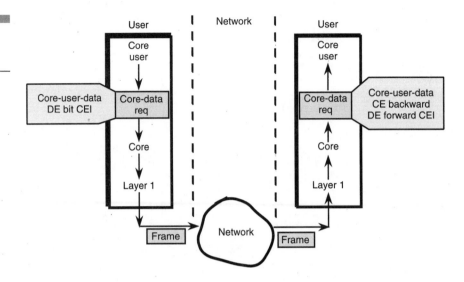

tion encountered backward parameter indicates that the provider has experienced congestion in transferring these units from the sending user.

The *connection endpoint identifier* parameter is used to further identify a connection endpoint. For example, this parameter would allow a DLCI to be used by more than one user, and each user would be identified with a connection endpoint identifier value.

ANSI T1.617, Annex C

Annex C of ANSI T1.617 describes how OSI connection mode network services (CONS) are provided over a Frame Relay bearer service. It shows the relationship between OSI CONS service definitions and Q931 messages and the fields in these messages. Since Q931 and its relationship to Frame Relay are described in Chap. 10, we defer discussion of Annex C and pick it up later in that chapter.

SUMMARY

Frame Relay utilizes conventional layered protocols for its U-plane and C-plane operations. The ITU-T provides guidance on the use of OSI services for implementing the Frame Relay operations, although the ANSI does not define these operations.

Both the ITU-T and ANSI publish performance criteria relating to throughput, transit delay, committed burst rates, excess burst rates, committed information rates, and other important measurement criteria. In addition, ITU-T publishes guidance for congestion management in Recommendation I.370.

Core Aspects of
Frame Relay

This chapter examines the core aspects of a Frame Relay network. The issue of congestion control is revisited and explained in more detail in relation to the consolidated link layer management (CLLM) procedure. The DLCI is also reexamined, with a discussion of the use of extended DLCI values.

The Five Core Functions

The ITU-T Q921 and ANSI T1.602-1988 core functions are organized around five elementary procedures. First, a Frame Relay system must provide services to delimit and align frames, and provide transparency of the frame flags with zero-bit stuffing and unstuffing. Second, the Frame Relay system must support virtual circuit multiplexing and demultiplexing through the use of the DLCI field in the frame. Third, the system must inspect the frame to make certain it aligns itself on integer number of octets prior to the zero bit insertion and following the unstuffing of the zero bit. Fourth, the system must inspect the frame to ensure that it does not exceed the maximum and minimum frame sizes (these frame sizes are established by the network provider). Fifth, the system must be able to detect transmission errors through the use of the frame check sequence field (FCS).

As part of this fifth function, the system must check the frame for formatting problems and other operational errors.

These core functions translate into a minimal service in comparison to other layer 2 protocol stacks, but as we have discussed in earlier chapters, that is the intent of Frame Relay.

The use of core functions does not mean that other services are not provided by Frame Relay. For example, flow control and congestion notification are important components of Frame Relay, but are not part of the core functions.

Frame Relay Frame Formats

We learned in Chap. 6 that the DLCI field in the Frame Relay frame can vary in size, and can contain two, three, or four octets. This approach allows the use of more DLCI numbers. Figure 8-1 illustrates the three formats. The extended address (EA) bits that are set to 0 indicate that

Figure 8-1

Frame Relay header formats.

8	7	6	5	4	3	2	1
DLCI						C/R	EA=0
DLCI				FECN	BECN	DE	EA=1

(a) Two octet address/control field

8	7	6	5	4	3	2	1
DLCI						C/R	EA=0
DLCI				FECN	BECN	DE	EA=0
DLCI or DL-CORE control						D/C	EA=1

(b) Three octet address/control field

8	7	6	5	4	3	2	1
DLCI						C/R	EA=0
DLCI				FECN	BECN	DE	EA=0
DLCI							EA=
DLCI or DL-CORE control						D/C	EA=1

(c) Four octet address/control field

more octets follow in the header, and the EA bit set to 1 indicates the end of the header. Presently, only the two-octet format can be used on a D channel, in order to maintain compatibility with ISDN standards.

The D/C field is called DLCI or DL-CORE control indication. (The core services are described in ITU-T I.233, Chap. 7.) It is used to determine whether the remaining 6 bits of the DLCI are to be interpreted as DLCI bits or as DL-CORE bits. This bit is set to 0 if the last DLCI octet contains DLCI bits. It is set to 1 if it contains DL-CORE information.

The forward explicit congestion notification (FECN) bit is set by a network node that is experiencing congestion. It is used to notify the device that congestion avoidance procedures should be initiated at the machine that receives this frame. The use of this bit is optional, and it can be used by either the network or the user. However, a network is not allowed to reset this bit to 0 once it has been set to 1.

The backward explicit congestion notification (BECN) bit is also used by a congested network node to notify the originator of the traffic that congestion avoidance procedures should be implemented. This bit is also optional, and can be used by either the network or the user. Like the FECN, the BECN bit cannot be cleared by the network.

The discard eligibility (DE) indicator bit is set to 1 to indicate that a frame can be discarded in relation to other frames that do not have this bit set. The use of this bit is optional by either the network or the user. However, the network is not allowed to clear this bit to 0. It should also be noted that networks may discard frames other than frames in which the DE is set to 1 if congestion becomes excessive.

The command/response (C/R) bit is not used by the core Frame Relay procedure; its use is application-specific. It is used in CLLM, which is explained shortly.

DLCI Values

As we learned in earlier chapters, the DLCI field identifies a logical connection that is multiplexed across a physical channel. DLCIs with the same value always identify the same logical connection across a particular physical circuit.

The DLCI values and ranges depend on whether Frame Relay is being transmitted across the D channel or the B/H channels. For the use of B/H channels, the range of the DLCI values vary, depending on whether a two-octet, three-octet, or four-octet frame address format is being used. The values are listed in Table 8-1.

Congestion Control Management

Most of the discussions of congestion control in this book are grouped into Chap. 9. The exception to this organization is the present section, since it deals with CLLM, which is a fundamental part of the core aspects of Frame Relay.

Like any network, a Frame Relay network must be concerned with potential congestion. Therefore, a network must have some form of con-

Table 8-1

DLCI Values for
B-Channel or
H-Channel
Applications

DLCI Values	Function
(a) Two-octet address format:	
0	In channel signaling
1 to 15	Reserved
16 to 991	Assigned using Frame Relay connection procedures (see Note)
992 to 1007	Layer 2 management of Frame Relay bearer service
1008 to 1022	Reserved
1023	In-channel layer management
(b) Three-octet address format with D/C = 0	
0	In channel signaling
1 to 1023	Reserved
1024 to 63,487	Assigned using Frame Relay connection procedures (see Note)
63,488 to 64,511	Layer 2 management of Frame Relay bearer service
64,512 to 65,534	Reserved
65,535	In-channel layer management
(c) Four-octet address format with D/C = 0	
0	In channel signaling
1 to 131,071	Reserved
131,072 to 8,126,463	Assigned using Frame Relay connection procedures (see Note)
8,126,464 to 8,257,535	Layer 2 management of Frame Relay bearer service
8,257,536 to 8,388,606	Reserved
8,388,607	In-channel layer management

Note: Some of these values are assigned to VCs.

gestion control management. However, since the FECN and BECN bits
reside inside user frames, they cannot be issued to a user device unless
user traffic is flowing back to that specific device. In other words,
Frame Relay must provide for out-of-band network management messages. Otherwise, as shown in Fig. 8-2, the network has no method for
notifying an upstream user about congestion problems. To solve this
problem, the *Consolidated Link Layer Management* (CLLM) protocol was
developed.

Figure 8-2
Effect of the lack
of out-of-band
signaling.

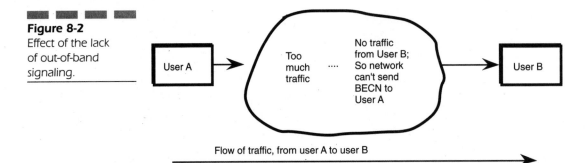

Figure 8-2
Effect of the lack
of out-of-band
signaling.

Consolidated Link Layer Management (CLLM)

To resolve the lack of flexible flow control messages previously discussed, the CLLM operation uses DLCI 1023 (as a reserved channel) to notify the user about problems. Figure 8-3 provides an example of how the CLLM message is used with both upstream and downstream user devices.

The CLLM operation supports the following modes of operation. First, it can identify more than one DLCI, if necessary. Second, it can identify active DLCIs that are problems. Third, it can identify inactive DLCIs that should not be activated.

In addition, the CLLM can be coded to identify problems other than congestion. As I explain shortly, equipment and failure problems can also be identified and reported.

Figure 8-3
CLLM operations.

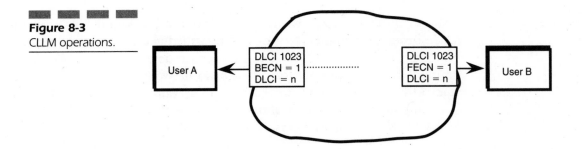

The CLLM Message

Since the high-level data link control (HDLC) and its subsets [for example, the link access control procedure for the D channel (LAPD)] are widely used throughout the industry, it is relatively easy to adapt parts of the protocol for use in other systems. In addition, the International Standards Organization (ISO) administers the use and registration of the exchange identification (XID) operation in HDLC, which allows XID to be applied to different networks and links in a systematic and known manner. CLLM uses the XID frame to carry its information. Figure 8-4 shows the format for the XID information and its relation to the Frame Relay frame.

The XID header contains the HDLC control field, which identifies an XID "frame." The format identifier is a registered number from the ISO. The group field is defined in ISO 8885, and for CLLM, indicates that "private" (CLLM-specific parameters) will be contained in the parameter fields of the frame.

Figure 8-4
CLLM format.

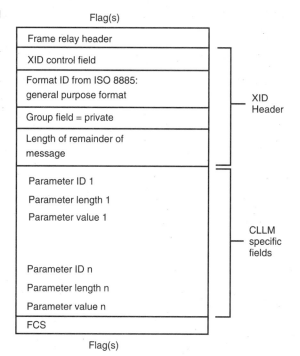

CLLM Message Formats for ISDN Channels. Figure 8-5 shows the format for a CLLM message to be used on a B or H channel with a two-octet header. The octets are shown on the left side of the picture, and the bit values are shown at the top part of the figure. The first two octets comprise the address format for a DLCI. The third octet is the HDLC exchange identifier (XID) control field. The *XID* is used widely throughout the industry to identify and convey diagnostic and setup information at the link layer. The fourth octet defines the format for the

Figure 8-5
The CLLM format.

Octet	Bits	Field description
	8 7 6 5 4 3 2 1	
1	1 1 1 1 1 0 R 0	Address octet 1 (R = response)
2	1 1 1 1 X X X 1	Address octet 2 (X = don't care)
3	1 0 1 0 1 1 1 1	XID control field
4	1 0 0 0 0 0 1 0	Format ID (130)
5	0 0 0 0 1 1 1 1	Group ID = 15 (private)
6		Group length octet 1
7		Group length octet 2
8	0 0 0 0 0 0 0 0	Parameter ID = 0
9	0 0 0 0 0 1 0 0	Parameter length = 4
10	0 1 1 0 1 0 0 1	Parameter value = 105 ("I")
11	0 0 1 1 0 0 0 1	Parameter value = 49 ("1")
12	0 0 1 1 0 0 1 0	Parameter value = 50 ("2")
13	0 0 1 1 0 0 1 0	Parameter value = 50 ("2")
14	0 0 0 0 0 0 1 0	Parameter ID = 2 (Cause Id)
15	0 0 0 0 0 0 0 1	Parameter length (1)
16		Cause value
17	0 0 0 0 0 0 1 1	Parameter value = 3 (DLCI ID)
18		Parameter length
19		DLCI value octet 1 (1st DLCI)
20		DLCI value octet 2 (1st DLCI)
2n+17		DLCI value octet 1 (nth DLCI)
2n+18		DLCI value octet 2 (nth DLCI)
2n+19		FCS
2n+20		FCS

remainder of the traffic. The fifth octet indicates that this message is for private use, that is, Frame Relay–specific.

Thereafter, the parameter IDs describe the contents of the fields. The first parameter ID in octet 8 has a value of 0, and is coded to identify I.122 as the relevant entity using this frame. Octet 14 contains the second parameter ID, with a value of 2, which identifies the cause ID. The *cause ID* contains diagnostic values that are coded in octet 16 (explained shortly). Finally, the last parameter value is defined in octet 17. Its value of 3 is used to signify the DLCIs that are being reported in the parameters that follow. The FCS follows the DLCI contents.

The *cause field* (octet 16 of the frame) contains the code that identifies the problem. The cause code enables a node that is experiencing congestion or other problems to report the type of problem, although it can be seen from Fig. 8-6 that the nature of the problem that can be reported is limited to a few codes.

One code is particularly interesting—the unknown cause. Of course, the use of such a code is not unusual in network operations, but to state that an unknown problem is "short term" or "long term" seems to indicate that the reporter of the problem suffers from a lack of clairvoyance and, at the same time, possesses an ample supply of it. It seems to say, "I do not know what the problem is, but it will last a long (short) time."

Whatever the rationale for this code may be, the Frame Relay protocol states that the cause code is to be coded "short term" if the sender anticipates a transient problem, and it is to be coded "long term" if the sender anticipates a problem that is not just transient. In any event, the decision of how to use this field is network-dependent.

Figure 8-6
Coding of the cause field (octet 16).

Octet	Bits 8 7 6 5 4 3 2 1	Cause description
16 Cause value	0 0 0 0 0 0 1 0	Network congestion, excessive traffic, short term
	0 0 0 0 0 0 1 1	Network congestion, excessive traffic, long term
	0 0 0 0 0 1 1 0	Facility or equipment failure, short term
	0 0 0 0 0 1 1 1	Facility or equipment failure, long term
	0 0 0 0 1 0 1 0	Maintenance action, short term
	0 0 0 0 1 0 1 1	Maintenance action, long term
	0 0 0 1 0 0 0 0	Unknown, short term
	0 0 0 1 0 0 0 1	Unknown, long term

Effect of Receiving a CLLM Congestion Notification

Upon receiving a CLLM message, the end user is to follow the procedures described in ANSI T1.618-1991, Annex A (see Chap. 9, section entitled "BECN Usage"). Figure 8-7 shows the CLLM message format for use on a D channel, using a two-octet header. Notice that the service access point identifier (SAPI) field and the terminal endpoint identifier (TEI) field are coded in the header. In CLLM, the setting of the C/R bit must indicate an HDLC-type response, which means that the sending of a CLLM message will not result in the sending of a related frame (which would simply compound the traffic congestion problem).

Figure 8-8 shows the format for the CLLM message for use over a B or H channel when three octets are used in the address field. Obviously, this format is quite similar to the format used with two octets in the B and H field. Therefore, the reader may wish to refer back to Fig. 8-4 for a discussion of the contents of the fields in this header.

Figure 8-9 is quite similar to Fig. 8-6, in that it shows the format of a CLLM message used on the D channel. In this example, though, there are three octets used for the address field.

Figure 8-10 shows the format of a CLLM message for a B or H field in which four octets are used for the address field. Finally, Fig. 8-11 shows a four-octet address field used on the D channel.

Figure 8-7
The CLLM message for a D channel (two octets in address field).

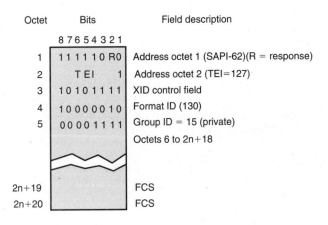

Figure 8-8

The CLLM message for a B or H channel (three octets in the address).

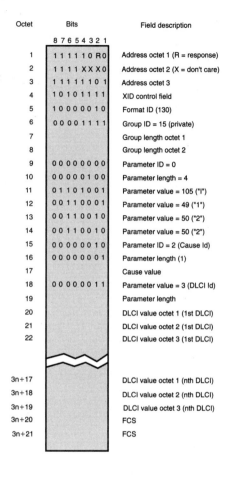

Octet	Bits 8 7 6 5 4 3 2 1	Field description
1	1 1 1 1 1 0 R 0	Address octet 1 (R = response)
2	1 1 1 1 X X X 0	Address octet 2 (X = don't care)
3	1 1 1 1 1 1 0 1	Address octet 3
4	1 0 1 0 1 1 1 1	XID control field
5	1 0 0 0 0 0 1 0	Format ID (130)
6	0 0 0 0 1 1 1 1	Group ID = 15 (private)
7		Group length octet 1
8		Group length octet 2
9	0 0 0 0 0 0 0 0	Parameter ID = 0
10	0 0 0 0 0 1 0 0	Parameter length = 4
11	0 1 1 0 1 0 0 1	Parameter value = 105 ("I")
12	0 0 1 1 0 0 0 1	Parameter value = 49 ("1")
13	0 0 1 1 0 0 1 0	Parameter value = 50 ("2")
14	0 0 1 1 0 0 1 0	Parameter value = 50 ("2")
15	0 0 0 0 0 0 1 0	Parameter ID = 2 (Cause Id)
16	0 0 0 0 0 0 0 1	Parameter length (1)
17		Cause value
18	0 0 0 0 0 0 1 1	Parameter value = 3 (DLCI Id)
19		Parameter length
20		DLCI value octet 1 (1st DLCI)
21		DLCI value octet 2 (1st DLCI)
22		DLCI value octet 3 (1st DLCI)
3n+17		DLCI value octet 1 (nth DLCI)
3n+18		DLCI value octet 2 (nth DLCI)
3n+19		DLCI value octet 3 (nth DLCI)
3n+20		FCS
3n+21		FCS

Figure 8-9

The CLLM message for a D channel (three octets in the address field).

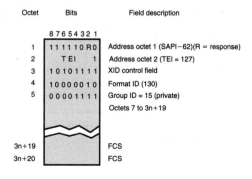

Octet	Bits 8 7 6 5 4 3 2 1	Field description
1	1 1 1 1 1 0 R 0	Address octet 1 (SAPI=62)(R = response)
2	T E I 1	Address octet 2 (TEI = 127)
3	1 0 1 0 1 1 1 1	XID control field
4	1 0 0 0 0 0 1 0	Format ID (130)
5	0 0 0 0 1 1 1 1	Group ID = 15 (private)
		Octets 7 to 3n+19
3n+19		FCS
3n+20		FCS

Figure 8-10
The CLLM message for a B or H channel (four octets in the address field).

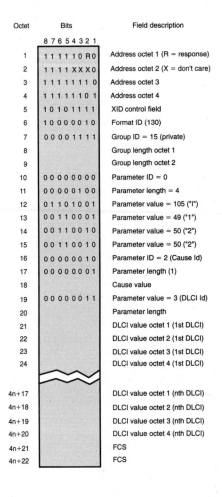

Octet	Bits	Field description
	8 7 6 5 4 3 2 1	
1	1 1 1 1 1 0 R 0	Address octet 1 (R = response)
2	1 1 1 1 X X X 0	Address octet 2 (X = don't care)
3	1 1 1 1 1 1 1 0	Address octet 3
4	1 1 1 1 1 1 0 1	Address octet 4
5	1 0 1 0 1 1 1 1	XID control field
6	1 0 0 0 0 0 1 0	Format ID (130)
7	0 0 0 0 1 1 1 1	Group ID = 15 (private)
8		Group length octet 1
9		Group length octet 2
10	0 0 0 0 0 0 0 0	Parameter ID = 0
11	0 0 0 0 0 1 0 0	Parameter length = 4
12	0 1 1 0 1 0 0 1	Parameter value = 105 ("I")
13	0 0 1 1 0 0 0 1	Parameter value = 49 ("1")
14	0 0 1 1 0 0 1 0	Parameter value = 50 ("2")
15	0 0 1 1 0 0 1 0	Parameter value = 50 ("2")
16	0 0 0 0 0 0 1 0	Parameter ID = 2 (Cause Id)
17	0 0 0 0 0 0 0 1	Parameter length (1)
18		Cause value
19	0 0 0 0 0 0 1 1	Parameter value = 3 (DLCI Id)
20		Parameter length
21		DLCI value octet 1 (1st DLCI)
22		DLCI value octet 2 (1st DLCI)
23		DLCI value octet 3 (1st DLCI)
24		DLCI value octet 4 (1st DLCI)
4n+17		DLCI value octet 1 (nth DLCI)
4n+18		DLCI value octet 2 (nth DLCI)
4n+19		DLCI value octet 3 (nth DLCI)
4n+20		DLCI value octet 4 (nth DLCI)
4n+21		FCS
4n+22		FCS

Figure 8-11
The CLLM message for a D channel (four octets in the address field).

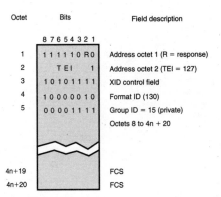

Octet	Bits	Field description
	8 7 6 5 4 3 2 1	
1	1 1 1 1 1 0 R 0	Address octet 1 (R = response)
2	T E I 1	Address octet 2 (TEI = 127)
3	1 0 1 0 1 1 1 1	XID control field
4	1 0 0 0 0 0 1 0	Format ID (130)
5	0 0 0 0 1 1 1 1	Group ID = 15 (private)
		Octets 8 to 4n + 20
4n+19		FCS
4n+20		FCS

SUMMARY

The core description specifications for Frame Relay are quite terse, reflecting the philosophy of keeping the user-to-network interface simple, with few options. This approach makes the operation quite efficient and very fast. Both ANSI and ITU-T now support congestion control management techniques published by the CLLM. In addition, ANSI has published recommended algorithms for the use of the BECN and FECN bits, both by the user and the network. As Frame Relay networks mature through this decade, it is likely that the CIR, committed burst rates, and excess burst rates will be used in a more sophisticated fashion for performance and pricing than they are today.

Traffic Management

This chapter explains how Frame Relay user and network devices manage traffic at the UNI or NNI. The performance parameters established by ANSI and ITU-T are defined in the first part of the chapter, with emphasis on the committed information rate (CIR), the committed burst rate (B_c), and the excess burst rate (B_e). The last part of the chapter provides ideas on how the BECN and FECN signals can be made known to end-user protocols.

Recommendation I.370 for Congestion Management

ITU-T Recommendation I.370 provides guidance for flow control and congestion management at the U-plane. It explains the operations at both the user and network interfaces for channel access rates of 2.048 Mbps or less.

The goal of congestion management is to maintain a very high QOS for each user at the U-plane. Congestion management includes congestion control, congestion avoidance, and congestion recovery. *Congestion control* provides for recovery from congestion during periods of high traffic activity and/or traffic overloads. It includes both congestion avoidance and congestion recovery.

Congestion avoidance seeks to detect congestion and to take remedial actions to prevent or recover from congestion. It attempts to provide high throughput and low delay for each DLCI. As shown in Fig. 9-1, congestion management attempts to avoid congestion by taking actions before or at point A, and to prevent the situation from deteriorating to point B. Of course, at point B, congestion avoidance cannot be performed. At this point, *congestion recovery* operations must be executed. These operations attempt to "minimize the damage" to user traffic and network operations. Nonetheless, any operations within region II might entail a deterioration of QOS to the network subscriber. At point B, frames might be discarded to prevent further congestion.

Any congestion avoidance operations should, as far as possible, minimize the discarding of user frames. After all, these discards will be regenerated by the user transport layer (or some other retransmission protocol), and create more "offered load." Next, the user should be given

Figure 9-1
Congestion
avoidance and
throughput.

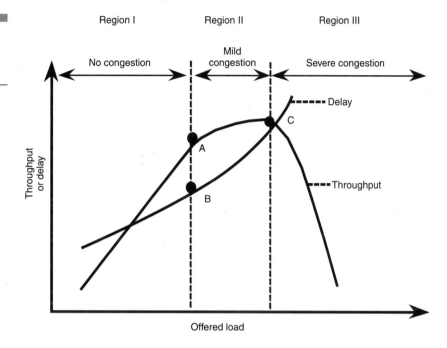

the expected QOS with minimal variance. This QOS includes the discarding of frames, which contributes to the residual error rate (RER).

Obviously, congestion avoidance operations should not generate overhead that leads to further congestion. Therefore, the operations should not create undue additional traffic. Insofar as possible, congestion warnings (such as explicit congestion notification) should be piggybacked onto ongoing traffic.

One end user should not monopolize network resources at the expense of other users, and the network load should be distributed fairly among users. Any type of congestion should be limited in its spread to other components of the network. What these other components are is not defined in the standards. However, they should include other Frame Relay nodes, as well as end-user devices at the customer premises equipment (CPE), such as routers.

Congestion avoidance also attempts to operate equally well in both directions on all virtual circuit connections. In other words, congestion avoidance seeks to maintain smooth network operations, and attempts to provide symmetric behavior in view of bursty traffic conditions in an asymmetric environment.

Performance Criteria

Annex A of I.233 and Section 4 of T1.606 contain several definitions of Frame Relay performance parameters. Several of these parameters, such as throughput and committed information rate, are used by commercial networks in establishing contracts with their customers. These parameters are summarized in this section.

Throughput

Throughput is defined as the number of protocol data units (PDUs) that have been successfully transferred in one direction per unit time over a virtual connection. The virtual connection can include any number of intermediate components between two user devices (data terminal equipment or DTEs).

In this definition, the PDU is considered to be all bits between the flags of the Frame Relay frame. These bits include the bits between the address field, the information field (I field), and the FCS field (see Fig. 9-2). The term *successful transfer* means that the frame check sequence (FCS) check indicates that the frame transfer has been completed successfully.

Transit Delay

Transit delay is the time taken to send a frame across a link between two machines. Strictly speaking, it is a function of the access rate of the link,

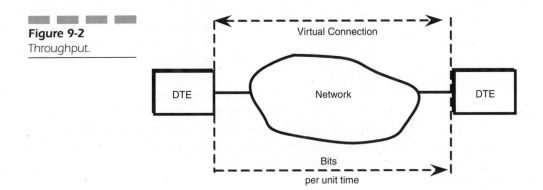

Figure 9-2
Throughput.

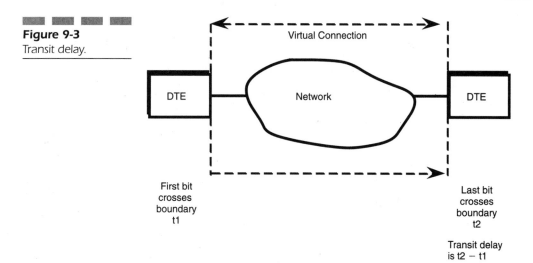

Figure 9-3
Transit delay.

Virtual Connection

DTE

Network

DTE

First bit
crosses
boundary
t1

Last bit
crosses
boundary
t2

Transit delay
is t2 − t1

the link distance, and the size of the frame. Link distance is usually ignored since it is a small value. Thus, transit delay is calculated as frame size (in bits)/link access rate (in bps).

Transit delay is measured between pairs of boundaries. The boundaries can be defined in a number of ways, although ITU-T uses the following definition (see Fig. 9-3): a boundary separates a network section from the adjacent circuit section, or it separates an access circuit section from the adjacent DTE.

Transit delay can define a boundary between two DTEs, or between two international networks, or between national networks, and so forth. Whatever the boundary is, transit delay starts at the time T_1, when the first bit of the PDU crosses the first boundary. It ends at time T_2, when the last bit of the PDU crosses the second boundary. In other words, transit delay = T_2/T_1. Transit delay through each boundary is summed to equal the total transit delay across a virtual connection.

Virtual Circuit Transit Delay

The *virtual circuit transit delay* is the sum of all the section delays. The decision to sum all delays (and each section delay) depends upon the agreements between network administrations. Figure 9-4 illustrates virtual circuit transit delay.

Figure 9-4
Transit delay across
the virtual connection.

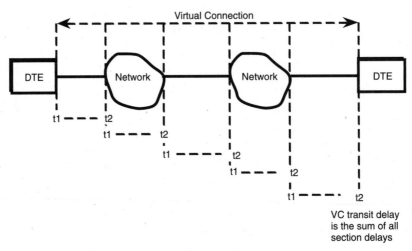

Residual Error Rate (RER)

Residual error rate is measured through the exchange of the Frame Relay SDUs (FSDUs) during a specified period and across a specified boundary—typically, between the core functions of Q922 and the protocol implemented above Q922. Figure 9-5 illustrates the operations of RER. The RER is defined as R = 1−(total correct SDUs delivered)/(total offered SDUs).

Without question, parameters such as throughput and delay are important in obtaining bandwidth on demand. Therefore, a user should pay close attention to these parameters when examining network offerings. The RER is equally important. After all, it is important for the user to know the relationship of traffic submitted to the network to that of traffic successfully delivered by the network.

The RER should be correlated with the users' actual throughput and committed burst rates. As an example, if users exceed their throughput agreement (contract), it should be expected that their traffic will be discarded and the RER will suffer. However, these matters should be examined in relation to the user-to-network contract. For example, if a user stays within the contract, a better RER should be expected, as well as a more attractive billing plan from the network. Conversely, the more a user violates the contract limits, the worse the RER.

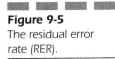

Figure 9-5
The residual error
rate (RER).

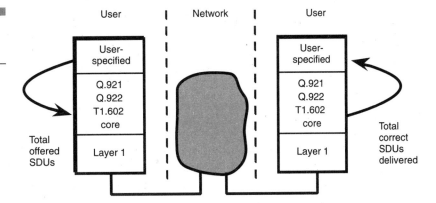

Other Parameters Defined by the ITU-T

The ITU-T has also defined other performance and QOS parameters. They are summarized in this section, and in Table 9-1.

A *delivered errored frame* is defined as a frame that is delivered when the values of one or more of the bits in the frame are discovered to be in error.

The *delivered duplicate frames* value is determined when a frame received at a destination is discovered to be the same frame as one previously delivered.

The *delivered out-of-sequence frame* describes the arrival of a frame that is not in sequence relative to previously delivered frames.

A *lost frame* is so declared when the frame is not delivered correctly within a specified time.

A *misdelivered frame* is one that is delivered to the wrong destination. In

Table 9-1

Other Statistics
and Performance
Criteria

- Delivered errored frames
- Delivered duplicate frames
- Delivered out-of-sequence frames
- Lost frames
- Misdelivered frames
- Switched virtual call establishment delay
- Switched virtual call clearing delay
- Premature disconnect
- Switched virtual call clearing failure

this situation, DLCI interpretation may be in error, the routing table may be out of date, and so on.

The *switched virtual call establishment delay* and *clearing delay* refer, respectively, to the time taken to set up a call and clear a call across the C-plane.

The *premature disconnect* describes the loss of the virtual circuit connection, and the *switched virtual call clearing failure* describes a failure to tear down the switched virtual call.

Using the CIR, B$_c$, and B$_e$ for Traffic Management

Committed Burst Rate (B$_c$) and Excess Burst Rate (B$_e$)

Several terms and definitions are key to understanding the basis for traffic management in a Frame Relay network. The *committed burst rate* (B$_c$) describes the maximum amount of data that a user is allowed to offer to the network during the time interval T$_c$. The B$_c$ is established (perhaps negotiated) during a call setup or pre-provisioned with a PVC. T$_c$ is sometimes called a *bandwidth interval,* in that it can be used to govern the interval for a burst of traffic to enter the network.

The *excess burst rate* (B$_e$) describes the maximum amount of data that a user may send, which exceeds B$_c$ during the time interval T$_c$. The value B$_e$ can also identify the maximum number of bits that the network will attempt to deliver in excess of B$_c$ during an interval T$_c$. B$_e$ is also negotiated during the call setup or preprovisioned with a PVC. The idea is for B$_e$ traffic to be subject to a lower probability of delivery than B$_c$ traffic. Figure 9-6 shows the relationships between B$_c$ and B$_e$.

Committed Information Rate (CIR)

The *committed information rate* (CIR) describes the user information transfer rate that the network supports during normal network operations. For an SVC, the CIR is negotiated during call setup under the C-plane. The CIR works in conjunction with the *committed rate measure-*

Figure 9-6
Committed and
excess burst sizes.

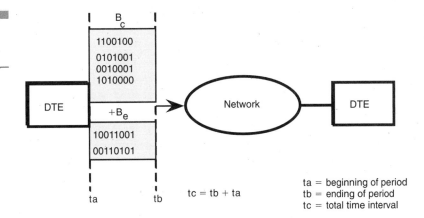

ment interval (T_c). This measurement defines the time interval in which the user can send only B_c and/or B_e.

The CIR is computed over the minimum increment of time T_c as $CIR = B_c/T_c$. For example, assuming a time interval of $T_c = 1.125$ s, a CIR of 64 kbps permits a B_c of 72 kbps (72/1.125 = 64). As another example, a CIR of 128 kbps permits a B_c of 144 kbps (144/1.125 = 128). Later discussions show more examples of CIR and B_c.

It is important to emphasize that each user's frames are sent at wirespeed (the access rate). A user may have a CIR of 128 kbps on a T1 link of 1.544 Mbps, but the traffic is burst across the link at 1.544 Mbps, which gives the user low latency into and out of the network.

The Measurement Interval and User/Network Reaction to Congestion

One issue that must be addressed is how the network and user determine a measurement interval (and agree on it). I.370 also provides guidance for the setting of T_c. The I.370 recommendation defines the measurement interval shown in Table 9-2. In addition to the parameter value definitions in Table 9-2, the ITU-T describes or implies two other conditions:

- When CIR equals the access rate (T1, E1, etc.), the access rates at the entrance and exit of the network (the end-to-end virtual circuit) must be equal.
- When CIR = 0, B_c = 0, B_e must be > 0, and $T_c = B_e$/access rate.

Table 9-2

Measurement
Intervals

CIR	B_c	B_e	T_c
>0	>0	>0	$T_c = (B_c/CIR)$
>0	>0	=0	$T_c = (B_c/CIR)$
=0	=0	>0	$T_c = (B_e/\text{access rate})$

The ITU-T recommends that end-user terminals should have the ability to receive explicit congestion notifications and react to them. Of course, what is considered to be an end-user terminal is important. In most Frame Relay systems, a router acts as the user terminal, and the actual end-user device (such as a workstation) is not aware of Frame Relay operations. Therefore, it has no knowledge of congestion notification. A Frame Relay network does not care about this aspect of flow control. From the standpoint of Frame Relay, the router is the end-user device.

In addition to a user responding to congestion notification, the user is not supposed to block its own data if networks are operating without problems, even though the user's load might exceed its own CIR. Additionally, it is expected that the user will immediately control data flow with fast slowdown measures and then gradually return to the negotiated transfer rate with slow startup measures.

I.370 provides a useful diagram and explanation of the relationships among B_c, B_e, and the CIR over the measurement period T_c. Figure 9-7 shows these relationships. Frames 1 and 2 should be delivered through the Frame Relay network with the guaranteed QOS. These frames are sent at the raw access rate within the B_c agreement. Notice that the line representing CIR represents the slope determined by B_c/T_c. Indeed, both CIR and B_c (and B_e) are slopes (gradients). However, the frames' gradient is the same as the access rate, and not the CIR, since CIR is less than B_c (and B_e).

In Figure 9-7b, frame 3, taken together with frames 1 and 2, is greater than B_c, but does not exceed B_c plus B_e. The user's QOS can be met, and frame 3 would most likely be delivered—although it could be marked as a possible discard if unusual conditions exist in the network.

In Figure 9-7c, frame 4 (and the accumulation of frames 1, 2, and 3) violates the B_c plus B_e provision, and could be marked for probable discard or could be discarded at the entrance to the network.

Figure 9-7
Relationships of
the Frame Relay
parameters.

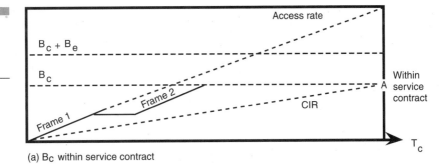

(a) B_C within service contract

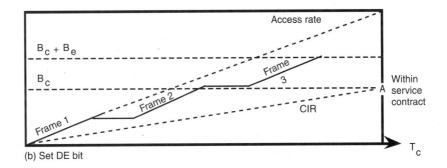

(b) Set DE bit

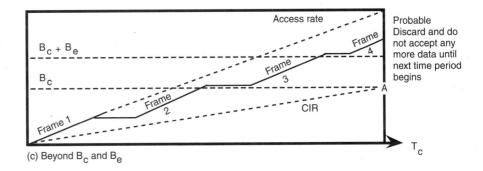

(c) Beyond B_c and B_e

In an ideal world, the last bit of the last frame of a user's burst would be sent to the network during interval T_c exactly at point A in Fig. 9-7. This means that the user would send $CIR \times T_c$ bits, which is not likely to happen. For example, for a time interval of $T_c = 1.125$ s and a CIR of 64 kbps, the total burst would be exactly 72 kilobits (64 kbps $\times$ 1.125 s).

Congestion, Throughput, and Delay

The Frame Relay specifications provide guidelines and rules on how the user and network can react to receipt of FECN = 1, receipt of BECN = 1, or loss of traffic. Before we examine this subject, a few comments about congestion should prove helpful.

The Frame Relay switch at the ingress UNI must exercise prudence in the amount of traffic that it allows to enter into the network. For example, due to the effect of queuing and its potentially severe consequences on network throughput, flow-control measures must be undertaken at the UNI before congestion becomes severe. In other words, the network UNI switch must have the capability to know when to flow-control the user traffic. Since traffic in a data network is bursty, the software at the switch must be somewhat "smart," in that it must be able to predict the time at which the traffic load will become a problem. Certainly, the software must not be so unintelligent that it waits too long before taking remedial action. The consequences of serious network congestion and the precipitous drop in throughput only result in unhappy users.

The buildup of excess queues and the resultant severe effect on network throughput also holds true for its effect on response time and delay. One might think that there is a one-to-one relationship between degraded throughput and degraded response time. While congestion degrades the QOS of both of these features, overall network throughput may actually benefit from longer queues because the network can build these queues and use them to smooth traffic conditions over a period of time. However, achieving superior performance relating to delay-and-response time requires the network to keep the queues small. Indeed, the smaller the queues, the better the response time. However, in the final analysis, congestion eventually degrades QOS for both throughput and delay.

ANSI has published Annex A to its T1.618 specification, which provides guidelines for the use of the BECN and FECN bits by both the user and the network. I will first discuss some ideas for FECN usage, and follow that with some ideas for BECN usage. I include in these discussions how window-based mechanisms can be employed, and how the detection of lost traffic can affect flow control.

The following material is organized as follows:

- FECN usage
  User
  Network

- BECN usage
  User
  Network
- Use of windows
  With FECN with no traffic loss
  With FECN when traffic loss is detected
  With BECN with no traffic loss
  With BECN when traffic loss is detected

FECN Usage

The user device compares the number of frames in which the FECN bit is set to 1 to the number of frames in which the FECN bit is set to 0 over a measurement period. During this period, if the number of FECN bits = 1 is equal to or exceeds the number of FECN bits = 0, the user device should reduce its throughput to .875 of its previous throughput value. Conversely, if the number of FECN bits = 0, the user device is allowed to increase transmissions by $1/16$ (0.0625) of its throughput (a slow start operation). The measurement interval is to be equal to approximately four times the end-to-end transit delay.

For the network use of the FECN bit, the Frame Relay node continuously monitors the size of each queue, based on what is known as a *regeneration cycle*. This cycle begins when a queue on an outgoing channel goes from idle (the queue is empty) to busy (the queue has traffic). During a measurement period, which is defined by the start of the previous regeneration cycle and the present time within the current measuring cycle, the average size of the queue is computed. When this average size exceeds a predetermined threshold value, this circuit is considered to be in a state of "incipient congestion." At this time, the FECN bit is set to 1 and remains set to 1 until the average queue size falls below this preestablished threshold.

ANSI T1.618 defines an algorithm to compute the average queue length. The algorithm consists of computing a queue length update, a queue area update, and an average queue length update, making use of the following variables:

t = Current time
t_i = Time of the ith arrival or departure event
q_i = Number of frames in the system after the event

T_0 = Time at the beginning of the previous cycle
T_1 = Time at the beginning of the current cycle

The algorithm consists of three components:

- Queue length update:

   Beginning with $q_0 = 0$,
   If the ith event is an arrival event, $q_i = q_i + 1$
   If the ith event is a departure event, $q_i = q_i - 1$

- Queue area (integral) update:

   $$\text{Area of the previous cycle} = \sum_{t1 \in T1,t} q_i - 1(t_i - t_i - 1)$$

   $$\text{Area of the current cycle} = \sum_{t1 \in T1,t} q_i - 1(t_i - t_i - 1)$$

- Average queue length update:

   Average queue length over the two cycles =

   $$\frac{\text{Area of the two cycles}}{\text{Time of the two cycles}} = \frac{\text{Area of the two cycles}}{t - T_0}$$

BECN Usage

If a user receives n consecutive frames with BECN = 1, the traffic should be reduced from the user by a step below the current offered rate. The step count (S) is defined in this order:

0.675 times throughput

0.5 times throughput

0.25 times throughput

Likewise traffic can be built up after receiving n/2 consecutive frames with BECN = 0. The rate is increased by a factor of 0.125 times the throughput.

The value of S is computed as follows:

$$IR_f = \frac{TH_f}{8} + \left(\frac{Be_f}{Be_f + Bc_f}\right) \frac{Ar_f}{8}$$

$$IR_b = \frac{Th_b}{8} + \left(\frac{Be_b}{Be_b + Bc_b}\right) \frac{Ar_b}{8}$$

$$S = \frac{F_b}{F_f} \left(IR_f \frac{EETD}{N202_f} + IR_b \frac{EETD}{N202_b} \right)$$

where IR_f = information rate in the forward direction
$\quad IR_b$ = information rate in the backward direction
$\quad\quad S$ = step function count
$\quad Th_f$ = throughput in the forward direction agreed during call establishment
$\quad Th_b$ = throughput in the backward direction agreed during call establishment
$\quad EETD$ = end-to-end transit delay
$\quad N202_f$ = maximum information field length in the forward direction
$\quad N202_b$ = maximum information field length in the backward direction
$\quad Ar_f$ = access rate forward
$\quad Ar_b$ = access rate backward
$\quad Be_f$ = excess burst size forward
$\quad Be_b$ = excess burst size backward
$\quad Bc_f$ = committed burst size forward
$\quad Bc_b$ = committed burst size backward
$\quad F_b/F_f$ = ratio (either expected or measured over some implementation-dependent period of time) of frames received to frames sent

For network use of the BECN bit, it is recommended that the network begin setting the BECN to 1 prior to encountering serious congestion and having to discard frames. However, it is clear that if congestion reaches a point of creating severe throughput and delay problems, the network should start to discard frames, preferably frames with the DE bit set to 1.

Use of Windows

FECN with No Traffic Loss. If the user device employs a protocol that uses windows for flow control (see Chap. 6, section entitled "Managing Congestion with Sliding Window Procedures"), it compares the number of frames received with FECN = 1 and FECN = 0 during a measurement interval equal to two window turns (the maximum number of frames that can be sent before an acknowledgment is required represents one window turn). If the number of frames with FECN = 1 is greater than or equal to the number of frames with FECN = 0, the user reduces the window size to 0.875 of its current value. Otherwise (number of FECN = 1 frames less than the number of FECN = 0 frames), the user increases the window size by one frame (not to exceed the maximum window size for the virtual circuit). With each adjustment, the process begins anew.

FECN When Traffic Loss Is Detected. Assuming the user device can detect the loss of traffic, upon the detection of nonreceipt of a frame the user reduces the window size to 0.25 of its current value. However, if it is known that the network is providing congestion notification and no FECN = 1 frames were received during the measurement interval, it is likely that congestion is not the problem. After all, the network would normally send FECN = 1 frames if problems were occurring. Therefore, it is assumed that frame loss is due to errors (noise on the line, etc.) and not congestion. In this situation, the working window size is reduced by a factor of 0.625 instead of 0.25.

BECN with No Traffic Loss. In this situation, the step count S (discussed earlier) is used to govern the user's traffic flow. For this discussion, S is defined as one window turn. If a frame with BECN = 1 is received, the user reduces the window size by 0.625, and continues to reduce the window size if S consecutive frames of BECN = 1 are received. The window cannot be reduced to less than one frame.

As soon as BECN = 0 frames are received, the user increases the window by one frame after receiving a total of S/2 FECN frames.

BECN When Traffic Loss Is Detected. Assuming the user device can detect the loss of traffic, upon detection of the nonreceipt of a frame the user reduces its sending rate to 0.25 of the current rate if either the rate is being reduced due to congestion notification, or the network does not provide BECN = 1 operations.

The CIR and Network Pricing

The majority of Frame Relay networks provide the user with a guaranteed service (relating to throughput) if the user's input rate is below a specified CIR. If the user exceeds the CIR for some period of time, the network may discard traffic. The phrase "may discard" means that the

Figure 9-8
The CIR gauge.

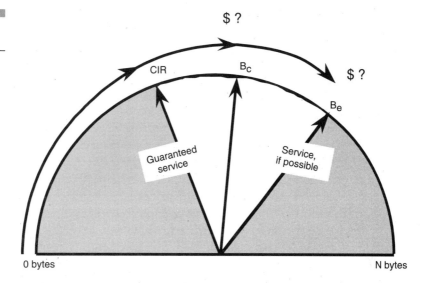

network will most likely not discard traffic if it has sufficient resources to transport the user traffic during the time the CIR is exceeded. After all, discarding traffic is tantamount to discarding revenue.

Figure 9-8 illustrates a CIR gauge that is used to show the relationship between CIR and network pricing. The vector moves to the right as traffic increases and to the left as traffic decreases. This figure is useful because it permits us to visualize the possible services of a Frame Relay network in relation to possible discard requirements. As we have learned throughout this book, a Frame Relay network attempts to guarantee service as long as the user traffic falls within the CIR value and, as we have also learned, as long as it falls within a committed burst rate (and perhaps even an excess burst rate). Beyond the CIR, service is provided, if possible.

If the network cannot support the traffic load, it will first discard traffic tagged with DE = 1. In addition, it is certainly conceivable that a network might charge more when the vector of the gauge moves past CIR. We could then hypothesize that some maximum rate (typically traffic beyond both burst and excess rate) would allow the network to discard more traffic.

The public Frame Relay networks provide a wide variety of prices and services in relation to CIR, B_c, and B_e. Several examples are provided in Chap. 15.

Approaches to Frame Relay Data and Congestion Management

Who Acts on the FECN and BECN Bits?

Frame Relay networks rely on the user machine (the router or the user workstation) to flow-control traffic at the UNI. In many installations, the transport layer in the user workstation assumes this responsibility. If the FECN/BECN bits are to be acted upon by the transport layer, some means must be devised for the FECN/BECN = 1 frames to be received and presented to the transport layer, or some other layer that can issue flow control against a user's traffic.

This approach, while simple in concept, may not be so easy to implement. It requires modification to user layers in the workstation, as well as additional coding.

Nevertheless, it is technically possible to make the user machine aware of the BECN and/or FECN operation. But be aware that it requires modifying or adding code to the existing protocols.

In addition, for many transport layer protocols, the nonreceipt of acknowledgments from the destination device will result in time-outs at the sender, with the resulting retransmission of discarded traffic. Thus, the network congestion problem is compounded, because valid traffic is thrown away due to congestion, yet this same traffic is reintroduced into the network, usually by the transport layer.

Clearly, a potentially vexing problem results from this approach. What is needed is for the originating workstation (and not just the router) to adjust the rate at which it sends traffic. Consequently, the BECN and FECN bits are important components for efficient Frame Relay operations.

The designer must give serious consideration to how FECN and BECN operate in conjunction with the origination and destination protocols. The next section provides ideas about this issue. The following cases are discussed with regard to the FECN and BECN bits.[1]

Case 1: Using X.25's layer 3 with receive not ready (RNR)

---

[1]These cases reflect discussions I have had with some of my clients on the use of end-to-end flow control using the Frame Relay UNI. In some cases, I have recommended that they not be used, and/or have pointed out the potential problems with their implementation. I shall take the same approach here. I have also created this section to give the reader information on how difficult it is to combine one technology (Frame Relay) with other existing technologies (other protocols, such as TCP, X.25). You will see why many network designers and administrators are reluctant to "enhance" existing systems.

Case 2: Using X.25's layer 3 with receive ready (RR)

Case 3: Using TCP or TP4 with their credit fields

Case 4: Using TCP or TP4 with delayed ACKs

Case 5: Using LLC type 2 with RNR

Case 6: Using IP and ICMP with source quench

Protocol Stacks and PDUs

In order to understand the operations of these cases, it is necessary to take a brief detour and examine the layers of the Internet and OSI protocols, their protocol data units (PDUs), and the headers within these PDUs. Figure 9-9 is used during this discussion, and shows an example of the names and addresses used in the Internet and OSI layers at an intermediate (router) or destination (end-user) machine. These identifiers are used to pass the PDU to the proper processing entity, such as a protocol (residing in the machine), and to determine (in the case of a router) the next node that is to receive the PDU.

The sending machine creates the various names and addresses at different layers; they are used by the peer layer of the receiving machine to identify the destination address and/or protocols to invoke at each layer, and/or functions to perform within the layer.

The destination link address is used by the link layer (layer 2) to determine whether the traffic is to be received at this station. If so, the link layer accepts the traffic and passes the traffic (after stripping off the layer 2 header and trailer) to an appropriate layer 3 protocol (at the network layer), making use of the EtherType or destination link service access point (LSAP) field. This latter field is used for all 802-based LANs in conjunction with the logical link control (LLC) layer.

After the traffic is passed to the network layer, the Internet Protocol (IP) or Connectionless Network Protocol (CLNP) address is used by IP or CLNP to determine the next route through the network. If the traffic has arrived at the final destination (the intended workstation), the protocol identifier in the IP or CLNP header is used to determine which transport layer protocol (or other layer 3 protocol) is to receive the traffic. The PDU is passed to this entity for processing. In this example, the protocol ID can identify TP4, TCP, or Internet Control Message Protocol (ICMP).

After the PDU is processed by the transport layer [Transmission Control Protocol (TCP) or Transport Protocol 4 (TP4)], the destination port number [or PSAP (presentation SAP) for TP4] in the transport layer PDU

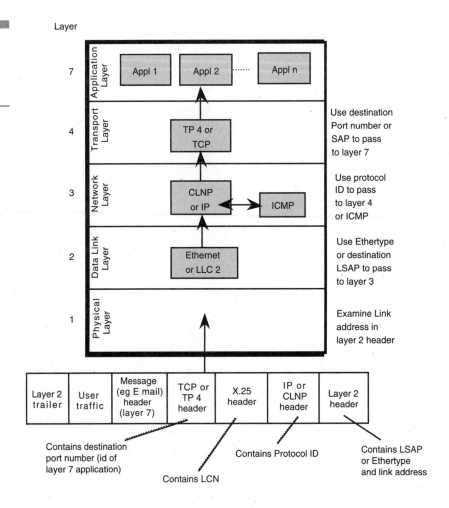

header is used to determine which layer 7 application entity (such as file transfer, email, etc.) is to receive the traffic. (For TP4, the SAP identifies the entity in layer 5 that is to receive the traffic. This operation is not shown in this example.)

Figure 9-10 shows that the router contains software that examines the FECN or BECN bits (in this example, the BECN bit) and the DLCI value(s) in the frame. It is the responsibility of the router to associate the DLCI with the appropriate user identifier. For cases 1–4, the router must be able to correlate (map) the DLCI with the user X.25 logical channel numbers (LCNs) or TCP/TP4 port (for TP4, the "port" is usually called a

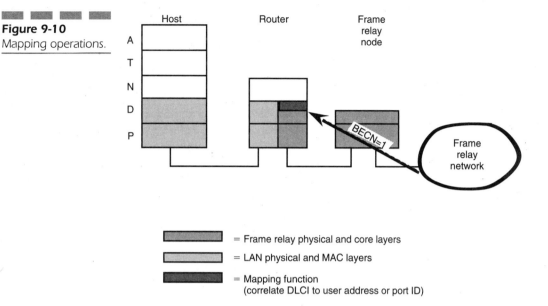

Figure 9-10
Mapping operations.

= Frame relay physical and core layers

= LAN physical and MAC layers

= Mapping function
(correlate DLCI to user address or port ID)

service access point or SAP). For case 5, a correlation must be made between the DLCI and the user LLC LSAP. For case 6, a correlation must be made between the DLCI and user IP or CLNP address. The mapping operations for FECN and BECN are provided in Table 9-3, which should be used as a reference during these discussions. Additionally, the router must be able to create the proper PDUs for this activity. Table 9-3 also shows the PDUs that the router must send to the downstream and upstream user.

These correlations and mapping operations are technically feasible, but their support is dependent upon how specific routers handle end-user traffic. For example, in the past, many routers were not designed to examine the layer 4 headers. Since their function was to act as a "pass through" machine for this traffic, the router did not examine this part of the PDU. For the layer 3 X.25 header, some routers also passed this header transparently to another machine, which supported the X.25 user-to-network interface (UNI), and processed this header.

Nowadays some routers have the capability to process these headers, and their associated fields, and identifiers. For example, some routers examine the TCP destination port numbers of the PDU arriving from attached workstations in order to filter (block) traffic destined for applications whose traffic the network administrator does want on the network.

The reader should thoroughly check out the "behavior" of the routers

Table 9-3

Mapping DLCIs
and Invoking
Proper PDUs at
Router

Case	*For FECN:* DLCI Mapped to Users	*For FECN:* Router Generates to Downstream User	*For BECN:* DLCI Mapped to Users	*For BECN:* Router Generates to Upstream User
1	Downstream LCN	Diagnostic* or RNR	Upstream LCN	Diagnostic* or RNR packet
2	Downstream LCN	RR packet	Upstream LCN	RR packet
3	Downstream port	Altered credit†	Upstream port	Altered credit†
4	(No action)	(No action)	(No action)	(No action)
5	Destination LSAP	LLC RNR	Source LSAP	LLC RNR
6	Destination IP address	ICMP source squench	Source IP address	ICMP source squench

*User-specific diagnostic should be used (X.25 diagnostic packet numbers 188–255, "Reserved for Network-Specific Information").
†Use with great care, see explanation in text.

and workstations in relation to their ability to accommodate to the operations described in these cases. In addition, these cases must be evaluated in terms of their interaction with the algorithms discussed in the previous section entitled "Congestion, Throughput, and Delay."

Case 1

The first case uses X.25 at the end-user workstations to issue flow-control packets. The packets are receive not ready (RNR) or a diagnostic packet (see Fig. 9-11). This operation assumes that X.25 is used jointly with Frame Relay. From the standpoint of performance, the stacking of X.25 and Frame Relay creates a few redundant operations. For example, two virtual circuit connections must be managed by the router with a user machine and the Frame Relay network. But this approach may be needed because X.25 is embedded into the system to provide services to an end-user application (call redirect, closed user groups, etc.), and Frame Relay is employed in order to connect to a public Frame Relay network.

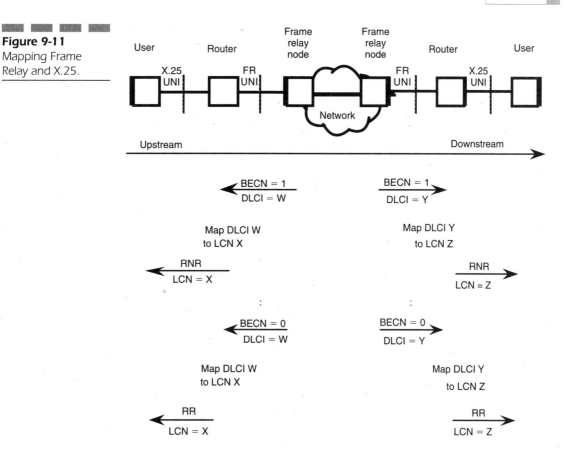

Figure 9-11
Mapping Frame
Relay and X.25.

While X.25 and Frame Relay are both UNIs, in this situation, X.25 is not invoked at the Frame Relay UNI, but at the end-user machines. The configuration is established by a workstation emulating the user device node (DTE), and the router emulating the X.25 network node (DCE). ISO 8208 specifies this DTE/DCE emulation operation.

As shown in Fig. 9-11, the FECN = 1 and/or BECN = 1 frames' DLCIs are mapped to associated X.25 logical channel numbers (LCNs) by the router. The router then sends X.25 RNR (receive not ready) packets to the user station. This action completely closes the flow of traffic.

While Fig. 9-11 shows that the traffic is flow-controlled in both directions, it may be that only the upstream user needs the RNR. The actual operation depends on how much traffic is flowing in each direction.

The flow-control restriction is released when the router receives FECN/BECN = 0 frames from the network. These frames are used to send X.25 RR (receive ready) packets to the user(s), which can continue their ongoing operations.

Case 1 can use X.25 diagnostic packets in place of the RNR and RR packets. In this situation, the router uses network-specific diagnostics (diagnostic codes #128–255), which requires the addition of software in the user's X.25 layer 3 software. The diagnostic packets perform the same functions as the RNR and RR packets depicted in Fig. 9-10.

Case 2

For case 2, the router acts upon the FECN/BECN = 1 frames by sending only RR packets to the user. However, these packets do not rotate the acknowledgment numbers [the P(R) field] in the packet header. By not turning the window, the user must flow-control itself until the router decides to send packets with the P(R) field indicating a window turn.

The router must make certain it maintains the accuracy of the sequencing operations. For example, assume the upstream user has sent to the router three packets with the packet send sequence numbers [P(S) of 0, 1, 2, respectively]. At this time, the router receives BECN = 1 from the network. As with case 1, the router must map the DLCI to an associated LCN, hold packets 0, 1, 2, and send to the user an RR packet with P(R) = 0.

The user interprets this packet from the router to mean "I am still expecting a packet with P(S) = 0." Depending on specific implementations, one of two events will then occur. For the first possibility, the user will do nothing until the router rotates the window with a packet of P(R) = 3, which means "I accept packets 0, 1, and 2, so send me the next packet(s), with the very next beginning with P(S) = 3." Of course, this event will not occur until the router receives BECN = 0 from the network. Therefore, the user is flow-controlled.

For the second possibility, the user may retransmit packets 0, 1, 2 to the router, because it interprets the received of P(R) = 0 as a negative acknowledgment from the router. The router ignores this traffic, since it has copies of these packets in its buffer.

Cautionary Notes Regarding Cases 1 and 2. The good news about case 1 and case 2 is that X.25 has no provision for a retransmission timer or a retry limit for data packets. Therefore, unless the user X.25 software contains vendor-specific timers and retries, the router can dictate the flow of the X.25 traffic, and the user must obey.

The bad news is that the layer above X.25's layer 3 may not be so obedient. Since layer 4 with TCP or TP4 uses retransmission timers and retries, it may attempt to resend its PDUs, which requires passing them to X.25 at layer 3. The problem must be solved by the vendor (and its operating system), by deciding how and when traffic is released from layer 4 to layer 3.

As far as possible, it is a good idea to keep layer 3 passive and rely on layer 4 to accommodate congestion problems. Let us now take a look at cases 3 and 4.

Case 3

The third case can be implemented with TCP/TP4 by issuing an acknowledgment for previously received traffic, but flow-controlling the source machine by setting the credit window to 0 or a number less than the previous credit value (the credit window is a field in the TCP/TP4 PDU header). This approach must also be used with some forethought, because the source machine may already have sent traffic before receiving the new credit. If this traffic is in the network, the destination receiver should receive it. After all, in fairness, the traffic was sent before the source device received the reduced credit (= 0).

It is once again instructive to know that this illustration assumes the end-user device receives some type of congestion notification. This operation requires that the router map the DLCI value of the frame to the destination port number for FECN, and the source port number for BECN.

In general, it is not a good idea to have the router involved in the flow control of layer 4 traffic. First, it places a great burden on the router. Second, most layer 4 protocols are designed for end-to-end (user-to-user) flow-control operations. Nonetheless, most high-end routers have this capability with their support of "local ACKs" for IBM Token Ring traffic. My preference is to use case 4. Let's see why.

Case 4

The fourth case assumes that either the receiving user delays sending acknowledgments back to the sending user, or the network is congested and acknowledgments to the receiver are delayed. In either situation, layer 4 can be programmed to delay sending its traffic when it notices

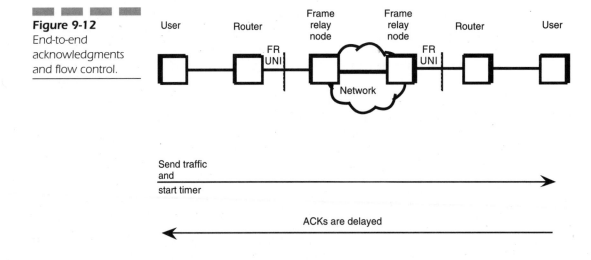

Figure 9-12
End-to-end
acknowledgments
and flow control.

that it is not getting responses back from the receiver in a timely manner. This method can be implemented with several transport layer protocols, such as TCP or TP4. The operation is shown in Fig. 9-12.

These operations rely upon retransmission timers that are turned on when traffic is sent to the network. Upon expiration, if an acknowledgment has not been returned from the receiver to the sender, the sender will time-out and resend the traffic, perhaps adjusting the timer to reflect nonreceipt of the traffic, or the delay in receiving acknowledgments. In the event that network congestion begins to occur, resulting in increased delays, the replies will arrive beyond the bound on the timer value. After the appropriate time-out occurs and the traffic is resent, the sending entity will adjust its timer to a longer value. In this manner, the traffic is not sent to the network so often, and the network can begin to adjust and drain its buffers. In this example, the transmitter increases its timer and continues to build profiles on the responses. As congestion diminishes and the round trip delay decreases, the timer values can decrease.

Choosing Values for Timers. Frame Relay users can implement TCP's approach to estimate a value for the time-out and retransmission function. This section starts with a discussion of some earlier TCP approaches to time-outs, and concludes with recent changes to the TCP retransmission algorithm.

Choosing a value for the retransmission timer is surprisingly complex. This complexity stems from the fact that (a) the delay in receiving acknowledgments from the receiving host varies in an internet; (b) segments sent from the transmitter might be lost in the Internet, which obviously invalidates any round-trip delay estimate for a nonoccurring acknowledgment; and (c) (and consistent with b) acknowledgments from the receiver might also be lost, which also invalidates the round-trip delay estimate.

Because of these problems, TCP does not use a fixed retransmission timer. Instead, it utilizes an adaptive retransmission timer that is derived from an analysis of the delay encountered in receiving acknowledgments from remote hosts.

The round trip time (RTT) is derived by adding the send delay (SD), the processing time (PT) at the remote host, and the receive delay (RD). If delay were not variable, this simple calculation would suffice for determining a retransmission timer. However, as stated earlier, since delay in the Internet is often highly variable, other factors must be considered.

The approach taken with earlier versions of TCP was to analyze each round-trip sample and develop an average RTT for the delay. This simple formula for RTT is a weighted value based on the following:

$$SRTT = (a \cdot OSRTT) + ([1 - a \cdot NRTT),$$

where SRTT is the smoothed round-trip time; a is a smoothing factor (ranging close to 1 to accommodate the changes that last for a short period); OSRTT is the old smoothed RTT (close to 0 to respond quickly to delays); and NRTT is the new RTT sample.

The next step in computing the timer value is to apply a weighting factor to RTT as follows:

$$VT = b \cdot SRTT,$$

where VT is the value for time-out, and b is a constant weighting factor that must be greater than RTT.

In addition, some implementations have varied this formula as follows:

$$VT = \min (Ubound, \max [Lbound, \{b \cdot SRTT\}]),$$

where Ubound is an upper bound on the time-out, and Lbound is the lower bound on the time-out.

This method of calculating the variable for the time-out did not work well, due to the variable delay and the loss of acknowledgments in an internet. Ideally, one would wish the time-out timer to be quite close to RTT. However, due to the variable nature of RTT, it was discovered that the time-out timer often expired too quickly, and resulted in unnecessary segments being reintroduced into the Frame Relay network. On the other hand, with a small time-out value, segment loss is handled more quickly.

One solution to the problem was provided by Phil Karn, and is known as Karn's algorithm. The approach is twofold: (1) TCP does not modify its estimate for any retransmitted segments, and (2) the time-out is increased each time the timer expires and initiates a retransmission. The reader might recognize that this approach is quite similar to the Ethernet back-off algorithm, except that Ethernet uses an exponential back-off in the face of increased traffic collisions on the network.

The Karn formula is

$$NVT = MF \cdot VT$$

where NVT is the new time-out value, and MF is a multiplicative factor (usually a value of 2, or a value taken from a table).

The approach is to recalculate the RTT on a segment that was not retransmitted. It works well enough, except in an internet with large variations in RTT.

The Internet Request for Comments (RFC) 1122 concedes that the original TCP approach to time-out and retransmission is inadequate. With new systems, Van Jacobsen's slow start approach is used: when a time-out occurs, TCP shuts its window down to a width of 1. Upon receiving an ACK, it opens its window to half the width it had before the time-out occurred.

Finally, the new TCP implementations take advantage of Poisson statistics and network utilization factors vis-à-vis RTT. This approach uses additional calculations that take into account varying delay as a function of network utilization.

Here are two more ideas before we move on to case 5. First, the fast back-off and slow-start operations discussed in this chapter (section entitled "Congestion, Throughput, and Delay") should be considered if you are designing a layer 4 protocol. Second, a simple solution is to restrict layer 4 to a window of one PDU. Thus, the sending user cannot send a second PDU until it receives an acknowledgment of the first PDU. This simplicity must be weighed against the reduced throughput that results in this half-duplex mode of operation, but many applications will tolerate this type of setup.

Case 5

Another possibility for providing flow control is to use the logical link control (LLC) layer of the IEEE 802 LAN stack. This layer is actually a sublayer of the data link layer, and it runs on top of the lower link sublayer called *media access control* (MAC). LLC can be configured as a type 2 operation, which uses HDLC's *set asynchronous balanced mode extended* (SABME) procedure. With this procedure, HDLC's receive not ready (RNR) frame can be sent to a station on the LAN to flow control a source link service access point (LSAP) at that station.

For this operation to work, there must be additional software stored in the router that understands that a BECN = 1 associated with a DLCI can be mapped to an LLC session residing on the LAN. How this mapping might occur depends entirely on how (and even whether) the LLC type 2 sessions are set up on the LAN. One problem is that many LANs, with IBM being a notable exception, choose not to use LLC type 2, with all its flow-control features. Instead, they adopt LLC type 1, which provides no flow control operations. Therefore, this idea will come to nought if the implementations are not using LLC type 2. Even if they are, the designer should give careful consideration before moving this type of control function behind the Frame Relay node. In any event, the illustration is provided not to suggest that it is an ideal solution, but to give the reader some ideas about how protocol stacks can be utilized.

Case 6

Finally, another possibility is for the router to correlate the DLCI in the FECN/BECN = 1 frames with an associated IP address, which is not a difficult procedure since IP addresses must be correlated with DLCIs during a system configuration. The BECN = 1 DLCI is mapped to a source IP address, and the FECN = 1 DLCI is mapped to a destination IP address. The router then issues ICMP source quench messages to the upstream and/or downstream IP modules. When the network starts sending FECN/BECN = 0 frames, the router stops sending ICMP source quench messages.

The continuous sending of source quench messages from the router to the workstation may exacerbate an existing congestion problem. One solution to the problem is for the workstation to reduce its throughput by a certain percentage upon receiving one source quench message, and increase its traffic flow after a time limit in which no source quench messages are received. With this approach, the router need not send continuous source quench messages.

SUMMARY

While the Frame Relay standards provide specific rules and algorithms for congestion management, most of them are optional and do not describe which user machine (router or workstation) or layer is affected. Vendors vary in their implementation of traffic management.

Signaling for Switched Virtual Calls

This chapter examines the Frame Relay signaling specification published in ANSI T1.617 and ITU-T Q933 for setting up and clearing switched virtual calls (SVCs). The procedures covered include both B-channel and D-channel frame-mode connection operations. We also examine operations for local frame handlers and remote frame handlers based on ISDN Q931 procedures.

Some of these procedures are used with the network-to-network interface (NNI), so the reader should review this chapter before reading Chap. 11, which discusses the NNI.

The reader of this chapter is expected to have a knowledge of the basic operations of ISDN, as provided in Chap. 4.

Scope of Signaling System Number 1 (DSS1)

The signaling specifications establish the procedures for the interactions between the user and the network for ISDN support of Frame Relay. The specifications define procedures for S, T, and U reference points and the B, H, and D channels. This specification is entitled Signaling System (DSS1) and applies to two cases (see Fig. 10-1). In the first, which is called case A, the procedures define circuit switched access through ISDN exchange termination points to a remote frame handler (RFH). In case A, connection is established through two steps. In step 1, a circuit-mode bearer service is established using Q931, then in step 2, the Frame Relay bearer connection is established in accordance with the documents, explained in this chapter. Case A is restricted solely to B and H channels. Case A also permits the connection to be initiated by the remote frame handler or by the local user.

For case B, the call is established to a local frame handler with either B, H, or D channels. Case B permits connections to be initiated by the local frame handler or the local user. There is only one step involved. A D-channel service is used, applying the procedures explained in this chapter.

The user device for either case is assumed to be an ISDN terminal equipment type 1 (TE1) or network termination 2 (NT2). The reader might recall from the ISDN chapter that an NT2 device is an ISDN functional grouping roughly equivalent to OSI layers 1, 2, and 3. Consequently, it supports machines such as PBXs, cluster controllers, and so forth. The ISDN TE1 is a user device that supports ISDN protocols.

Figure 10-1
DSS case A and case B.

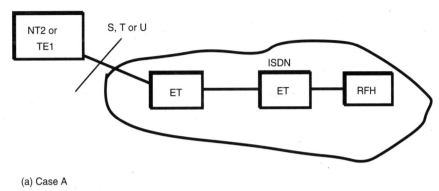

(a) Case A

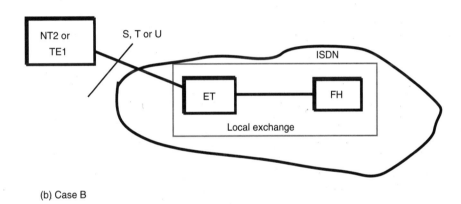

(b) Case B

Messages for Frame Relay Connection Control

Establishing the Call

As mentioned earlier, Frame Relay uses the ISDN Q931 specification for frame connection control messages. These messages are summarized in Table 10-1 and explained in this section. Figure 10-2 provides an example of the call setup procedure and clear procedures, with the most commonly used messages with these operations. Other messages not shown in Fig. 10-2 are also explained in this section.

The *setup* message is sent by the Frame Relay originator to the Frame Relay network to establish a Frame Relay call. On the other side of the

Table 10-1

Frame Relay
Connection
Control Messages

Call Establishment
CONNECT
CALL PROCEEDING
PROGRESS
CONNECT ACKNOWLEDGE
SETUP
ALERTING

Call Clearing
DISCONNECT
RELEASE
RELEASE COMPLETE

Miscellaneous
STATUS
STATUS

Figure 10-2
Example of a call
setup.

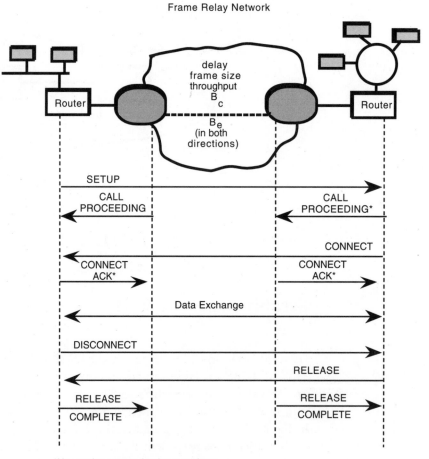

*Use varies among implementations

network, it is sent by the network node to the called user to initiate the Frame Relay establishment at the remote side. The setup message contains a number of fields that describe the type of message, the type of capabilities that will be established with the call, the relevant DLCIs, the suggested end-to-end transit delay, the parameters for core operations, any OSI network features that are to be provided, calling and called party addresses, and a number of other features. We have more to say about the specific content of the messages later in the chapter. Be aware that many of the parameters just described are optional.

If the setup message is accepted by the called user, the user responds with a *connect* message. This message is sent to the local node and relayed through the network to the initiating Frame Relay caller. It contains various identifiers in the message, as well as parameters dealing with transit delay, DLCIs, and so forth.

The *connect acknowledge* message is sent by the network to the called Frame Relay user to notify the user that a call can take place. As an option, it can also be sent by the calling Frame Relay user upon receiving a connect message.

While not shown in Fig. 10-2, the *alerting* message may be sent by the called user to the network and forwarded to the calling user to indicate that a call to the called user has indeed been initiated. In turn, the *call proceeding* message is sent by the called user to the network and forwarded to the calling user to indicate that a call establishment procedure has begun. It also indicates that additional call information for this call is not necessary and will not be accepted.

The *final call setup* message is the progress message (also not shown in Fig. 10-2). It is sent by the network or the user to give status about the progress of the call. This call is intended to be used for internetworking environments between networks.

Clearing the Call

Three messages are used to clear the Frame Relay call (also see Fig. 10-2). First, either party can issue a *disconnect* message, which requests the network to clear the Frame Relay call. In turn, a *release* message is sent by the user or the network indicating that the connection has occurred and, if a DLCI has been used, it is released for further use. Finally, the *release complete* message clears the call and establishes whether the channel is available for reuse. During the disconnect operations, the call reference shall be released.

Other Connection Control Messages

There are two other connection control messages that can be used for Frame Relay call management. A *status* message invokes a *status enquiry message*, which is simply a response to the status message. The status enquiry message can be sent by the user or the network to solicit information about various operations and procedures occurring in the Frame Relay network. Status and status enquiry messages are also used to report certain error and diagnostic messages, which are explained later in this chapter.

DSS1 Message Formats

Now that we have developed a general understanding of the Frame Relay messages, it will be helpful to examine the contents of the fields of the messages to gain a better understanding of how the messages are used for Frame Relay connection control. Figure 10-3 illustrates the format and fields of the message.

Figure 10-3
The DDS1 message.

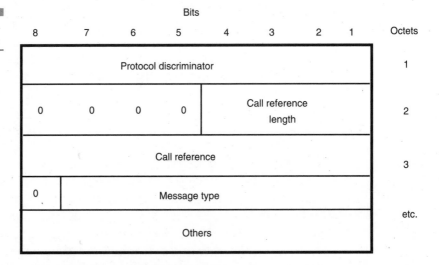

Protocol descriminator: Distinguishes call control messages from others
Call Reference: Identifies each call
Message type: Identifies function message
Others: Contains other fields specific to the message type

Required Fields. The *protocol discriminator* field occupies the first octet of the message. Its purpose is to distinguish user-to-network call control messages from other messages. For the purposes of Frame Relay, the protocol discriminator's value for both the ITU-T and ANSI specifications is 00001000. This value is defined in Q931 to identify user-to-network call control messages. It is also defined in the same manner in the ITU-T and ANSI Frame Relay specifications.

The second octet contains four bits for the length of the *call reference* field. The call reference field occupies octet 3 of the message. The purpose of this field is to identify uniquely each call at the Frame Relay interface. The call reference field is quite similar to an X.25 logical channel number, in that it has only local significance at the Frame Relay interface.

The call reference field likely contains a different value at the remote interface. Therefore, the call reference value does not have end-to-end significance. How two call reference values are mapped to each other for an end-to-end connection is not defined in any of these standards. The network is free to implement any procedures deemed appropriate.

The last required field for all Frame Relay DDS1 messages is the *message type* field. It occupies the first 7 bits of the fourth octet of the message. This field identifies the type of message that is being sent across the interface. These message types were explained in the last section and summarized in Table 10-1.

Fields (Information Elements) for Specific Messages. The other fields, following the mandatory fields, are coded based on what type of message is being processed. This section describes these fields in relation to the specific message type. The fields are referred to as *information elements*, a term that we use from here onward. Table 10-2 lists the information elements and the messages in which they are used. For the purposes of the following discussion, the ANSI documents will be used, with references to the ITU-T documents if notable exceptions exist.

The protocol discriminator, call reference, and message type information elements were described in Chap. 4.

The *cause* information element is used to generate messages, which principally contain diagnostic information. The information element contains a field to describe the location of the relevant point relating to the cause. As examples, the location field can contain an identifier of a user, a private network serving a local user, a public network serving a local user, a transit network, an international network, and so forth.

The cause information element contains the cause value. This value is

Table 10-2

Messages for
Frame Relay
Connection
Control

This table itemizes the information element for each of the messages for Frame Relay connection control. There are six messages for call establishment numbered from 1 to 6, three messages for call clearing numbered 7 to 9, and two miscellaneous messages numbered 10 and 11. The table identifies all the information elements and the Xs mark the appropriate elements for each message.

1. ALERTING
2. CALL PROCEEDING
3. CONNECT
4. CONNECT ACKNOWLEDGE
5. PROGRESS
6. SETUP

7. DISCONNECT
8. RELEASE
9. RELEASE COMPLETE
10. STATUS
11. STATUS ENQUIRY

Information Element	Connection Control Messages										
	1	2	3	4	5	6	7	8	9	10	11
Protocol discriminator	X	X	X	X	X	X	X	X	X	X	X
Call reference	X	X	X	X	X	X	X	X	X	X	X
Message type	X	X	X	X	X	X	X	X	X	X	X
Cause					X	X	X	X		X	
Bearer capability									X		
Channel identification	X	X	X						X		
Data link connection ID	X	X	X						X		
Progress indicator	X	X	X			X			X		
Network specific facilities									X		
Call state										X	
Display	X	X	X	X	X	X	X	X	X	X	X
End-to-end transit delay			X						X		
Packet binary parameters			X						X		
Link core parameters			X						X		
Link protocol parameters*			X						X		
Calling party number									X		
Calling party subaddress									X		
Called party number									X		
Called party subaddress									X		
Connected number			X		X		X	X			
Connected subaddress			X		X		X	X			
Transit network selection									X		
Repeat indicator									X		
Low layer compatibility			X						X		
High layer compatibility									X		
User-user	X		X		X		X	X	X		

*Link and Packet notations refer to link layer and packet layer information elements.

somewhat of a generic field to describe the general aspect of the event being reported. Consequently, events such as a normal event, resource unavailable, protocol error, and the like, are identified in this field. Over 50 diagnostic codes can be placed in this information element as well. Notifications such as *call rejected, facility rejected, network out-of-order, call blocked, bearer capability not authorized, invalid call reference value, incompatible destination* are all available for the cause information element. In addition, for Frame Relay operations, two other cause values are available: *permanent virtual connection out-of-service* and *permanent virtual connection operational.*

The *bearer capability* information element is used to identify an ITU-T I.122 bearer service. This element is used by the network only to identify a network service. The value in this field identifies a transfer mode as the frame mode. An important subfield within this information element identifies a layer 2 protocol. For the ANSI standard, this identifies T1.618 core aspects of Frame Relay. For the ITU-T implementation, it defines Annex A of Q.922.

The bearer capability field contains some other minor subfields to indicate that standardized ITU-T coding is used for the field, and that the information transfer capability should be unrestricted digital information.

The *channel identification* information element identifies the type of channel being used with the interface. Coding options are available to identify a wide variety of channel options. As examples, this information element can identify the channel as supporting speech, carrying 64-kbps synchronous traffic, carrying 56-kbps traffic, using ITU-T E.110 or X.30, taking advantage of various options with B channels, H channels, and so on.

The *data link connection identifier* (DLCI) identifies the assigned or requested DLCI for this connection. This information element must be in the *call proceeding* message in response to the *setup* message. In addition to the DLCI, another field in this information element enables the requestor to indicate that a particular DLCI is preferred, or that only the DLCI so indicated can be used. If the network cannot assign the requested DLCI, it will allocate another value.

The *progress indicator* information element is used to describe an operation that has occurred during a connection. It contains the *location* field described earlier in this section. It also contains a *progress description* field. This field contains status information that can indicate, for example, that the call is not an end-to-end ISDN call, that the destination address is non-ISDN or the origination address is non-ISDN, that a delay has been detected in responding at the called interface, and so on.

The *network specific facilities* information element is used to indicate which, if any, network layer facilities are being invoked. It also indicates whether these facilities are user-specified, or are required by a national or international network. The network identification plan is also identified—for example, the ITU-T X.121 data network identification code (DNIC). For Frame Relay, this field enables layer 3 OSI facilities for connection-oriented facilities to be used with the call. This information is not processed by the Frame Relay network, which passes it transparently between OSI users.

The *call state* information element contains information about the status of a call. Since the call setup operations of Frame Relay use the ISDN Q931 standards, the call states are based on the ITU-T specification. While a description of each call state is beyond the scope of this book, it should be emphasized that most connection-oriented systems have states such as *connect request, call delivered, call present, call initiated, disconnect request,* and the like. For purposes of the Frame Relay operations, only one state has been added, which is the call *independent service.*

The *display* information element can be used by the user to display data such as ASCII characters. Whatever resides in this field is not described in the standard, although the maximum permitted field length is 82 ASCII octets.

The *end-to-end transit delay* information element enables the user to request a maximum transit delay on each Frame Relay call. Transit delay is defined as end-to-end, one-way only. It involves only the data-transfer phase, and not call setups. It also includes the total processing time in the user systems.

The end-to-end transit delay information element contains three values: cumulative delay, request delay, and maximum end-to-end delay. The cumulative delay defines the greatest delay that should be experienced by 95 percent of the traffic; therefore only 5 percent of the frames for this call should exceed this value. The other two fields (requested delay and maximum delay) are used to check whether the call can be set up to meet these values. This information element is used in the setup message when the call is being connected.

The general format for this information element is depicted in Fig. 10-4. (Be aware that octet and bit positioning, as well as unused bits, are not shown here.)

The *packet-layer binary parameters* information element is used to support the OSI connection-mode network service (CONS) that is to be associated with this call. It contains fields to request an expected data transfer and confirmation of message receipt. It is not processed by the Frame Relay network.

The *link layer core parameters* information element is used to negotiate and agree upon the Frame Relay link layer core parameters for the call. These parameters identify permissible Frame Relay frame sizes,

Figure 10-4
End-to-end transit
delay information
element.

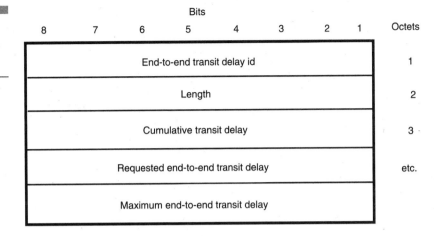

Bits								Octets
8	7	6	5	4	3	2	1	
End-to-end transit delay id								1
Length								2
Cumulative transit delay								3
Requested end-to-end transit delay								etc.
Maximum end-to-end transit delay								

throughput, committed burst rate, and excess burst rate. Figure 10-5 shows the general format of this information service element (be aware that octet and bit positioning, as well as unused bits, are not depicted in this figure). The Frame Relay information field is defined to be the number of octets that follow the address field and precede the FCS field in a frame. Both incoming and outgoing maximum Frame Relay information field (FRIF) size can be negotiated. The outgoing FRIF size identifies the maximum number of user octets that can be sent from the called to the calling user. The incoming FRIF size is the maximum number of octets sent from the calling to the called user. The number of octets is measured between the control field and the FCS field. Certain restrictions are placed on this size based on using D channels, with 262 octets being the maximum size. For B and H channels the FRIF can be up to 4096 octets long.

The *throughput* field allows a throughput in bit/s to be negotiated across the interface; it is equivalent to CIR. In addition, a minimum acceptable throughput can be specified. The latter field defines the lowest throughput value that a calling user can accept. If either the network or the called user cannot support this minimum acceptable throughput, the call will not be set up. The magnitude and multiplier fields are coded to reflect a magnitude ($100 - 10^6$) and an integer multiplier. For example, 128 kbps is represented as 128×10^3.

The committed burst size (both incoming and outgoing) indicates the maximum number of bits the network will transfer over a measurement interval. These fields are equivalent to B_c, and are computed in accordance with the rules explained in Chap. 9.

Figure 10-5
The core parameters
information element.

			Bits					Octets
8	7	6	5	4	3	2	1	

Field	Octets
Link layer core parameters ID	1
Length	2
Outgoing & incoming max FRIF sizes	3
Throughput ID	etc.
Outgoing magnitude & multiplier	
Incoming magnitude & multiplier	
Maximum acceptable throughput ID	
Outgoing magnitude & multiplier	
Incoming magnitude & multiplier	
Committed burst size ID	
Outgoing committed burst size value	
Incoming committed burst size value	
Excess burst size ID	
Outgoing excess burst size	
Incoming burst size	

Note: Some fields are variable in length.

The excess burst size (both incoming and outgoing) indicates the maximum number of uncommitted bits that the network will attempt to deliver over a field measurement period. These fields are equivalent to B_e, and they are also explained in Chap. 9. For both committed burst size and excess burst size, data may not be interrupted with extraneous signals such as flags. To do so would be unfair to the end user, since it would misrepresent the number of user bits sent.

The point has been made several times in this book that Frame Relay is not designed with extensive data management capabilities. However, the use of the signaling standards does provide an option for obtaining end-to-end sequencing, window size negotiations, and retransmissions.

This is performed with the *link layer protocol parameters* information element, but it should be noted that this service is available only if the implementation uses an additional link layer feature that handles these features, such as LAPB, or X.75 link layer procedures. If this feature is supported, this information service element contains a value to indicate the number of outstanding frames permitted, a retransmission timer, and whether sequencing must be carried out Modulo 8 or Modulo 128.

Four information elements in a message are used to identify the called and calling parties. These are the *calling party number, calling party subaddress, called party number,* and *called party subaddress.* The four fields contain a number and a subaddress for both the called and calling parties. The numbers are based on international numbering plans. Thus, several address formats are permitted, such as X.213-based network service access points (NSAPs), X.121, E.164, private addresses, and the like.

The *connected number* information element is used to identify the responding party of the call. The information element contains a field to identify the type of number, such as an international number, a national number, subscriber number, and so on. It also has a field to identify the numbering plan, such as X.212, E.164, Telex, E.163, and so on.

The *connected subaddress* information element is used to identify the subaddress of a responding party. This is coded in conformance with ITU-T I.330 and I.334. It can also indicate whether a network service access point (NSAP) is based on ITU-T 213 or ISO 8348 AD2.

The *transit network selection* information element enables a user to specify one transit network to be used in the end-to-end transmission process. The information element contains a field to identify the network as a national, international, or user-specified network, as well as a specific network identification plan for the network number.

The *repeat indicator* information element is used to indicate whether information elements are repeated and, if so, how many times they are repeated.

The *low layer compatibility service* information element is a rather extensive set of fields that identifies the type of interfaces and protocols that will be used for the call. Fields are provided to identify digital or speech traffic, circuit or packet mode services, and line speeds in bits per second. Fields are also provided to indicate whether various types of ITU-T recommendations are being used for synchronous/asynchronous formats, the use of network independent clocks, flow control mechanisms, rate adaptation, start bits for asynchronous operations, parity information, and several other features. Fields are also available to identify the type of modem, if needed. Additional fields are available to provide more information about the information layer 2 protocol, such as the IEEE LLC, HDLC's normal response mode or asynchronous response mode, LAPB, and LAPD. Finally, information is available to identify the type of user layer 3 employed, such as X.25 or ISO's 8473 connectionless service.

The *high layer compatibility* information element is used to determine whether the two users are compatible with regard to services offered and services provided. The information element contains fields to identify protocols operating over Frame Relay that can be used by the two users. As examples, higher-level identifications can identify facsimile transmission, teletext, Telex messages, X.400, and OSI-type protocols.

The *user/user* information element is used by the end user only as a means to convey information between two users. This traffic is not acted upon by the network, instead being carried transparently through the network. The field has a maximum size of 131 octets. It also contains a protocol discriminator, which can be used to indicate a high level protocol that is operating at the end-user stations. This field is somewhat similar to the field discussed previously in the high layer compatibility information element. As examples, the protocol discriminator might identify the Internet Protocol (IP), DECnet network layer, SNA network layer, and so on.

Proposals for Modification to Q.933

As of this writing, a rather extensive modification to Q.933 has been proposed, and is wending its way through the standardization process. The rationale for the proposed change is that Q.933 is unnecessarily complex for a Frame Relay SVC. Table 10-3 reflects this proposed change. Also, be aware that many of the information elements shown in Table 10-2 will be eliminated with the implementation of this proposal.

Frame Relay Forum Recommendations for a Switched Virtual Call (SVC) Capability

The Frame Relay Forum has also developed a proposal for an SVC. It differs from the X.933/T1.617 specifications in that it is simpler, uses an

Table 10-3

Proposed Frame
Relay Connection
Control Messages
for a Revised
Q.933

Call Establishment
CONNECT
CALL PROCEEDING
PROGRESS   proposal deletes this message
CONNECT ACKNOWLEDGE   proposal deletes this message
SETUP
ALERTING   proposal deletes this message

Call Clearing
DISCONNECT
RELEASE
RELEASE COMPLETE

Miscellaneous
STATUS
STATUS ENQUIRY

and
Many information elements listed in Table 10-2 would be deleted.

unchannelized interface (a channel that is not subdivided into subchannels—e.g., B and D subchannels), and is also appropriate for both UNI and NNI. It also differs slightly from the proposed changes to Q933 that were summarized in the previous section.

The reader should refer to the appropriate specifications if more detail is needed.

ANSI's Provision for OSI Connection Mode Network Services over Frame Relay

ANSI T1.617, Annex C describes the procedures for the use of the OSI connection mode network services (CONS) over Frame Relay. This section provides a summary of these services.

The CONS Interface

The interconnections between the transport and network layers delineate the distinction between the network (lower three layers) and the

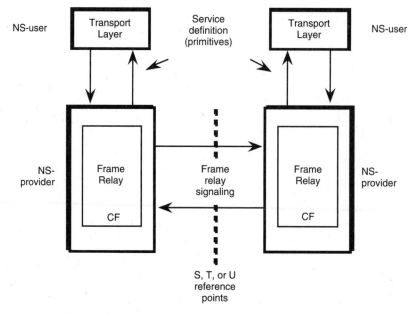

Figure 10-6
OSI CONS and Frame
Relay.

user (upper four layers). The relationship of the layers is shown in Fig. 10-6. In this section, we learn how the layers communicate. ITU-T X.213 is used as the example for this subject. The ISO publishes a similar document designated as DIS 8348.

As with other OSI layers, the network layer enables the network service user to request certain qualities of service (QOS). In addition, the network service provides addressing schemes that enable network service users to refer to one another unambiguously.

Network Service Primitives

As with all OSI layers, the network services are invoked via *primitives*. The primitives used by the network service for Frame Relay are illustrated in Table 10-4. The parameters are also shown with the primitives. In addition, the table also shows the relationship between the primitives and parameters and the Q931 messages and information elements. These primitives are used in various sequences to perform network establishment and network release.

Each of the QOS parameters listed in Table 10-4 (throughput, transit delay, and—eventually—protection and priority) also contains a set of subparameters. These parameters are necessary to allow the Frame Relay

Table 10-4

OSI CONS
Primitives and
Frame Relay
Signaling Messages
(for Connection
Setup)

Primitive	Frame Relay Messages
N-CONNECT.request	SETUP (user to network)
N-CONNECT.indication	SETUP (network to user)
N-CONNECT.response	CONNECT (user to network)
N-CONNECT.confirm	CONNECT (network to user)

Parameters in Primitive	Information Elements
Called address	Called party number
	Called party subaddress
Calling address	Calling party number
	Calling party subaddress
Responding address	Connected party number
	Connected party subaddress
Receipt confirmation selection	Packet layer binary parameters
Expedited data selection	Packet layer binary parameters
QOS	
Throughput	Link layer core parameters
Transit delay	End-to-end transit delay
Protection	For further study
Priority	For further study
NS-user data	User-data

software to create the fields in message signaling information elements shown in this chapter in Table 10-2.

The subparameters are listed in Table 10-5, along with their associated primitives. In addition, the list shows the field within the signaling protocol message. The direction of the message from user-to-network (U-to-N) or network-to-user (N-to-U) is also shown.

Figure 10-7 shows an example of how the primitives are used between the user and the Frame Relay entity, as well as how these primitives are mapped to *setup* and *connect* messages. For ease in following this figure, events are marked with numbers in bold parentheses.

To establish a connection, the NS user (usually a transport layer, unless this entity is located in a router) issues an N-CONNECT request primitive. Associated with this primitive is the term *Tgt*, which is an abbreviation that asks for a target throughput and a target committed burst size for this connection. Also associated with this primitive is the term *LQA*, which stands for lowest quality acceptable. This parameter in

Table 10-5

The QOS Subparameters and Their Relationship to the Frame Relay Messages

Sub-parameter	Associated Primitive	Field in Message	Direction
Target	N-CONNECT.request	Throughput/CBS req	SETUP U-to-N
LQA	N-CONNECT.request	Minimum acceptable TP	SETUP U-to-N
Available	N-CONNECT.indication	Throughput/CBS ava	SETUP N-to-U
LQA	N-CONNECT.indication	Minimum acceptable TP	SETUP N-to-U
Selected	N-CONNECT.response	Throughput/CBS agreed	CONNECT U-to-N
Selected	N-CONNECT.confirm	Throughput/CBS agreed	CONNECT N-to-U

Legend:
CBS	Committed burst size
req	requested
LQA	Lowest quality acceptable
TP	Throughput
ava	available
U-to-N	User-to-network
N-to-U	Network-to-user

the primitive signifies to the Frame Relay entity what the minimum acceptable throughput would be for the connection. Frame Relay uses this information to create the SETUP message in event 2. The parameter *TP req* reflects the requested throughput, the parameter labeled *CBS req* represents the requested committed burst size, and the parameter *Min TP* establishes the minimum acceptable throughput. As the figure shows, this SETUP message is sent through the Frame Relay network.

In event 3, the Frame Relay network acts upon this message and relays the message to the Frame Relay entity at the remote side of the network. The event 3 SETUP message contains the parameter *TP ava*, which describes the throughput available for the session. It can be seen that the throughput requested in event 2 can be changed to reflect the throughput available in event 3. The same holds for the event 3 setup message. The parameter labeled *CBS ava* establishes the committed burst size available for this session, and the *min TP* parameter establishes the minimum acceptable throughput.

The message is mapped in event 4 to the N-CONNECT indication primitive. It contains the *Ava* parameter, which reflects the throughput availability and committed burst size availability, as well as the parameter labeled LQA, which reflects the minimum acceptable throughput.

Events 1, 2, 3, and 4 complete the first half of the virtual communications setup. The transport layer, in event 5, returns the N-CONNECT

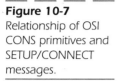

Figure 10-7
Relationship of OSI
CONS primitives and
SETUP/CONNECT
messages.

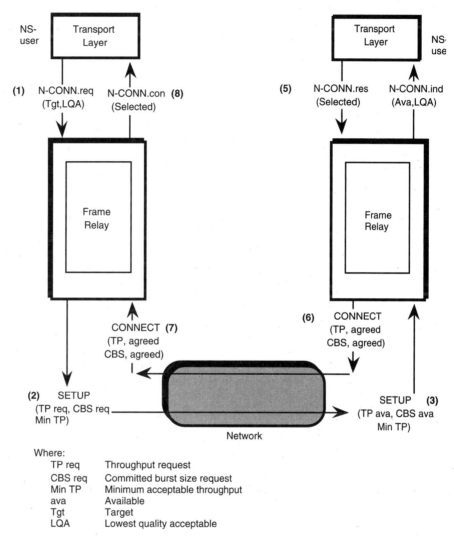

Where:
TP req	Throughput request
CBS req	Committed burst size request
Min TP	Minimum acceptable throughput
ava	Available
Tgt	Target
LQA	Lowest quality acceptable

request primitive with a parameter entitled *Selected,* which contains
information that is mapped to the CONNECT message in event 6. The
values selected are used to create the fields in event 6 labeled *TP, agreed*
(upon throughput) and *CBS, agreed* (upon burst size). This traffic is then
relayed through the Frame Relay network. The fields are not changed
from event 6 to event 7. Thus, the fields in the CONNECT in event 7 are
used to create the parameters labeled *Selected* in event 8, N-CONNECT
CONFIRM primitive. Once all these actions have been completed, a network connection has been established.

When the network entity receives the N-CONNECT request primitive, it checks the parameters in the primitive to see whether they can meet the requirements. If these parameters are unspecified, it is anticipated that their default values will be supplied. The term *anticipated* is used because as of this writing, this service has not been established commercially. If the values in the subparameters are specified, the entity must check the lowest quality accepted value. If it cannot support this level of service, it is required to return an N-DISCONNECT indication to the user. This effectively terminates any further operations. If the service can be met, the entity then uses these parameters to encode the fields in the SETUP message and, of course, sends the SETUP message through the Frame Relay network. The remote entity receives the SETUP message and, if it is unable to provide the services established in the message, it must create a release complete message with a diagnostic indicating that the quality of service (QOS) requested is not available. Assuming all goes well, as suggested in the previous discussion, the operations occur through the events described in Fig. 10-2.

Connection release is obtained through the use of the N-DISCONNECT request and N-DISCONNECT indication primitives. As illustrated in Table 10-6, the relationship of these primitives to the DISCONNECT RELEASE, and RELEASE messages are shown, as well as the

Table 10-6

OSI CONS Primitives and Frame Relay Signaling Messages (for Disconnects)

Primitive	Frame Relay Messages
N-DISCONNECT.request	DISCONNECT (user to network) RELEASE (user to network) RELEASE COMPLETE (user to network)
N-DISCONNECT.indication	DISCONNECT (network to user) RELEASE (network to user) RELEASE COMPLETE (network to user) RESTART (network to user)

Parameters in Primitive	Information Elements
Responding address	Connected party number Connected party subaddress
Originator	Cause
Reason	Cause
NS-user data	User-user

relationship of the parameters and primitives to the information elements in the message. The messages can contain a number of diagnostics to indicate the reason for the N-DISCONNECT.

SUMMARY

The Frame Relay signaling specifications are published in ANSI T1.617 and ITU-T Q933. These specifications define the procedures for the user-to-network signaling to support Frame Relay calls. The procedures include both B-channel and D-channel frame-mode connection operations.

The NNI, ICI, and LMI

This chapter examines several Frame Relay interfaces. Some operate at the UNI and some at the NNI, but all are designed to be enhancements to the basic Frame Relay services. The topics to be discussed are the network-to-network interface (NNI), the intercarrier interface (ICI), and the local management interface (LMI). It will be evident as you read this chapter that the NNI and LMI have many similarities.

The NNI

The initial thrust of the Frame Relay work focused on the user-to-network interface (UNI). Subsequent work resulted in the publication by the Frame Relay Forum (based on ANSI's T1.617, Annex D) of a network-to-network interface (NNI). This interface is considered instrumental to the success of Frame Relay, since it defines the procedures for different networks to interconnect with each other in support of Frame Relay operations.

The relationship between the UNI and NNI is illustrated in Fig. 11-1. Obviously, the UNI defines the procedures between the user and the Frame Relay network, and the NNI defines the procedures between the Frame Relay networks.

A PVC operating across more than one Frame Relay network is called a *multinetwork PVC.* Each piece of the PVC provided by each network is a PVC *segment.* Therefore, the multinetwork PVC is a combination of the relevant PVC segments. In addition, the NNI uses the bidirectional network procedures published in ANSI T1.617 Annex D, and also requires that all networks involved in the PVC support NNI procedures and UNI procedures. Thus, a PVC segment can exist between a UNI and NNI, or between two NNIs.

Main Purpose of NNI

The main purpose of NNI is to provide a standardized procedure for users and networks to provision PVCs end to end. This purpose is met by having the parties inform each other that their respective PVC segment has been configured and is ready for use. After ongoing PVCs are active and operational, NNI is then used to keep all parties informed about the status of the PVCs. If a network or user encounters problems, it informs its respective UNI or NNI neighbor about the problem, and

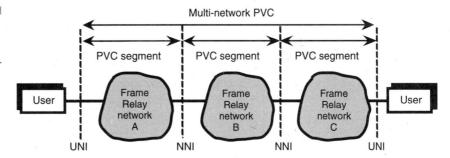

Figure 11-1
Frame Relay internetworking with NNI.

remedial action is taken (which is not defined in the NNI). Additionally, the NNI is used by the user and networks to verify periodically that the physical link between the UNI or NNI is operating properly.

Congestion Management.   Congestion management at the NNI is quite similar to the UNI operations discussed in Chap. 9. The reader can refer to Table 9-2 for a refresher. The only difference in this table for the NNI is that in the last row, where CIR = 0, $B_c = 0$, and $B_e > 0$, T_c is a network-defined value.

NNI Message Exchange

Full internetworking operations between Frame Relay networks requires that the procedures stipulated in ANSI T1.617 Annex D be used at the UNI and the NNI. This concept means that a user sends a status enquiry (SE) message to the network and the network responds with a status (S) message (see Fig. 11-2). The SE message, as the name suggests, is used to query the receiver about the status of PVC segments. In turn, the S provides information about PVC segments. Bidirectional procedures at the NNI require that a network be allowed to send status enquiry and status messages.

Messages sent across the NNI are encapsulated into an HDLC unnumbered information frame (UI). The default size of the information field is 1600 octets. Other sizes must be negotiated. Since the UI does not have any timers or sequence numbers associated with it, these features are added into the SE and S messages. The messages are sent on DLCI 0, with the UI poll bit (P bit) set to 0. The BECN, FECN, and DE bits are not used and are set to 0.

Figure 11-2
The NNI messages.

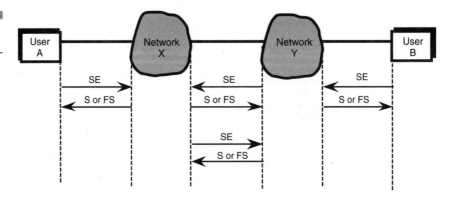

Where:

FS   Full status message
S   Status message
SE   Status enquiry

NNI Operations

The principal operations of NNI involve these services:

- Notification of the addition of a PVC
- Detection of the deletion of a PVC
- Providing for notification of UNI or NNI failures
- Notification of a PVC segment availability or unavailability
- Verification of links between Frame Relay nodes
- Verification of Frame Relay nodes

These operations take place through the exchange of status (S), full status (FS), and status enquiry (SE) messages that contain information about the status of the PVCs. With this thought in mind, we now explore the principal NNI operations.

Parameters for the NNI/UNI Interfaces

As explained earlier, the NNI uses the procedures established by ANSI T1.617 Annex D for the UNI. Therefore, periodic polling takes place between user equipment and network equipment to determine the status of PVCs, links, and Frame Relay nodes. The information associated with these polling operations deals with status enquiry messages, the responses with status messages, and full status messages (information on all PVCs).

Like any conventional polling operation, the behavior is determined through the use of timers. In addition, periodic messages are issued based on every few polling events that occur. The NNI stipulates that two sets of timers, sequence numbers, and polling cycles must exist with both the UNI and the NNI.

The procedures at the user side must include support for T391, N391, N392, and N393. The procedures at the network side must support T392, N392, and N393. Table 11-1 describes the purpose of the NNI parameters and the permissible ranges for these values at the NNI.

Every T391 seconds, the user side sends a status enquiry message to another network. Upon issuing this message, it resets this timer. Typically, the status enquiry message only requests a link integrity check. Every N391 polling cycles (a polling cycle is the interval between the status and status enquiry messages), the user side asks for a full status of all the PVC segments with a full status enquiry message. In turn, the responder (network side) reacts to each status enquiry message with a status message and also resets its T392 timer. The information in the status enquiry

Table 11-1

NNI Parameters

Name	Purpose
N391	Polling cycles for full status of all PVCs
N392	Number of errors occurring during N393 monitored events
N393	Monitored events counter
T391	Link integrity verification polling timer
T392	Polling verification timer

Name	Range	Default	User or Network Side
N391	1–255	6 polling cycles	Both*
N392	1–10	3 errors	Both
N393	1–10	4 events	Both
T391	5–30 secs.	10 secs.	User
T392	5–30 secs.	15 secs.	Network

*Always on user side and may be on network side if bidirectional procedures are in place.

message contains DLCIs and the status of the DLCIs. The N392 counter is used to indicate the number of errors occurring during the N393. The N393 is the monitor count. These latter two parameters are discussed in more detail later in the chapter.

The NNI access is not considered operational until an agreed-upon number of N393 polling cycles have occurred.

NNI Messages

NNI messages were briefly discussed earlier; we now continue that discussion. Three messages are used for the following operations:

- *Status Enquiry (SE):*   Message that requests the status of a PVC or PVCs, or requests the verification of the status of a physical link
- *Status (S):*   Message that reports on the status of a PVC, or reports on the status of a physical link. Sent in response to a status enquiry message
- *Full Status (FS):*   Message that reports on the status of all PVCs on the physical link

The formats for these messages are shown in Fig. 11-3 (you can study ANSI T1.617, Annex D for more detail on the messages, as well as Frame Relay Forum document number FRF92.62). For the status enquiry mes-

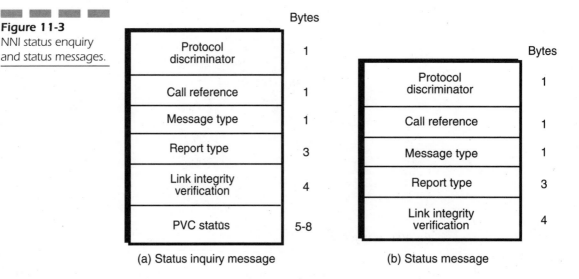

Figure 11-3
NNI status enquiry and status messages.

(a) Status inquiry message

(b) Status message

sage, six fields are used. The header consists of three fields: *protocol discriminator, call reference,* and *message type.* These fields are coded in accordance with ANSI T.607. Thereafter, the message contains the *report type, link integrity verification,* and *PVC status fields.* The following discussion explains the contents of the messages as they relate to the NNI.

The header contains the protocol discriminator, call reference, and message types. The contents of these fields were discussed in Chap. 10. The message type is coded to indicate a status message (01111101) or a status enquiry message (01110101).

The report type is coded to indicate a full status message (00000000), a link integrity verification only (00000001), or a single PVC status (00000010).

The link integrity verification field actually consists of four octets. The identifier in the first octet is used to tag the remainder of the octets. The second octet contains the length of the verification contents. The next two octets contain the send sequence number and the receive sequence number. The purpose of these fields is to ensure that both sides of the NNI receive all the traffic, and to be sure that the link and NNI nodes are also operating properly. The send sequence number contains the number of this message, and the receive sequence number contains the value of the send sequence number that was received in the last message.

The last field in the status message is the PVC status field, which actually consists of six octets (when the default address format of two octets is used). The first octet identifies the information element as the PVC status when it is set to 01010111. The second octet is the length of the remainder of the contents. The next two octets contain the DLCI. The fifth octet contains a number of bits that are not used, and the new bit (N), delete bit (D), and the active bit (A). These bits are set to the following values:

New bit

0 PVC is already present

1 PVC is new

Delete bit

0 PVC is configured

1 PVC is deleted

Active bit

0 PVC is inactive

1 PVC is active

A network can only report a multisegment PVC active if four conditions hold:

- all PVC segments have been configured
- N393 consecutive polling cycles have occurred
- all relevant UNIs and NNIs are operational
- the user (at the UNI) sets the active bit = 1 in a status message

The last octet contains two fields, the network count and the inactive reason. The inactive reason is used to determine why problems may exist regarding DLCI(s). It is coded to indicate the following situations:

- Adjacent NNI or UNI does not support inactive reason
- NNI or UNI channel is inactive
- PVC segment deleted in adjacent network
- PVC segment failure has occurred in a network

The network count field is used to provide the relative location of a fault by using the number of networks between the fault and the reporting NNI along the multisegment NNI.

Examples of NNI Operations

The following examples provide explanations of several NNI operations. The reader should refer to Frame Relay Forum FRF92.62 for more detailed information (from which these examples are derived).

I made brief mention earlier of the link integrity verification procedures. Recall that the send sequence and receive sequence numbers are used between the two entities to verify that all is well across the channel. This procedure is quite similar to many other verification procedures that use sequence numbers. The send sequence number is simply acknowledged by the receive sequence number. Since both the send and receive sequence numbers reside in the message, one entity can transmit a send sequence number and simultaneously piggyback the receive sequence number in the message to acknowledge previously received traffic from the transmitter. These messages are issued periodically across the interface. Both machines send status enquiry (SE) messages, and both machines respond to those messages with status (S) messages.

In addition, one of the principal jobs of the NNI interface is to use periodic polling to notify the user side of new PVCs. When a new PVC is added, the new bit is set to 1 in the NNI message to inform the user side about this PVC. Initially, a new PVC is so identified with a new bit set to 1 and the active bit set to 0. As we shall see, the next step is to set the active bit to 1 in order to accommodate the lag effect of notifying various sides about the PVC creation and its availability. NNI also provides procedures for deleting PVCs and/or making them inactive.

Adding a PVC. PVCs are added at the NNI either by having the Frame Relay network inform the user of the addition, or having the Frame Relay network inform another network of the addition. Since PVC segments belong to a network, multiple networks cannot add PVCs simultaneously. Instead, messages are sent between networks at the NNI, and between the user and the network at the UNI, to add the full multi-network PVC, with the segments being added one at a time. Figure 11-4 shows an example of the addition of a multinetwork PVC.

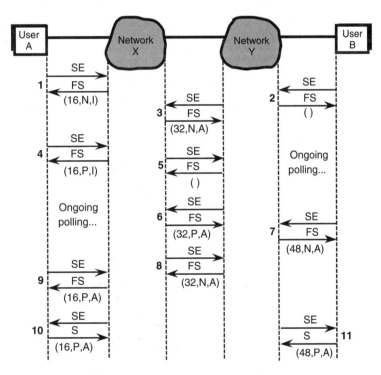

Figure 11-4
Adding a PVC.

Where:

A	Active bit set to 1
FS	Full status message
I	Active bit set to 0
N	New bit set to 1
P	New bit set to 0, PVC is not new
S	Status message
SE	Status enquiry message

In the context of the link between user A and network X, DLCI 16 is added. In the context of the link between network X to network Y, DLCI 32 is added. In the context of the link between user B and network Y, DLCI 48 is added. You will notice that end-to-end configuration occurs by making each segment "active," one step at time.

Let's examine the bottom part of the figure first to illustrate the point. The user-A-to-network-X segment executes an active status (event 9) after the network-X-to-network-Y interface is made active (event 8). In turn, the X-to-Y segment interface waits for the active notification of the segment between network Y and user B (event 7) before it assumes an active status in event 8. Therefore, the provisioning process can begin at the upstream interface, with A-X acting as the upstream interface. The final activation of each PVC segment, however, occurs from the downstream interface, with B-Y acting as the downstream interface.

The multinetwork PVC cannot be used until all PVC segments have been configured and link integrity has been successfully verified on all UNIs and NNIs. With these thoughts in mind, the events in Fig. 11-4 can now be explained. First, all parties (users and networks) have prior agreements that a PVC is to be established. Each party knows beforehand which DLCI value will be used at the interface. Thus, the NNI is invoked to "bring up" the PVC connection at each interface.

Event 1   User A periodically polls network X through status enquiry (SE) messages. After network X has performed the necessary provisioning and bandwidth allocation operations within its network, it responds to the SE message with a full status (FS) message, which indicates PVC 16 is new (N) and inactive (I). The inactive status prevents user A from using the connection at this time.

Event 2   User B also repeatedly polls network Y, which returns an FS message reporting nothing about this particular PVC. The notation ( ) in the figure is used to symbolize this action. In actual practice, this particular SE message solicits information on all PVCs, so the FS response would contain information about other connections, if any exist.

Event 3   Upon receiving an SE poll from network Y, network X returns an FS message. This message contains fields that indicate PVC 32 is new and active. Network X is responsible for correlating PVC 16 at the user A–network X UNI with PVC 32 at the network X–network Y NNI.

Event 4   User A continues its polling of network X, which now informs the user that PVC 16 is present (P) but is still inactive. User A must therefore continue to defer using the connection.

Event 5   Network X also polls network Y, which responds with no relevant information about PVC 32, because network Y has not yet activated its part of the connection to user B (which is achieved in event 7).

Event 6   Network Y will continue to receive status information on PVC 32 from network X, but the new/present bit is set to present (P) to indicate that the PVC is not new. Network X knows it cannot use the connection until it receives an activation message from network Y (which is achieved in event 8).

Event 7   When network Y is ready to support the connection, it responds to user B's SE message with an FS message containing fields indicating that PVC 48 is new and active. Network Y is responsible for correlating PVC 48 at the user B–network Y UNI with PVC 32 at the network Y–network X NNI.

Event 8   Since network Y knows that its PVC 48 to user B is activated, it informs network X that PVC 32 can now be used.

Event 9   Since network X knows that all PVC segments downstream are activated, it informs user A that PVC 16 can now be used. The PVC provisioning is complete, and traffic can now be exchanged.

Event 10   The UNI part of the PVC can be used upon the user returning an S message with A = 1.

Event 11   Same as event 10.

Deleting a PVC.   A PVC is taken out of commission in a manner similar to its creation, on a step-by-step basis. Figure 11-5 shows an example of a PVC deletion, which consists of the following events. These operations assume all parties have agreed to the deletion and removal of the services at all affected UNIs and NNIs.

Event 1   Network X informs user A that PVC 16 has been deleted by sending A an FS message with the D bit set to 1 (noted as D in the figure).

Event 2   Network X makes PVC 32 inactive across the X-Y NNI as soon as possible, by sending network Y an FS message with the active bit set to 0 (noted as I in the figure).

Event 3   Network Y informs user B about the deletion of PVC 48 by sending B an FS message with the D bit set to 1.

Event 4   Network X now deletes the PVC across the NNI by sending network Y an FS message with the D bit set to 1.

Figure 11-5
Deleting a PVC.

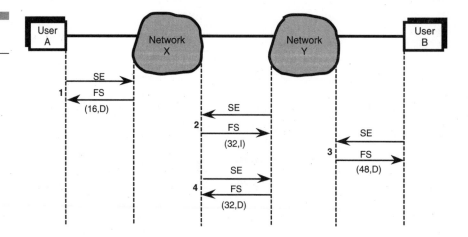

Where:

D   Delete bit set to 1
FS Full status message
I   Active bit set to 0
SE Status enquiry message

Notification of UNI Failure and Restoration. The NNI also establishes a procedure for a network to detect an inoperative UNI and to notify the PVC users associated with the UNI of the problem. This operation is depicted in Fig. 11-6. It also shows how the DLCIs are restored.

Event 1   Network X has issued SE messages to user A, but A's S messages are not delivered successfully to X. There can be many reasons for the problem. Perhaps A's transmit capability and/or X's receive capability are down; the link might be noisy, creating garbage on the line, and so forth.

Event 2   Network X makes the decision to take the PVC down at the NNI, at least temporarily. This operation is not the same as deleting the PVC, which was described in Fig. 11-5. The temporary take-down is performed by exchanging an FS message with the active bit set to 0 (shown as I in the figure).

Event 3   Network Y takes down its part of the PVC by issuing an FS message with the active bit set to 0 for PVC 48.

Event 4   At a later time, SE and FS/S messages are exchanged successfully between user A and network X.

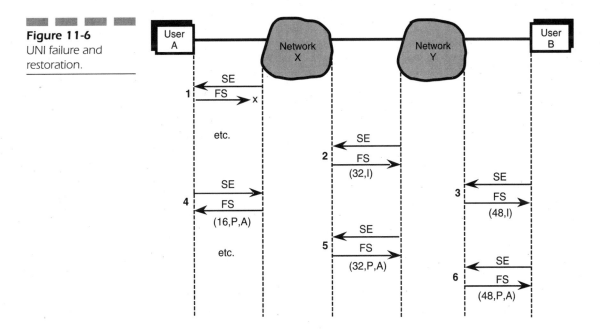

Figure 11-6
UNI failure and
restoration.

Events 5 and 6   As a result of user A and network X activating their PVC
segment, the other segments are activated.

Notification of PVC Segment Failures. Upon detecting an NNI
interface failure, each affected network must notify the affected users
that the PVC is inactive. If the notifying network sits between other networks, these networks are required to relay this information to the affected users at the UNI. These operations are the same as those depicted in
Fig. 11-6, except that the initial time-out occurs at one of the NNIs,
instead of the UNI.

Example of the Interactions Between Messages and Timers

Figure 11-7 shows how T391 and N391 are used. T391 initiates a status
enquiry message upon its expiration. A status message is returned, carrying link integrity information. The link integrity information is simply
a heartbeat operation to ensure that the interface is up and the other
machine is functioning properly.

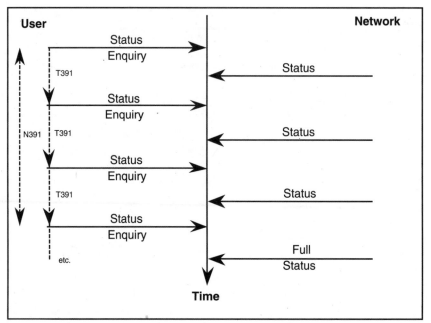

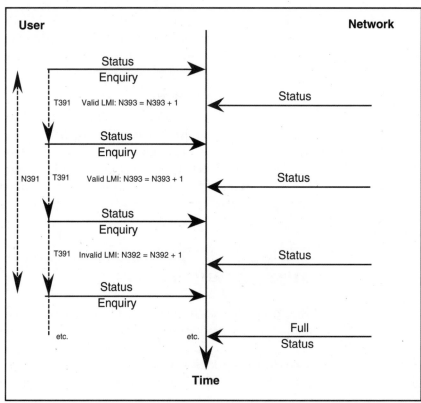

With each invocation of the status enquiry message, N391 is incremented by 1. After a set value of N391 has been reached, the next status enquiry message results in a full status message being returned, with information on each PVC that exists on the physical interface.

N392 is incremented by 1 for each error detected at the interface for each monitored event. A *monitored event* is simply the receipt of a message across the interface, and N392 is a count of errors occurring during those monitored events, such as an invalid message. These two counters are used to determine whether a UNI is in a failure state.

The T392 is used by the network to ascertain whether the user side is responding in a timely fashion to the network's status enquiry messages. If the user does not respond within T392, N392 is incremented by 1.

SVC Operations at the NNI

Chapter 10 describes the Frame Relay proposal for the SVC capability at the UNI. The proposal also includes specifications for SVC capability at the NNI. Figure 11-8 shows the operations for a connection setup and release. In the Chap. 10 section entitled "Frame Relay Forum Recommendations for a Switched Virtual Call (SVC) Capability," the timers involved in this operation, as well as other nuances, are discussed in more detail.

The ICI (FR_ICI)

The Bellcore Frame Relay Intercarrier Interface (FR_ICI) is also called the Exchange Access Frame Relay Service (XA-FR). I will use both terms in my explanations of this interface. This specification is available from Bellcore in Technical Reference TR-TSV-001270, Issue 1, May 1993, "Generic requirements for exchange access Frame Relay PVC service." The abbreviated notation of this specification is *XA-FR PVC service*.

Main Purpose of ICI

As depicted in Fig. 11-9, FR_ICI is designed to provide consistent service vis-à-vis the end-to-end PVC, that is, from UNI to UNI. In so doing, the XA-FR defines operations between interexchange carriers (ICs) and local

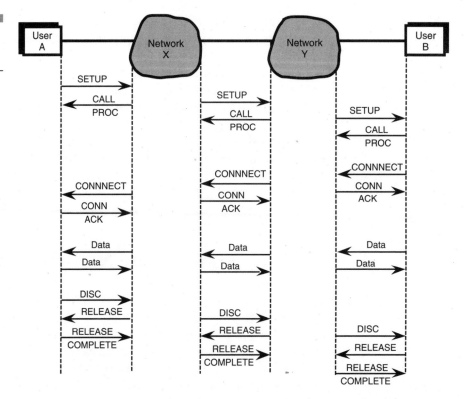

Figure 11-8
NNI SVC connection setup and release.

exchange carriers (LECs). The operations are called the *Frame Relay Inter-carrier Interface* (FR_ICI).

The FR_ICI supports BECN, FECN, and DE in accordance with the LEC network conventions. However, CIR is not policed again at an ICI, since it is assumed to have been policed at the ingress UNI. It is moni-

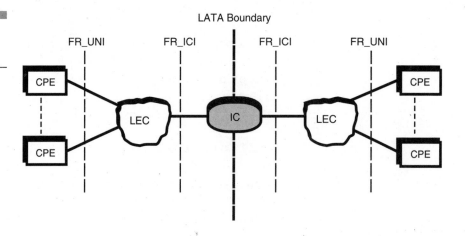

Figure 11-9
The Bellcore XA-FR service.

tored, however, by the LEC network that terminates the XA-FR service.

PVC status signaling is also supported at the ICI, in accordance with T1.606, Annex B, which is based on ITU-T Q933 (Annex A). Lastly, both LECs must exchange the parameter values of CIR, B_c, B_e, and T in accordance with the Frame Relay Forum document *Intercarrier Frame Relay services: recommendations and guidelines.*

XA-FR PVC Service Objectives

The XA-FR PVC service establishes several *service performance parameters* that must exist at the FR_ICI, and some of these parameters stipulate performance from the FR_UNI to the FR_ICI. See Table 11-2. The service parameters are relevant only to the *compliant frames*—this term describes those frames that are sent within the limits of the B_c. Any frames marked with DE = 1 are considered to be noncompliant. The performance objectives described in this section include three categories: *delay objectives, accuracy objectives,* and *availability objectives.*

Table 11-2

Bellcore Frame
Transfer Delay
Requirements
(Milliseconds)

ICI Rate	FR_UNI Access Rate for 512 Octet Frames				
	56	64	384	768	1536
56	161	152	99	94	91
64	152	143	90	85	82
1536	91	82	29	23	21
44210	89	80	27	22	19

ICI Rate	FR_UNI Access Rate for 1600 Octet Frames				
	56	64	384	768	1536
56	473	444	278	261	253
64	444	415	249	232	224
1536	253	224	57	40	32
44210	245	218	52	35	27

ICI Rate	FR_UNI Access Rate for 4096 Octet Frames				
	56	64	384	768	1536
56	1185	1112	686	643	622
64	1112	1039	613	570	549
1536	622	549	122	79	58
44210	601	528	102	59	38

Delay Objectives. The XA-FR delay objectives are described in relation to the FR_UNI access rate (in kbps), the FR_ICI access rate (in kbps), and the frame size (in octets). Delay is measured from the time the first bit of the frame (address field) is placed on the FR_UNI link to the time the last bit of the trailing flag is received at the FR_ICI. At least 95 percent of all frames should incur a delay no greater than the delay shown in this figure.

Accuracy Objectives. The XA-FR accuracy objectives specify performance goals for frames not delivered, frames with errors, and extra frame rate. The following notation is used to describe the accuracy objectives, which are provided in Table 11-3:

Ne Number of errored frames [frame arrives within a maximum time, and the cyclic redundancy check (CRC) computes correctly, but I field is different from that of the original frame]

Nl Number of lost frames (frame arrives late, or does not arrive, or the CRC does not compute correctly)

Ns Number of successful frames (frame arrives within a maximum time, the CRC computes correctly, and the I field is the same as in the original frame)

Nx Number of extra frames (frames misdelivered or duplicated)

Given this notation, the accuracy objectives are computed as shown in this table.

Availability Objectives. XA-FR PVC service specifies six availability objectives. Four parameters describe availability, and are measured as long-term averages. Two other parameters pertain to congestion notification, and are measured beginning with the receipt of BECN or FECN, and terminated after a time interval that is still "under study." The availability objectives are measured as shown in Table 11-4.

Table 11-3

Performance
Objectives—
Accuracy

- Frame not delivered ratio (should be $<1 \cdot 10^{-5}$):
  $$Nl{:}N_s + N_e + N_l$$
- Errored frame ratio (should be $<5 \cdot 10^{-13}$):
  $$Ne{:}N_s + N_e$$
- Extra frame ratio (should be $<5 \cdot 10^{-8}$ frames per second):
  Total N_x observed on a connection per connection second

Table 11-4

Availability
Objectives

- Scheduled hours of service: 24 hours per day, 7 days per week
- Service availability: Ratio of actual service time to schedule service time (criteria for outage is under study) with an objective of at least 99.95%
- Mean time to service restoral (MTTSR): Sum of all time between service unavailability and its restoral, with an objective of ≤3.5 hours
- Mean time between service outages (MTBSO): At least 3500 hours
- Fraction of time in noncongestion notification state: Time spent in noncongestion notification state, with an objective of at least 99%
- Mean time between congestion notification states: Arithmetic average of continuous time intervals in which no congestion state is entered, with an objective of at least 100 hours

Measurements and Billing

The XA-FR also defines procedures for the generation and reporting of network statistics for OAM and billing. Guidance is provided on when to perform measurements, in what increments, and when the measurements are stored and formatted for network management use. To ensure compatibility across the differing LECs and IC, all traffic must be formatted in accordance with Bellcore's Document TR-NWT-001100, which lists the well-known Bellcore Automatic Message Accounting Format (BMAF) requirements.

Information recorded for traffic measurement and billing must include the following data shown in Table 11-5.

Table 11-5

Billing and Usage
Information

- The date that the measurement began
- The time the measurement began
- The elapsed time of the measurement interval
- Identifier of the destination interface
- Identifier of the source interface
- Destination DLCI
- Source DLCI
- Unit of measurement and appropriate counts that pertain to that measurement

The LMI

In its most basic implementation, Frame Relay is a simple interface that offers bandwidth on demand, low delay, and high throughput to its users. It is designed deliberately to offer few additional services. Nonetheless, it is recognized that some users and networks wish to have information about the Frame Relay connections at the UNI. To that end, ANSI and the ITU-T define a standard to define these operations. This standard is called the local management interface (LMI). It is published in ANSI T1.617, Annexes B and D, and in ITU-T Q.933, Annexes A and B.

Main Purpose of LMI

The LMI enables both the user and the network to gather information about the UNI (see Fig. 11-10), and to signal each other about several activities pertaining to the virtual circuits on the link, and the status of the physical link itself.

LMI is quite similar to NNI. Indeed, the two are more alike than they are different. They use the same timers and parameters as well as the same messages. The principal difference is that LMI operates only at the UNI, whereas NNI operates at the UNI and an NNI. I have provided additional examples in this section of LMI operations, with illustrations of the use of the timers. Be aware that these examples are applicable also to NNI.

Like the NNI, the LMI is rather restricted in what it does. It provides these services:

- A polling function to test whether the user or network machine is connected to the interface

- A set of operations that inform the user of the addition or deletion of virtual circuits at the interface

Figure 11-10
The local management interface (LMI).

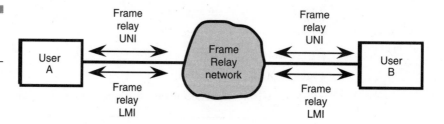

- A report on the status of all virtual circuits on the interface that states whether or not a virtual circuit is active
- A report on the availability of a new virtual circuit

The LMI contains two common extensions and a number of optional extensions. The optional extensions deal with global addressing and multicasting, which were introduced earlier in this book. The common extensions are explained in this section.

DLCI Values for the LMI

The DLCI values for the LMI are identical to those allocated for the NNI. These values are listed and described in Table 11-6. DLCI 0 is used to carry LMI traffic; the other DLCIs are available for the user, or are reserved for other management operations, or are reserved for future use.

The LMI Frame

Figure 11-11 shows the format of the LMI frame and the LMI information field (I field), which contains the LMI message. The Frame Relay header requires that DLCI = 0. Additionally, the command/response bit (C/R) and the BECN/FECN bits are set to 0. The LMI frame uses the well-known high level data link control (HDLC) unnumbered information (UI) control field, which is so named because it contains no sequence numbers. As such, UI frames cannot be sequenced or flow

Table 11-6

DLCI Values for the LMI

DLCI Values	Function
0	LMI channel
1–15	Reserved
16–991	For user virtual circuits
992–1007	Layer 2 management of Frame Relay bearer service (OAM, etc.)
1008–1022	Reserved
1023	In-channel layer management

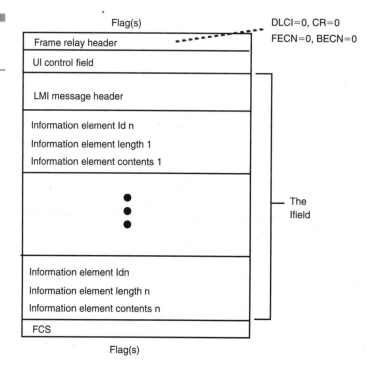

controlled, since no method exists to associate these operations with a specific frame.

The LMI message header contains several fields (explained shortly) to identify the specific type of LMI message. Thereafter, depending upon the type of message, the remaining parts of the message contain the LMI parameters, which are called *information elements.*

Each information element has three parts: a unique ID identifier, a field that specifies the length of the information element contents, and the information contents field itself. This set is repeated as necessary to convey the needed information.

Types of Messages

LMI provides for two types of message: a status (S) message and a status enquiry (SE) message (see Fig. 11-12). Within certain rules, these messages can be issued by the network or user. The status enquiry message is invoked to poll for an enquiry message. The issuance of the status enquiry message is governed by a timer, which is configurable within an

Figure 11-12
Contents of LMI
frame.

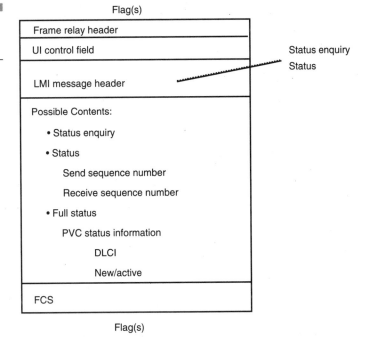

upper and lower limit. When the timer expires, a status enquiry message is sent onto the link. Upon receiving a status enquiry message, the receiving machine responds with a status message.

The status message reports on the status of the virtual circuits at the UNI or on the status of the link connecting the user and network machines. In reporting on virtual circuits, the message describes whether these circuits are active, new, inactive, or deleted. For reporting on the status of the link, the message contains a send and receive sequence number. As I explain shortly, these sequence numbers are used to ensure that all messages are being sent and received without loss or corruption.

LMI Operations

Like the NNI, periodic polling takes place between user equipment and network equipment to determine the status of PVCs. The parameters associated with these polling operations deal with status enquiry messages, their responses with status messages, and full status messages (inquiring about information on all PVCs). Table 11-6 lists these timers and their functions.

Like any conventional polling operation, behavior is determined through the use of timers. In addition, periodic messages are issued based on every few polling events that occur. The NNI parameters (Table 11-1) are quite similar to the LMI parameters, except that LMI uses different notations:

$$LMI\ nN3 = NNI\ N393$$

$$LMI\ nT2 = NNI\ T392$$

$$LMI\ nN2 = NNI\ 392$$

Also, LMI defines nN4, which is the maximum received network-side status enquiry value, and a network side nT3 timer (for nN4 SEs received).

SUMMARY

The network-to-network interface (NNI) is published by the Frame Relay Forum. The NNI defines the procedures required for different networks to interconnect with one another to support Frame Relay operations.

The principal operations of NNI involve notifying users and other networks of the addition and deletion of PVCs, UNI failures, NNI failures, and PVC segments in an end-to-end PVC. NNI is now being deployed in Frame Relay networks in the United States.

The local management interface (LMI) is almost identical to the NNI, except that it is supposed to operate only at the UNI.

The intercarrier interface (ICI) defined by Bellcore is designed to provide consistent service from UNI to UNI. In so doing, the XA-FR defines operations between interexchange carriers (ICs) and local exchange carriers (LECs).

Internetworking Frame Relay and Other Systems

This chapter describes several Frame Relay internetworking operations. The emphasis is on how Frame Relay relates to ATM and X.25, and how traffic from other protocols can be transported through the Frame Relay network.

As the Asynchronous Transfer Mode (ATM) becomes more prevalent, it will become necessary to internetwork Frame Relay systems with ATM networks. Until 1993, this interface was being developed without guidance from the standards organizations, and left a lot of choice to vendor-specific solutions. Therefore, the Forums have published a standard for interworking between Frame Relay and ATM. It is called the *ATM Data Exchange Interface* (ATM DXI).

A related standard, called the *Frame User-to-Network Interface* (FUNI), is based on DXI. Both specifications are described in this chapter.

The chapter concludes with an examination of the relationships of (1) the Internet Protocol (IP) and Frame Relay, and (2) X.25 and Frame Relay.

The reader should have an understanding of ATM and the ATM adaptation layer (AAL) before reading this chapter. Appendix B of this book provides a tutorial on these subjects. You should also review Chap. 9 and Fig. 9-9 if you are not familiar with EtherType and LLC LSAPs.

RFC 1490: Running Multiprotocol Families over Frame Relay

The Internet standard Request for Comments (RFC) 1490 (which makes RFC 1294 obsolete) establishes the rules for how protocols are encapsulated within the Frame Relay frame and transported across a network. This proposal is based on the encapsulation standards published in ANSI T1.617, Annex F. The Frame Relay Forum has used these documents as the basis for its Implementation Agreements (IAs) on this matter.

The Network Level Protocol ID

The *network level protocol identifier* (NLPID) contains values to identify common protocols that are used in the industry, such as ISO CLNP, the Internet's IP, and so forth. It is administered by the ISO and ITU-T. The purpose of this field is to inform the receiver which protocol is being carried inside the Frame Relay frame. This field is ignored by the Frame Relay network, and is examined only by user CPE.

The reader can obtain ISO/IEC TR9577 for the values that are currently administered by the ISO. Examples of NLPID values are:

0X00	Null network layer (not used by Frame Relay)
0X80	IEEE SNAP
0X81	ISO CLNP
0X82	ISO IS-IS
0X83	ISO IS-IS
0XCC	IP
0X8	ISDN Q933

Frame Format

As shown in Fig. 12-1, all traffic (and protocols) are carried in the Frame Relay frame, with the NLPID field used to identify which pro-

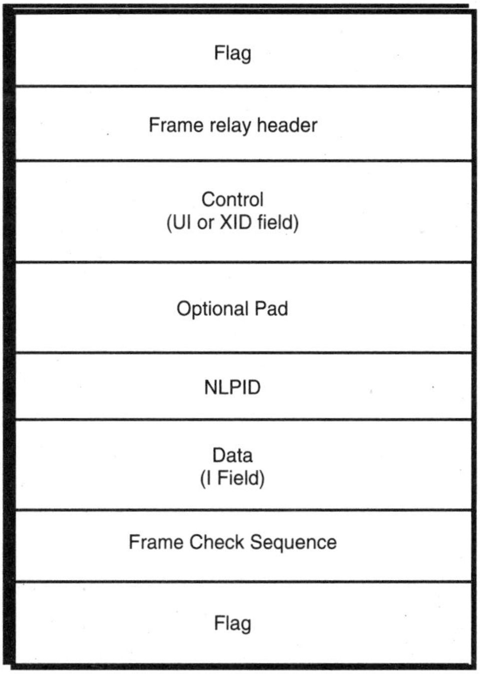

Figure 12-1
Using the NLPID field.

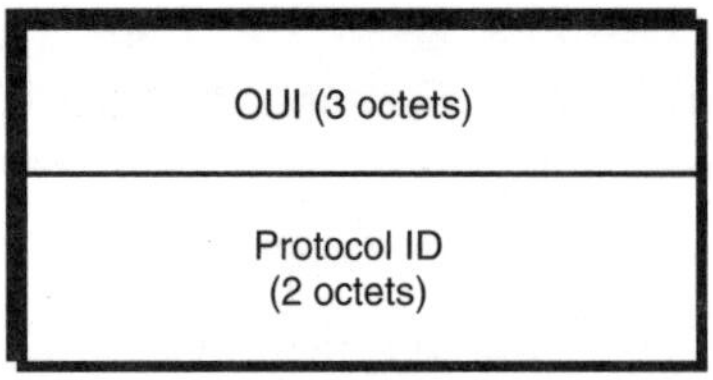

Figure 12-2
PDUs for multiproto-
col encapsulation
with SNAP.

| OUI (3 octets) |
| Protocol ID (2 octets) |

tocol family is contained in the I field of the frame. The control field contains the HDLC unnumbered information (UI) field or the XID field. The pad field is used to align the full frame to a two-octet boundary.

For ongoing traffic, the UI control field is used. The XID control field can be employed during an initialization operation between the user stations to negotiate the maximum frame size, the retransmission timer, and the window size (maximum number of permitted outstanding I frames allowed).

Some protocols do not have an assigned NLPID. In this situation, the *subnetwork access protocol* (SNAP) header is used, and the NLPID is set to indicate that a SNAP header is present. Figure 12-2 shows the format of the SNAP header. The *organizationally unique identifier* (OUI) is a registered number that identifies the organization that administers the *protocol ID field* (PID). Taken together, they identify a specific protocol. If the SNAP is used, it is placed in the frame immediately following the NLPID field.

Routed Frames and Bridged Packets

Two types of PDUs are sent through a Frame Relay network: *routed* PDUs and *bridged* PDUs. For routed PDUs, the traffic residing in the I field of the frame is identified by either an EtherType field as part of SNAP, or a conventional NLPID field.

For bridged PDUs, the SNAP header is used, and follows the NLPID header. In addition, the NLPID header indicates whether the original FCS is preserved within the bridged PDU. An organizational unique code of 0x00-80-C2 is reserved for this operation, and the PID field is coded to indicate the following:

With Preserved FCS	Without Preserved FCS	Traffic Type
0x00-01	0x00-07	802.3/Ethernet
0x00-02	0x00-08	802.4
0x00-03	0x00-09	802.5
0x00-04	0x00-0A	FDDI
0x00-0B		802.6

Only one choice exists for the PID field for 802.6 traffic, since the presence of an 802.6 CRC-32 field is indicated inside the 802.6 header.

Fragmentation

A Frame Relay network is supposed to support a frame size as small as 262 octets in the I field. Consequently, RFC 1490 defines the procedures for the fragmentation of larger PDUs into smaller frames. The fragments are identified with the SNAP header, with an OUI of 0x00-80-C2, and a PID of 0x00-0D. As shown in Fig. 12-1, these fields are followed by a *sequence number* for each frame, which is used to detect lost fragments, and an *offset field*, which shows the relative position of the fragment in the original, nonfragmented frame. Recently, the Frame Relay Forum published a specification for fragmentation operations, which is explained in Chap. 14.

Address/DLCI Resolution

Procedures are also available to use SNAP to identify the traffic in the frame as *address resolution protocol* (ARP) data. This operation can be invoked to obtain a DLCI value for a user station, as well as to correlate a DLCI with an address.

For the uninitiated, ARP is widely used throughout the industry to seek an unknown address and/or correlate one type of address with another. For example, a higher-layer network destination address (such as an IP address) can be associated with a lower-layer physical destination address (such as an Ethernet address).

Generally, ARP works with mapping tables (referred to as the *ARP cache*). Such a table provides the mapping between one address and another. In a LAN (like Ethernet or an IEEE 802 network), ARP takes the target IP address and searches for a corresponding physical address in a mapping table. If the 48-bit address is found, it is returned to the requester, such as a device driver or server on a LAN. However, if the desired address is not found in the ARP cache, the ARP module sends a broadcast onto the network.

The broadcast is called the *ARP request.* The ARP request contains an IP address. Consequently, if one of the machines receiving the broadcast recognizes its IP address in the ARP request, it will return an ARP reply to the inquiring host. This reply contains the physical hardware address of the queried host. Upon receiving this datagram, the inquiring host enters this address into the ARP cache. Thereafter, datagrams sent to this particular IP address can be translated to the physical address.

Address resolution in a Frame Relay network works in much the same way as in a conventional environment such as the one just described. Figure 12-3 shows how ARP is used with Frame Relay. Be aware that the

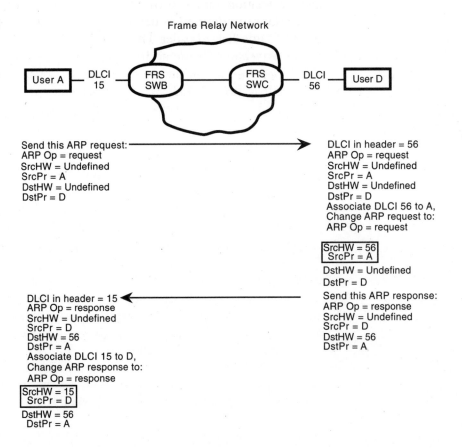

Figure 12-3
Frame Relay ARP operations.

approach described here does not use ARP in the conventional manner. The hardware address fields in the ARP messages are used to contain DLCIs, and pure modular-OSI layering concepts are not used.

To begin the process, user A forms an ARP request message. Since hardware addresses are not used in this process, the hardware address fields are undefined in the request message. The source and destination protocol addresses (for example, IP addresses) are filled in as usual. In this example, the source IP address is A (for user A) and the destination IP address is B (for user B). When user D receives the ARP request, it is encapsulated into the Frame Relay frame, which contains the local DLCI value of 56 (placed in the frame by the Frame Relay network). User B extracts this value from the header and places it in the source hardware address of the incoming ARP request message. This process enables user B to associate protocol address A (in the source protocol address field) with DLCI 56. The box on the right-hand side of the figure shows where the correlation takes place.

Next, user B forms the *ARP response* message (interchanges the source and destination values in the message), but leaves the destination hardware address undefined. When user A receives this frame, it has DLCI 15 in the Frame Relay header. Thus, user A extracts this value and places it in the source hardware address field of the message. This operation enables user A to correlate DLCI 15 with protocol address D. Once again, the two boxes in Fig. 12-3 highlight where the correlations take place.

After these operations have taken place,

- user A knows that address D is correlated with DLCI 15;
- user D knows that address A is correlated with DLCI 56.

Reverse ARP (RARP)

Reverse ARP (RARP) will use the same procedures shown in Fig. 12-3. If we assume that user D is an RARP server, the ARP request and response will enable the two protocol addresses to be correlated with the two respective DLCIs.

Internetworking ATM and Frame Relay

The next part of this chapter defines the operations for internetworking Frame Relay and ATM networks. (Appendix B is provided for the reader who is not familiar with ATM.) We begin by comparing and contrasting ATM and Frame Relay. In this material, we examine the requirements for the support of each major Frame Relay "feature" by an ATM support network. The second part of the analysis explains the Data Exchange Interface (DXI). The next part explains the Frame UNI (FUNI) and compares it to DXI. To conclude the Frame Relay/ATM internetworking subject, we take a look at RFC 1483, an encapsulation specification.

Why Internetwork Frame Relay and ATM?

A reasonable question that could be posed by the reader is why should an organization wish to internetwork Frame Relay and ATM networks? Before we move to an analysis of Frame Relay and ATM internetworking, let us answer this question.

The intent of Frame Relay and ATM internetworking is to allow the continued use of a very effective technology, Frame Relay, and at the same time, provide a platform to migrate to ATM.

This approach assumes that Frame Relay is viewed by an organization as a transient technology—one that serves the enterprise for a while, and is then replaced by a more effective technology, in this case, ATM.

Since ATM is still an emerging technology, and in its place in the telecommunications marketplace is yet to be determined, the final scenario for the internetworking of Frame Relay and ATM is not known.

Nonetheless, the wide use of Frame Relay, and the emergence of ATM leads to situations where these two networks must be able to exchange user traffic. If one user is attached to a Frame Relay network, for example, and another is attached to an ATM network, then it makes sense to have a means for these users to be able to communicate with each other—thus the reason for internetworking Frame Relay and ATM.

Key Definitions

Two definitions that are used in this part of the chapter are *network interworking* and *service interworking* (see Fig. 12-4). For this discussion, interworking is used in the same context as internetworking, and the machine that performs these operations is called an interworking unit, an internetworking unit, or simply a gateway.

Network interworking entails the support of Frame Relay systems

Figure 12-4
Service and network
interworking.

Network Interworking:
Frame Relay operates on each side of ATM "backbone":

Service Interworking:
ATM backbone sits between Frame Relay and ATM:

Where:
IWF   Interworking function (also known as a gateway or internetworking unit)

through an ATM network, typically called a *backbone*. As we see in more detail later, network interworking is an operation in which the ATM service user performs Frame Relay functions by executing the *FR-service specific convergence sublayer* (FR-SSCS) functions of AAL5. These operations are performed by the user machine, known as the *broadband customer premises equipment* (B-CPE). The B-CPE must have knowledge of remote Frame Relay system.

Service interworking entails the support of a Frame Relay system with an ATM system, through an ATM backbone. Service interworking is similar to network interworking, but the ATM service user has no knowledge of the remote Frame Relay system. The Frame Relay service user performs no ATM services and the ATM service user performs no Frame Relay services. All interworking operations between the user are performed by the interworking function (IWF).

A Comparison of Frame Relay and ATM

We now pause and compare some of the major attributes of these two technologies. Table 12-1 provides information to make the comparison. It consists of three columns: the first column is labeled attribute, which describes the characteristics (attributes) of the technology in a short

Table 12-1

Major Attributes of
Frame Relay and
ATM

Attribute	Frame Relay	ATM
Application support?	Asynchronous data (with voice gaining in use [but not designed for voice])	Asynchronous, synchronous voice, video, data
Connection mode?	Connection-oriented	Connection-oriented
Congestion management?	Yes, congestion notification, traffic tagging (DE bit), and possibly traffic discard	Yes, congestion notification, traffic tagging (CLP bit), and possibly traffic discard
Method of identifying traffic?	Virtual circuit id: The DLCI	Virtual circuit id: The VPI/VCI
PVCs	Yes	Yes
SVCs	Yes	Yes
Congestion notification?	FECN and BECN bits	CN bits in the PTI field
Traffic tagging?	The DE bit	The CLP bit
LAN- or WAN-based?	WAN-based	Either
PDU size?	Variable "frame"	Fixed-length "cell"
Sequence numbers?	No, but sequencing preserved	No, but sequencing preserved
QOS?	Yes, but limited	Yes, extensive
ACKs/NAKs/Resends?	No	No
Encapsulation?	Yes	Yes

Where:
BECN	Backward explicit congestion notification
DLCI	Data link connection identifier
CLP	Cell loss priority
CN	Congestion notification
DE	Discard eligibility
FECN	Forward explicit congestion notification
LAN	Local area network
PDU	Protocol data unit
PTI	Payload type identifier
PVC	Permanent virtual circuit
QOS	Quality of service
SVC	Switched virtual call
VCI	Virtual channel identifier
VPI	Virtual path identifier
WAN	Wide area network

phrase; the next two columns, labeled Frame Relay and ATM, describe how these technologies use or do not use the attribute.

As these comparisons suggest, Frame Relay and ATM have many similar operating characteristics. But their differences are significant enough to require several protocol conversion operations at the machine that operates between them.

This machine is called an *internetworking unit* (IWU), an *interworking unit* (once again, an IWU), and in some circles, a *gateway.*

Figure 12-5 illustrates the headers for Frame Relay and ATM. They are more alike than different, in that each contains a virtual circuit id, which is called the *data link connection identifier* (DLCI) in Frame Relay and the *virtual path identifier/virtual channel identifier* (VPI/VCI) in ATM. Both contain bits to allow the traffic to be tagged; for Frame Relay this is called the *discard eligibility* (DE) bit and for ATM it is called *cell loss priority* (CLP).

Figure 12-5
The Frame Relay and ATM headers.

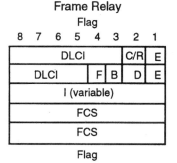
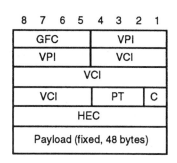

Where:
B   Backward explicit congestion notification bit (BECN)
C   Cell loss priority bit (CLP)
C/R   Command/response bit (C/R)
D   Discard eligibility bit (DE)
DLCI   Data link connection identifier (DLCI)
E   Address extension bit (EA)
F   Forward explicit congestion notification bit (FECN)
FCS   Frame check sequence field
GFC   Generic flow control field
HEC   Header error control
I   Information field (user traffic)
PT   Payload type identifier
VCI   Virtual channel identifier
VPI   Virtual path identifier

Both technologies provide for congestion notification. For Frame Relay this feature is provided in the *forward explicit congestion notification* (FECN) and the *backward explicit congestion notification* (BECN) bits. For ATM, this feature is provided in the bits residing in the *payload type identifier* (PTI), which is known generically as *congestion notification*. ATM provides no mechanism for identifying forward or backward congestion notification with these bits.

The figure provides other information that is pertinent to this discussion. Notice that the Frame Relay header is actually embedded into another *protocol data unit* (PDU), which is considered part of the overall Frame Relay header and trailer (*protocol control information* [PCI]). The flags are used to delineate the beginning and ending of traffic; and the *frame check sequence* (FCS) field is used to error check at the receiver to determine if any of the information between the flags was damaged while in transit.

In contrast, ATM does not contain flag-type fields and its error checking is performed with the fifth byte of the header called the *header error correction* (HEC) field. This field error corrects any one-bit error in the header and will detect most others. But it operates differently from the Frame Relay FCS field in that it does forward error correction. Keep in mind the Frame Relay FCS only does error detection.

Appendix B describes the basic operations of the ATM adaptation layer (AAL). For Frame Relay and ATM interworking (and other interworking relationships as well), the AAL is divided into several sublayers. The sublayers are: (1) *FR-SSCS* for the Frame Relay service specific convergence sublayer; (2) *CPCS* for the common part convergence sublayer; and (3) *SAR* for the segmentation and reassembly sublayer.

Figure 12-6 shows the relationship of the FR-SSCS PDU (protocol data unit: that is the Frame Relay frame) to the CP-AAL5 and the ATM layers. AAL5 performs its conventional segmentation and reassembly functions by delineating the traffic into 48-byte data units with the addition of an 8-byte trailer as part of the last data unit. The error-detection operation is provided by the AAL5 CRC-32 calculation over the FR-SSCS PDU.

How the ATM Backbone Supports the Frame Relay Operations

This section explains how ATM supports the major Frame Relay operations, and the implications of providing this support. Table 12-1 provides

Figure 12-6
FR-CPCS operations.

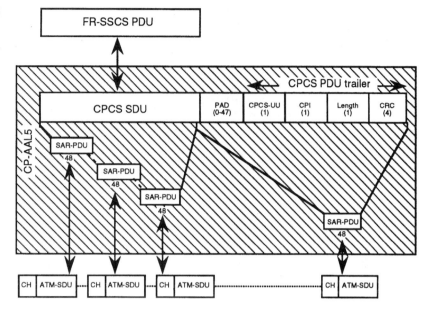

Note: Error detection is provided over the complete FR-SSCS PDU for the AAL5
CRC operation

Where:
ATM   Asynchronous transfer mode
CH   Cell header
CP-AAL5   Common part ATM adaptation layer type 5
CPCS SDU   Common part convergence sublayer service data unit
CPCS-UU   CPCS user to user
CPI   Common part indicator
CRC   Cyclic redundancy check
FR-SSCS   Frame Relay service specific convergence sublayer
SAR PDU   Segmentation and reassembly protocol data unit

a structure for this analysis. Each row of this table is discussed in this
analysis. To aid your following this discussion, one (or more) figures is
provided for each row of Table 12-1 and the specific row entry is repro-
duced in the figure for each analysis.

Implications Regarding Application Support. The support of
Frame Relay asynchronous data applications is performed by the
AAL5 operations just described. Figure 12-7 provides a summary of
this operation.

Implications Regarding Connection Mode. Since Frame Relay and
ATM are connection-oriented technologies, the mapping of their virtual

Figure 12-7
Application support.

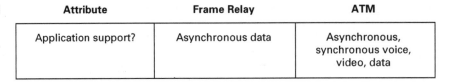

Attribute	Frame Relay	ATM
Application support?	Asynchronous data	Asynchronous, synchronous voice, video, data

Approach:

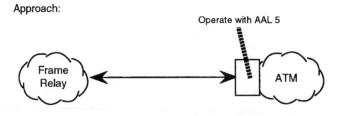

Where:
AAL5   ATM adaptation layer, type 5

circuits is a straightforward matter (see Fig. 12-8). Later discussions will focus on some options for mapping between Frame Relay data link connection identifiers (DLCIs), and ATM virtual channel identifiers/virtual path identifiers (VCIs/VPIs).

Implications Regarding Congestion Management. The IWF equipment must support two modes of operation for discard eligibility and cell loss priority bit mapping. Be aware that these modes operate in the Frame Relay to ATM direction. Figure 12-9 illustrates these modes.

For mode 1, the discard eligibility (DE) bit in the Frame Relay frame header must be copied without alteration into the DE bit that is coded in the FR-SSCS header. Next, this bit must be mapped into the cell loss priority (CLP) bit in the header of each ATM cell that is generated as a result of segmenting each specific Frame Relay frame.

For mode 2, the DE bit in the Frame Relay frame header must be copied without alteration into the DE bit in the FR-SSCS header and the ATM CLP bit shall be set to a constant value of 0 or 1. This value is decided when the connection is set up and must be used for all cells generated from the segmentation process for every frame. It must remain unchanged until such time that an ATM connection has its characteristics changed.

To support discard eligibility (DE) and cell loss priority (CLP) mapping in the ATM–to–Frame Relay mapping, the network provider can choose

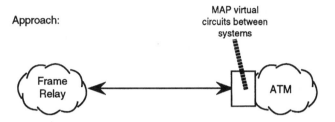

Figure 12-8
Connection mode
support.

Attribute	Frame Relay	ATM
Connection mode?	Connection-oriented	Connection-oriented

Approach:

between two modes of operations. For mode 1, if one or more ATM cells pertaining to a segmented frame have the CLP bit set to 1 or if the DE bit of the FR-SSCS PDU is set to 1, then the IWF must set the DE bit to 1 of the Frame Relay frame. For mode 2, the FR-SSCS PDU DE bit is copied without alteration into the Q922 DE bit. This operation is independent of any cell loss priority indications received by the ATM layer.

Figure 12-9
Congestion manage-
ment support.

Attribute	Frame Relay	ATM
Congestion management?	Yes, congestion notification, traffic tagging (DE bit), and possibility traffic discard	Yes, congestion notification, traffic tagging (CLP bit), and possibility traffic discard

Approach:

FR-to-ATM (Mode 1)			FR-to-ATM (Mode 2)			ATM-to-FR (Mode 1)			ATM-to-FR (Mode 2)		
from Q.922 Core	mapped to FR-SSCS	Mapped to ATM layer	from Q.922 Core	mapped to FR-SSCS	Mapped to ATM layer	from ATM layer	from FR-SSCS to	Q.922 Core	from ATM layer	from FR-SSCS to	Q.922 Core
DE	DE	CLP	DE	DE	CLP	CLP	DE	DE	CLP	DE	DE
0	0	0	0	0	Y	0	0	0	X	0	0
1	1	1	1	1	Y	1	X	1	X	1	1
						X	1	1			
Note 1			Note 2			Note 3					

Note 1: For all cells generaged from the segmentation process of that frame.

Note 2: Y can be 0 or 1.

Note 3: For one or more cells of the frame, X indicates that the value does not matter (0 or 1).

Implications Regarding Method of Identifying Traffic. Frames are identified at the Frame Relay interface through the 10-bit *data link connection identifier* (DLCI), which is an identifier with local significance only. The DLCI permits multiple logical connections to many destinations over a single access channel. Frames belonging to each logical connection are identified by distinct DLCI values, and are correlated with an ATM VCC, as shown in Fig. 12-10.

It may be desirable to map multiple Frame Relay connections to a single ATM connection. For the networking interworking specification, the FR-SSCS must support connection multiplexing on either a one-to-one basis (a single FR connection is mapped to a single ATM connection) or many-to-one basis (multiple FR connections are mapped to a single ATM connection). In both cases, a correlation must be made between the Frame Relay data link connection identifier (DLCI) and the

Figure 12-10

Supporting the virtual circuits.

Attribute	Frame Relay	ATM
Method of identifying traffic?	Virtual circuit id: The DLCI	Virtual circuit id: The VPI/VCI

Where:
DLCI Data link connection identifier
VCI   Virtual channel identifier
VPI   Virtual path identifier

Approach:

A one-to-one mapping is made between DLCIs and VPI/VCIs, unless connection multiplexing is applied

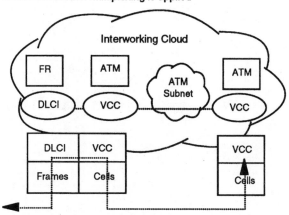

Where:
VCC Virtual channel connections

ATM virtual path identifier/virtual channel identifier (VPI/VCI). These operations are also described in ITU-T I.555. Let us now examine the two modes of connection multiplexing. (Refer to Figs. 12-10, 12-11, and 12-12 during this discussion.)

For the case of one-to-one multiplexing, the multiplexing is performed at the ATM layer using ATM VPIs/VCIs (see Fig. 12-11). The Frame Relay DLCIs can range from 16–991, and the values must be agreed upon between the ATM end systems (that is to say, IWFs or ATM end users). Otherwise, a default value of 1022 will be used for the operation. These rules apply for a two-octet Frame Relay header. If three- or four-octet headers are used, the DLCI value must be agreed upon between the two ATM end systems and the standards do not specify a default value.

Figure 12-11

Correlating VC IDs: One-to-one.

Attribute	Frame Relay	ATM
Method of identifying traffic?	Virtual circuit id: The DLCI	Virtual circuit id: The VPI/VCI

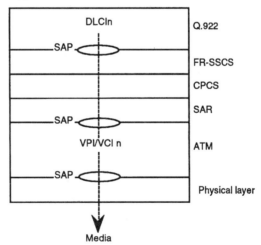

Approach:

Where:
ATM   Asynchronous transfer mode
CPCS   Common part convergence sublayer
DLCI   Data link connection identifier
FR-SSCS   Frame Relay service specific convergence sublayer
SAP   Service access point
SAR   Segmentation and reassembly
VCI   Virtual channel identifier
VPI   Virtual path identifier

For the case of the many-to-one multiplexing, the Frame Relay connections are multiplexed into a single ATM *virtual channel connection* (VCC) and identification of the Frame Relay traffic is achieved by using multiple DLCIs. The many-to-one operation is restricted to Frame Relay connections that terminate on the same ATM-based system.

The specification has no rules on the DLCI values that are to be used. Therefore, they must be agreed upon between the two ATM end systems.

For the case of the many-to-one multiplexing, the Frame Relay connections are multiplexed into a single ATM virtual channel connection (VCC) and identification of the Frame Relay traffic is achieved by using multiple DLCIs. The many-to-one operation is restricted to Frame Relay connections that terminate on the same ATM-based system. See Fig. 12-12. The specification has no rules on the DLCI values

Figure 12-12

Correlating VC IDs: Many-to-one.

Attribute	Frame Relay	ATM
Method of identifying traffic?	Virtual circuit id: The DLCI	Virtual circuit id: The VPI/VCI

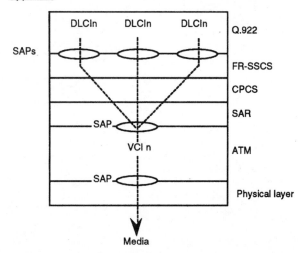

Where:

ATM	Asynchronous transfer mode
CPCS	Common part convergence sublayer
DLCI	Data link connection identifier
FR-SSCS	Frame Relay service specific convergence sublayer
SAP	Service access point
SAR	Segmentation and reassembly
VCI	Virtual channel identifier
VPI	Virtual path identifier

Figure 12-13
Support of PVCs.

Attribute	Frame Relay	ATM
PVCs	Yes	Yes

Where:
PVCs   Permanent virtual circuits

that are to be used. Therefore, they must be agreed upon between the two ATM end systems.

Implications Regarding PVCs.   The internetworking of similar features between systems is usually a relatively simple matter. This is the case in the mapping of *permanent virtual circuits* (PVCs) between Frame Relay and ATM. Figure 12-13 summarizes this situation.

Implications Regarding SVCs.   Both Frame Relay and ATM use signaling protocols that are based on the layer 3 ISDN Q931. Whereas Q931 is concerned with setting up, managing, and tearing down B channels (64 kbps slots on a channel), Frame Relay and ATM are concerned with setting up, managing, and tearing down virtual circuits.

The Frame Relay signaling specification, published in ANSI T1.617 and ITU-T Q933, is used for setting up *switched virtual calls* (SVCs) and explains the procedures for the user-to-network signaling to support Frame Relay calls. The procedures covered include both B channel and D channel frame-mode connection operations. The signaling specifications establish the procedures for the interactions between the user and the network for ISDN support of Frame Relay. The specifications define procedures for S, T, and U reference points and the B, H, and D channels. This specification is titled, "Digital Signaling System 1 (DSS1)."

As just stated, the ATM signaling operations at the UNI are also based on the ISDN layer 3, Q931, modified and published as Q2931. The operations deal with call and connection control procedures. The focus of Q2931 is placed on how connections are setup on demand between users and the ATM network.

As shown in Fig. 12-14, it is necessary to map between the two versions of Q931. Some of the mapping operations are easy and some are more complex. For example, mapping a Frame Relay SETUP message to an ATM SETUP message is simple, but mapping the parameters in the message is not a trivial task. To continue the example, the ATM sup-

Figure 12-14
Supporting the
signaling operations.

Attribute	Frame Relay	ATM
SVCs?	Yes	Yes

Where:
SVC Switched virtual call (a connection on demand)

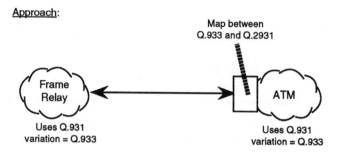

Figure 12-14
Supporting the
signaling operations.

porting backbone must support the Frame Relay performance parameters such as the CIR, Be, and so on. I show examples later in this part of the chapter on how these support operations can be accomplished.

Implications Regarding Congestion Notification. The rules for mapping the congestion notification bits vary slightly between service interworking and network interworking. This example (Fig. 12-15) shows the rules for service interworking:

In the Frame Relay to ATM direction, two modes of operation can be selected for mapping forward congestion indication. In mode 1, the FECN bit in the Frame Relay frame header is mapped to the ATM *explicit forward congestion indication* (EFCI) field of every cell generated from the SAR operation. In mode 2, the FECN field of the Frame Relay frame header is not mapped to the ATM EFCI field. The EFCI field is set to a constant value of "congestion not experienced."

In the ATM to Frame Relay direction, the ATM EFCI field (congestion or no congestion) is set to the FECN bit of the Frame Relay frame header.

Congestion Indication Backward (BECN has no equivalent function in AAL5 or ATM):

In the Frame Relay to ATM direction, the BECN bit is ignored.

In the ATM to Frame Relay direction, the BECN bit is always set to 0.

Attribute	Frame Relay	ATM
Congestion notification?	FECN and BECN bits	CN bits in the PTI field

Figure 12-15
Support of congestion notification operations.

Where:
BECN   Backward explicit congestion notification
CN   Congestion notification
FECN   Forward explicit congestion notification
PTI   Payload type identifier

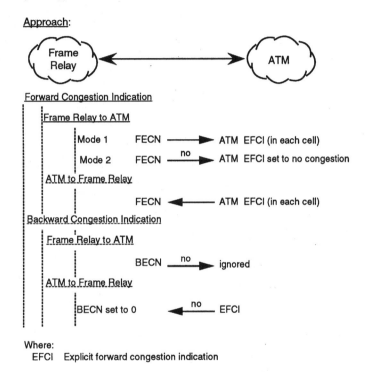

Where:
EFCI   Explicit forward congestion indication

Implications Regarding Traffic Tagging. The operations described for discard eligibility and cell loss priority mapping are organized in the Frame Relay–to–ATM direction and the ATM–to–Frame Relay direction. In both directions, two modes of operation are supported (see Fig. 12-16).

For the Frame Relay–to–ATM direction, mode 1 must be supported with mode 2 provisioned as an option. If both modes are supported in the IWF equipment, they must be configurable on a specific virtual connection basis.

In the mode 1 operation, the Frame Relay DE bit is mapped to the ATM CLP bit in every cell generated by the segmentation process. In the

Figure 12-16
Support of traffic tagging.

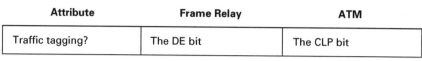

Attribute	Frame Relay	ATM
Traffic tagging?	The DE bit	The CLP bit

Where:
CLP   Cell loss priority
DE   Discard eligibility

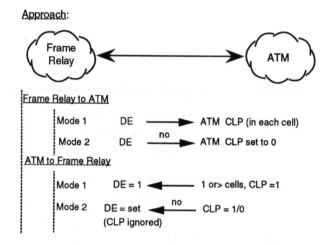

Approach:

Frame Relay to ATM

Mode 1   DE ――――→ ATM CLP (in each cell)
Mode 2   DE ――no――→ ATM CLP set to 0

ATM to Frame Relay

Mode 1   DE = 1 ←―――― 1 or> cells, CLP =1
Mode 2   DE = set ←―no―― CLP = 1/0
          (CLP ignored)

mode 2 operation, the DE bit of the frame header is set to a constant value. The value is configured on a PVC basis at subscription time.

For the ATM-to-Frame Relay direction, two modes of operations also are permitted with mode 1 required and mode 2 optional. Once again, if both modes are available, each must be configurable per virtual connection.

In the mode 1 operation, if at least one cell belonging to a frame has its CLP bit set, the IWF must set the DE bit of the resulting Frame Relay frame. In the mode 2 operation, the DE bit of the frame is set to a constant value. The value is configured on a PVC basis at subscription time.

Implications Regarding LANs and WANs.   As discussed earlier, Frame Relay is a wide area network technology, and ATM can be positioned in either a local or wide area network. This issue is not a factor in the internetworking of the two technologies, as summarized in Fig. 12-17. In effect, if ATM is being employed as a LAN backbone, and Frame Relay is used as a wide area network, then the physical layer at the LAN is likely based on one of the ATM Forum's twisted pair or fiber specifications. The physical layer at the Frame Relay network is

Figure 12-17
LAN and WAN
support.

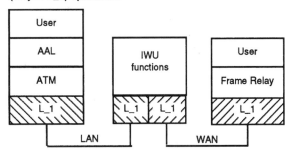

Attribute	Frame Relay	ATM
LAN or WAN based?	WAN based	Either

Where:
LAN   Local area network
WAN Wide area network

Approach: Run ATM or Frame Relay over LAN/WAN L_1
(maybe L_2) operations

Where:
AAL   ATM adaptation layer
ATM   Asynchronous transfer mode
IWU   Interworking unit
L_1   Layer one, the physical layer

likely based on the T1 or SONET technology. Whatever the case, as the traffic is passed through the IWU from one system to the other, the movement of the traffic from an input port to the output port effectively allows the traffic to use different physical layers.

Implications Regarding PDU Size. Figure 12-18 provides an example of the Frame Relay/ATM operations in relation to how ATM support the variable length Frame Relay frames. The interface between the Frame Relay entity and the AAL entity occurs through the Frame Relay core SAP (service access point) that is defined in the Frame Relay specifications. Therefore, the IWF must accommodate to the Frame Relay service definitions at this SAP. Ideally, the Frame Relay entity has no awareness of the AAL and ATM operations.

In accordance with the Frame Relay specifications, the service primitives contain up to five parameters: core user data, discard eligibility (DE), congestion encountered (CE) backward, congestion encountered (CE) forward, and connection endpoint identifier (CEI).

The *core user data* parameter is used to convey data between the end users in the Frame Relay service, and is represented by FR-SSCS PDU.

Figure 12-18
Support of Frame
Relay variable-length
frames.

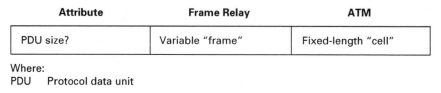

Attribute	Frame Relay	ATM
PDU size?	Variable "frame"	Fixed-length "cell"

Where:
PDU   Protocol data unit

<u>Approach</u>:

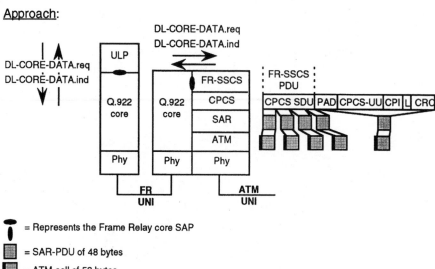

The *discard eligibility* parameter is sent from the core service user to the service provider (FR-SSCS), and is mapped into the ATM CLP bit.

The two congestion parameters supply information about congestion that is encountered in the network. The *congestion encountered forward* parameter is used to indicate that congestion has occurred in transferring data to the receiving user. The *congestion encountered backward* parameter indicates that the network has experienced congestion in transferring these units from the sending user.

The *connection endpoint identifier* parameter is used to further identify a connection endpoint. For example, this parameter would allow a DLCI to be used by more than one user and each user would be identified with a connection endpoint identifier value.

The AAL type 5 PDU is used to support Frame Relay and ATM interworking. As before, the CPI field is not yet defined. The CPCS-UU field

Figure 12-19
Sequencing support.

Attribute	Frame Relay	ATM
Sequence numbers?	No, but sequencing preserved	No, but sequencing preserved

<u>Approach</u>: Keep all traffic sequenced with first-in first-out operations

```
 ⎧ Frame ⎫        ⎧        ⎫        ⎧        ⎫
 ⎨ Relay ⎬  ──►   ⎨  ATM   ⎬  ──►   ⎨  ATM   ⎬
 ⎩       ⎭        ⎩        ⎭        ⎩        ⎭

 ┌───┐ ┌───┐    ┌─┬─┬─┬─┬─┬─┐      ┌───┐ ┌───┐
 │ 2 │ │ 1 │    │6│5│4│3│2│1│      │ 2 │ │ 1 │
 └───┘ └───┘    └─┴─┴─┴─┴─┴─┘      └───┘ └───┘

   Out of          Through            Into
 Frame Relay         ATM          Frame Relay
```

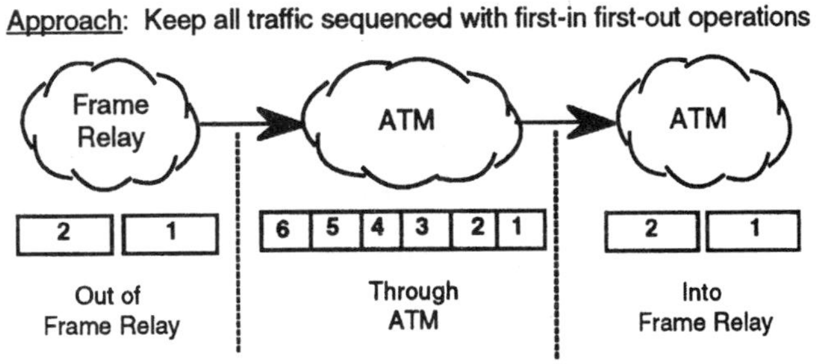

is passed transparently by the ATM network. The length field is checked for oversized or undersized PDUs. CRC violations are noted, and a reassembly timer can be invoked at the terminating endpoint.

Implications Regarding Sequencing of Traffic. Frame Relay and ATM do not use sequence numbers in their headers, so the issue of correlating sequence numbers between a frame and the cells is not an issue (see Fig. 12-19 for an example of traffic sequencing). The approach is to keep all traffic flowing through the network and the switch buffers on a first-in-first-out basis. If fixed routing is employed, the operation is relatively simple.

On another point regarding sequencing, Frame Relay and ATM require that the sequencing of the frames and cells for each connection be preserved through the networks. If a user submits traffic in a particular order to the networks, it must leave the network in the same order.

Implications Regarding QOS. The traffic management operations for Frame Relay–ATM service interworking are established in Q.933 Annex A, T1.617 Annex D, and vendor-specific operations. This section focuses on the service interworking operations implemented by Nortel in its Passport and Magellan products[1] (see Fig. 12-20). Traffic management across the FR-ATM IWF focuses on two areas:

---

[1] I thank Nortel for their information on this aspect of ATM internetworking. Further information is available in Nortel's various user and programming guides on Nortel's Magellan ATM family.

Figure 12-20
Support of QOS.

Attribute	Frame Relay	ATM
QOS?	Yes, but limited	Yes, extensive

Where:
QOS   Quality of service

Approach:

FR-ATM Typical Mapping between FR and ATM QOS Classes

Traffic Type	FR Emission Priority	FR Discard Priority	ATM QOS Class	ATM QOS Name
Packetized Voice	Class 0	Class 1	Class 2	VBR
Data	Class 1	Class 2	Class 2/3	VBR/CO
Data	Class 2	Class 2	Class 3	CO/CNLS
Data	Class 3	Class 3	Class 0	UBR

Note: Frame Relay discard priority Class 3 is not directly provisionable. Traffic can be forced to DE = 1 by provisioning CIR = 0.

Discard Priority Mapping

ATM CLP	Provisioned Frame Relay Discard Priority	Resulting FR Discard Priority	Frame Relay DE
0	Class 1	Class 1	0
0	Class 2	Class 2	0
1	Don't care	Class 3	1

Frame Relay DE	ATM Discard Priority (see Note)	Resulting ATM Discard Priority	ATM CLP
0	Class 1	Class 1	0
0	Class 2	Class 2	0
0	Class 3	Class 3	1
1	Don't care	Class 3	1

Note: Provisioned by selecting ATM QOS.

1. QOS class mapping between Frame Relay and ATM, to determine emission priority and discard priority
2. Traffic management

To provide maximum versatility, and recognizing that the selection of the mapping between the Frame Relay and ATM classes of service is dependent on network traffic types and engineering considerations, no restrictions are imposed on the selection of the available QOS classes. The network provider can tailor this mapping to best match network capacity.

The table in this figure shows a typical mapping between the Frame Relay and ATM QOS classes. Voice applications are assigned to the highest Frame Relay emission priority and the ATM variable bit rate (VBR) class. This table also differentiates between three types of data. This differentiation allows the best match of application demands to network performance.

The discard priority of the connection is also dependent on the settings of the Frame Relay DE and ATM CLP bits. Based on the assumption that the DE-CLP mapping option is enabled, this table shows the effect that these bits have on the connection discard priority that results from applying FR-ATM IWF for each direction.

Implications Regarding ACKs/NAKs/Resends. Frame Relay and ATM do not support the ACKing (positive acknowledgment), NAKing (negative acknowledgment), or resending of traffic at the Frame Relay core layer, and the ATM layer. Therefore, this feature (or the lack of the feature) is not an issue in their internetworking operations, as shown in Fig. 12-21.

Implications Regarding Encapsulation. Encapsulation operations are discussed in the beginning of this chapter. Figure 12-22 shows the location of the encapsulation headers in the Frame Relay and ATM protocol data units. Frame Relay carries the header in front of the payload, and just behind the Frame Relay header. In contrast, ATM carries the header as part of the CS-PDU header.

Figure 12-23 shows the formatting and identification conventions for the interworking of Frame Relay frames with the AAL5 CPCS PDUs.

Figure 12-21
Support of ACKs, NAKs, and resends.

Attribute	Frame Relay	ATM
ACKs/NAKs/Resends?	No	No

Approach:
Not an issue in the internetworking operations

Figure 12-22
Support of the encapsulation header.

Attribute	Frame Relay	ATM
Encapsulation?	Yes	Yes

Approach:

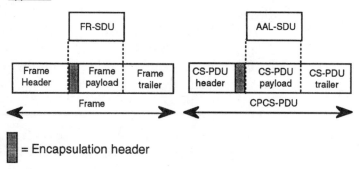

= Encapsulation header

Figure 12-23
Formatting and identification conventions.

Approach:

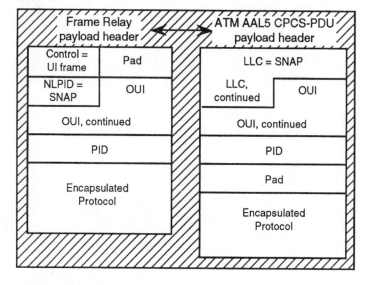

Where:
LLC   Logical link control
NLPID Network level protocol id
OUI   Organizationally unique id
Pad   Align to a two octet boundary (optional)
PID   Protocol id
SNAP   Subnetwork access protocol
UI   Unnumbered acknowledgment frame

The frame and the PDU use the ongoing standards for these operations. They are:

Control   The control field, as established in High Level Data Link Control (HDLC) standards

NLPID   The network level protocol id, as established in the ISO/IEC TR 9577 standard

OUI   The organizationally unique id, as established in RFCs 826, 1042, and several other RFCs

LLC   The logical link protocol, as established in the IEEE 802.x standards

The Data Exchange Interface (DXI)

The purpose of the ATM DXI is to offload some of the more complex operations of ATM from a conventional customer CPE, such as a router. An additional piece of equipment is installed to support ATM DXI. It is usually implemented with a *data service unit* (DSU). Once this equipment is installed, the CPE is relieved of the requirements needed to support all the features of the ATM *convergence sublayer* (CS) and the *segmentation/reassembly sublayer* (SAR). The CPE's principal job is to perform AAL3/4 or AAL5 *common part convergence* sublayer (CPCS) encapsulation. Its only other requirement is to encapsulate this protocol data unit in an ATM DXI frame. The DSU performs the SAR operations and acts as the interface to the ATM network at the ATM UNI. Figure 12-24 shows the DXI configuration.

Figure 12-24
ATM data exchange interface (DXI).

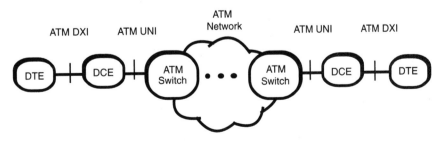

Note: The DTE is relieved of most of the AAL tasks.
Where:

    DTE   Data terminal equipment (a router for example)
    DCE   Data circuit terminating equipment (such as a data service unit)

Table 12-2

DXI Requirements
for ATM Support of
Frame Relay

- Frame Relay QOS will remain intact from end to end
- The Frame Relay user shall not be aware of the ATM operations
- The Frame Relay DLCI must be mapped to the ATM VPI/VCI and vice versa
- The Frame Relay DE bit must be mapped to the ATM CLP bit
- QOS remains intact end to end
- Order of frames will remain intact end to end
- Congestion and flow control operations must be consistent end to end

DXI Support for Frame Relay

Table 12-2, which is self-explanatory, lists the primary requirements that an ATM network must provide to a Frame Relay network.

DXI Modes of Operation

DXI operates with three "modes": mode 1a is used only for AAL5; mode 1b operates with AAL3/4 and AAL5; and mode 2 operates with AAL3/4 and AAL5. AAL5 is used with Frame Relay interfaces.

The principal differences among these modes are in how many virtual connections are allowed across the interface, and the size of the per-

Table 12-3

DXI Modes

- *Mode 1a*
  Up to 1023 virtual connections
  AAL5 only
  Up to 9232 octets in DTE SDU
  16 bit FCS between DTE and DCE

- *Mode 1b*
  Up to 1023 virtual connections
  AAL3/4 for at least one virtual connection
  AAL5 for others
  Up to 9232 octets in DTE SDU for AAL5
  Up to 9224 octets in DTE SDU for AAL3/4
  16 bit FCS between DTE and DCE

- *Mode 2*
  Up to 16,777,215 virtual connections
  AAL5 and AAL3/4: one per virtual connection
  Up to 65,535 octets in DTE SDU
  32 bit FCS between DTE and DCE

mitted user payload (SDU). Additionally, each mode defines slightly different headers and trailers, which are created by the DTE and/or DCE at the CPCS sublayer. Table 12-3 summarizes the major features of the three DXI modes.

DXI Layers

Figure 12-25 shows the relationship between the DTE layers and the DCE layers. The emphasis is on AAL5, since it is the AAL type that is preferred (over AAL3/4). The DTE DXI data link layer is closely related to an HDLC interface. Indeed, the use of HDLC-type frames eases the task of the DTE, because HDLC is well known and implemented in many products. The task of the DTE is a relatively simple one: to create a header that provides enough information for the DCE to create a virtual circuit in the ATM network. In essence, the DXI header contains a DXI frame address (DFA), which is used to convey the VPI and VCI values between the DTE and DCE. The DFA is 10 bits long in modes 1a and 1b, and 24 bits long in mode 2.

Figure 12-26 provides an example of the operations between the DTE and internetworking unit. The interface between the Frame Relay entity and the AAL entity occurs through the Frame Relay core SAP (service access point). Therefore, the IWF must accommodate to the Frame Relay

Figure 12-25
Layers for modes 1a and 1b for AAL5.

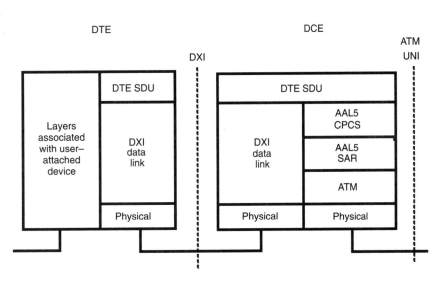

Figure 12-26
Frame Relay and ATM
interworking.

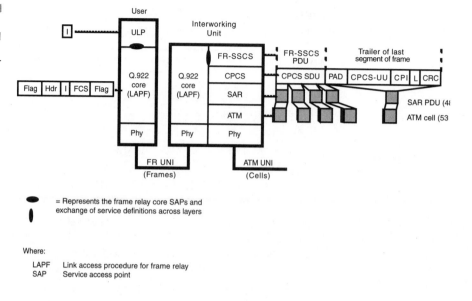

service definitions at this SAP. Ideally, the Frame Relay entity has no awareness of the AAL and ATM operations.

RFC 1483: Running Frame Relay over ATM

RFC 1483 defines two methods for carrying network interconnect traffic over an ATM network. The first multiplexes multiple protocols over a single ATM virtual circuit, and the second carries each protocol over a different ATM virtual circuit (VC). The RFC applies to Frame Relay running over ATM as well.

Use of FR-SSCS

An FR-SSCS (Frame Relay–service specific convergence sublayer) PDU consists of a Q922 (Frame Relay) address field followed by an information field (I). The Frame Relay frame flags and the FCS are omitted, since the FCS functions are provided by the AAL, and the flag operations are supported by the underlying physical layer. Figure 12-27 shows an FR-SSCS-PDU encapsulated in the AAL5 CPCS PDU.

Routed and bridged traffic is carried inside the FR-SSCS-PDU as

Figure 12-27
The AAL5 operations
for Frame Relay.

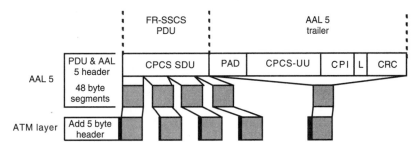

defined in RFC 1490, which was discussed earlier. The protocol of the carried PDU is identified by prefixing the PDU with a network layer protocol ID (NLPID).

The FR-SSCS supports variable-length frames at the FR UNI over preestablished connections (PVCs). Each FR-SSCS connection is identified with a Frame Relay data link connection identifier (DLCI: equivalent to the ATM VPI/VCI). Multiple FR-SSCS connections can be associated with one Common Part CS (CPCS).

The principal job of FR-SSCS is to emulate the FR UNI. In so doing, it supports Frame Relay forward and backward congestion notification (FECN, BECN), as well as the discard eligibility (DE) bit.

The CPCS is responsible for the following operations:

■ Support of *message mode* (fixed-length blocks) or *streaming mode* (variable-length blocks) operations

■ *Assured operations:* CPCS is responsible for traffic integrity (retransmission of lost or corrupted PDUs)

■ *Nonassured operations:* CPCS is not responsible for traffic integrity

The interface between the Frame Relay entity and the AAL entity occurs at the Frame Relay core SAP (service access point) defined in the Frame Relay specifications. Therefore, the gateway must accommodate to the Frame Relay service definitions at this SAP. Ideally, the Frame Relay entity has no awareness of the AAL and ATM operations.

The Frame User-to-Network Interface (FUNI)

The frame user-to-network interface (FUNI) is based on the DXI, which is explained earlier in this chapter. The main difference is that the ATM switches perform the SAR functions. In DXI, these operations are per-

Figure 12-28
The FUNI topology.

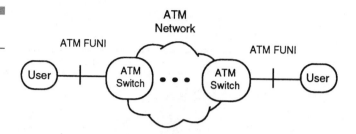

formed by the DSU. Therefore, by using FUNI, an organization can avoid acquiring expensive ATM-based DSUs.

The ATM switch must assume this operation (see Fig. 12-28), but I do not think this shift should be a problem, since most ATM switches run AAL5 anyway, due to the need to operate other protocols over AAL5 (for example, SNMP). An SSCS must be added for Frame Relay specific operations, but some of the code is available in other SSCS modules.

Table 12-4 compares the major features of DXI and FUNI. They are similar in their operations, but have some significant differences. FUNI is more flexible and does not require the installation of an SDU. It also allows the use of fractional T1.

Table 12-4

Differences Between DXI and FUNI

DXI	FUNI
DSU/CSU is required	DSU/CSU is not required
Cells operate on the link	Cells are created at the ATM switch
No Fractional T1	Supports Fractional T1
Does not support SVCs	Supports SVCs
Supports SNMP	Supports SNMP
Uses a MIB	Uses a MIB (a subset of the DXI MIB)
Uses AAL5 or 3/4	Requires AAL5 with 3/4 optional
Encapsulation supported	Encapsulation supported

Where:
AAL	ATM adaptation layer
ATM	Asynchronous transfer mode
CSU	Channel service unit
DSU	Data service unit
MIB	Management information base
SNMP	Simple network management protocol

For FUNI operations, the network is tasked with executing AAL to segment and reassemble the user's traffic. However, this arrangement allows the user link to/from the network to use frames, and takes advantage of the variable (potentially large) information field in the frame. Thus, the overhead of the small payload in the ATM cell is not visible at the UNI. The network must absorb this overhead as part of its operations.

Internetworking Frame Relay and X.25

The Frame Relay Forum has established procedures for using Frame Relay backbone networks to transport either X.25 or X.75 traffic between two user devices. The concept is implemented by encapsulating the X.25 layer 3 service data unit (an X.25 packet) and part of the LAPB service data unit into Q922A. This general summary is derived from studies conducted by Sprint, which is published by the Frame Relay Forum.

As illustrated in Fig. 12-29, a transmitting encapsulator is responsible for receiving end-user data and encapsulating this traffic into Q922A. An encapsulator at the receiving site reverses the process. The operations are transparent to the end user, who is unaware of the intermediate functions. The end user perceives that there is a virtual circuit end to end, and is not aware that the Frame Relay network stands between these operations.

The control procedures use LAPB to perform end-to-end acknowledgment between the Frame Relay X.25 encapsulators. Therefore, the end-user device is not aware of these operations. The purpose of the encapsulator-to-encapsulator services is to provide for congestion avoidance in the Frame Relay network. The LAPB control field is used between the two encapsulators to sequence and acknowledge traffic, using the conventional LAPB fields of N(S) and N(R) and the REJECT operation.

The encapsulator must react to the *backward explicit congestion notification* (BECN), because from the standpoint of the Frame Relay network, this encapsulator is a source-controlled device. Since LAPB is a full duplex protocol, it is easy to send BECNs frequently to the source.

Figure 12-30 illustrates how the X.25 packet and the LAPB frame control fields are carried inside the Frame Relay frame. As with most of the

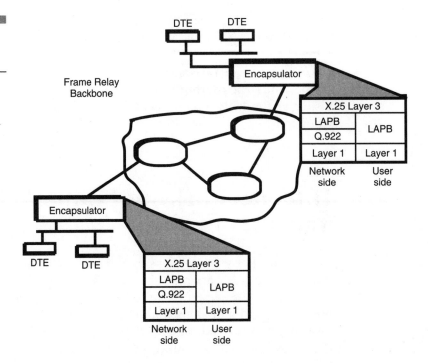

Figure 12-29
Interworking X.25
and Frame Relay.

other illustrations in this chapter, the X.25 protocol at layer 3 (or for that matter X.75) and layer 2's LAPB are simply encapsulated into the Frame Relay I field and transmitted across the Frame Relay network.

The Frame Relay X.25 interworking procedure makes use of several congestion management concepts, which are now briefly defined.

A *configured window size* is the maximum window that can exist between a transmitter and receiver. This window size can be established as a provisioning procedure. In contrast to the configured window size, the *working window size* identifies the number of frames that can be outstanding during a session. It may not exceed the configured window size.

The reader may recall the term *window turn,* which was discussed earlier in this book. *Window turn* is the time during which an LAPB frame is sent by the encapsulator and is acknowledged by the remote encapsulator. The *congestion monitoring period* (CMP) is the window turn time in which the encapsulator monitors what happens with a window size adjustment. The CMP always begins after a window turn, or when a window size adjustment takes place. The purpose of CMP is to give the encapsulator an opportunity to review the window reduction, as well as

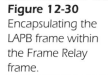

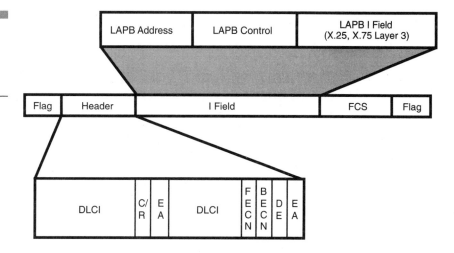

to expand the window size until the working window size is equal to the configured window size.

A window size adjustment can occur for a number of reasons, and the size of the window adjustment can vary. As an example, if all frames within a CMP have been received with BECN equal to zero and a frame loss has also occurred, and the working window is not equal to the configured window, then the working window must be reduced either to a value for which the working window is greater than 1, or to .625 times the current working window. As another example, if a frame loss has occurred, and during the last CMP one of the frames had BECN equal to 1, then the working window is reduced to the greater of 1 or .25 times the current working window. The purpose of these rules is to provide for "instant" window reduction to avoid congestion, instead of gradually reducing the window size.

Additionally, if BECN is received and no frame loss has occurred, the working window will be reduced to either 1 or .625 times the current working window, whichever is greater. Of course, it would not be fair to automatically reduce a working window if it is already small. Consequently, the working window need not be reduced if (a) no frame loss exists and the working window is less than the configured window; (b) BECN = 1 has been received among the transmitted frames; and (c) the number of frames with BECN = 1 is less than 50 percent of the total frames received. The idea behind this rule is not to penalize an entity that has already had its working window reduced below the provisioned configured window.

Interworking IP and Frame Relay

Since Frame Relay is a connection-oriented technology and uses labels (DLCIs) to identify traffic, a router must be able to translate an IP address to a DLCI, and vice versa. Although this operation is not complex, it does require the careful construction of mapping tables at the router. The Frame Relay standards do not describe how this mapping and address translation takes place. Typically, each router has a table that correlates IP addresses to DLCIs and vice versa, as depicted in Fig. 12-31.

Frame Relay and IP: Partners or Competitors?

Is IP a competitor to Frame Relay, or vice versa? The answer is yes and no. Let us start with the no answer first. IP does not define a transport mechanism for the transfer of IP datagrams through a network. IP operates at L_3 over L_1 and L_2. So, Frame Relay (a combination of L_2 and L_3) is a good choice as a transport mechanism for IP. In addition, IP runs on a user workstation, and Frame Relay runs at the user network interface (UNI), typically between a router and a Frame Relay switch.

Figure 12-31
Mapping IP addresses to DCLIs.

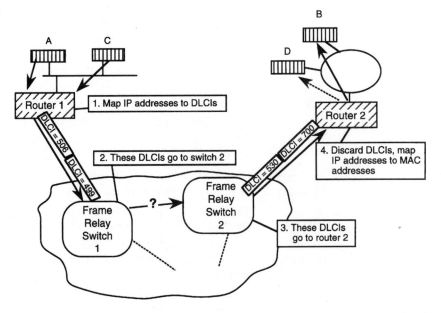

For the yes answer, IP is evolving toward a multiapplication technology, with the eventual support of voice and video. The new version of IP, called *IPv6*, and several supporting protocols perform the same operations as Frame Relay, such as the provisioning of QOS, the reservation of bandwidth, and so on. Much attention is focusing on voice over IP (VoIP), which is designed to perform the same services as voice over Frame Relay (VoFR, Chap. 14).

How IP and Frame Relay will incorporate to provide these same services (if indeed they do) is yet to be determined. But make no mistake, the fact that IP runs in the user machine, and is deeply embedded into the user's L_4, and L_7 operations means that IP gets the first shot at supporting the end-user applications. How this support is translated into Frame Relay (if indeed it is) is also to be determined. Clearly, redundant operations are defined in some of the Frame Relay and IP (and related protocols) features.

SUMMARY

With the publication of RFC 1490, a standard is available to define how to run multiprotocol families of a Frame Relay network. The ATM and Frame Relay Forums have published specifications on internetworking Frame Relay and ATM networks. One is called the ATM Data Exchange Interface (ATM DXI). A related standard is called the Frame User-to-Network Interface (FUNI), and is based on DXI.

Whereas X.25 is an older protocol, it is widely installed and its use is growing in some companies, often as part of an overall product. It will be used in Frame Relay transport networks for many years to come.

Network Management

This chapter examines Frame Relay network management operations. The use of object libraries and management information bases (MIBs), is covered with emphasis on the Bellcore management model and the Frame Relay MIB (published by the Frame Relay Forum). We also examine the use of the Simple Network Management Protocol (SNMP) and the Common Management Information Protocol (CMIP) for performing network management operations.

I assume that you have an understanding of these protocols, libraries, and MIBs. I recommend a book on these subjects entitled *Network Management Standards,* by Uyless Black (McGraw-Hill), if you need more information. Nevertheless, App. A will bring you up to speed on the basics needed to understand this chapter. I also assume that you have a sound knowledge of Frame Relay—at least that you have read Chaps. 6 and 12 of this book.

The term *virtual circuit* (VC) is used in parts of this chapter in place of the term *permanent virtual circuit* (PVC). The term *PVC* is used in all the current standards and specifications because *switched virtual call* (SVC) services were not available when these specifications were written. I have made this modification because many of the operations for PVC and SVC are identical in relation to the operations of the Frame Relay MIB. Some exceptions are required to my convention when PVC is only implied. Additionally, I do not change the name of an MIB object that has "PVC" embedded in its name.

The Frame Relay MIB

RFC 1604 defines the *management information base* (MIB) that is to be used with Frame Relay networks in TCP/IP-based networks. It was produced jointly by the Frame Relay Forum Technical Committee MIB Working Group and the Frame Relay Service MIB Working Group. The purpose of the MIB is to define the objects that are to be managed in Frame Relay systems. It defines objects for both UNI and NNI operations.

The MIB is registered under transmission 44. See App. A for information on registrations and naming.

The *Simple Network Management Protocol* (SNMP) is used to set and get the values of the MIB variables for the purposes of network monitoring and management. Additionally, an SNMP agent can issue traps for status reports and unusual conditions. The *Common Management Information Protocol* (CMIP) can also be used in conjunction with object libraries, but SNMP is the prevalent choice as of this writing.

The Frame Relay MIB Structure

The Frame Relay MIB consists of five major groups, a number of objects associated with the groups, and other objects that are not associated with groups. The major object groups with their associated objects are illustrated in Fig. 13-1. The objects in the groups in this figure are organized in tables, with columns and rows forming a two-dimensional table. The structure and content of each table are described in the next section.

frLportTable. This table is based on the Internet MIB (IMIB) interface table (ifTable), and describes the objects associated with logical ports. The term *logical port* is used to describe the interface at a Frame Relay machine, such as a DS1 line. (The section titled "Relationships of the IMIB II Interfaces Group to Frame Relay" has more information on this subject.) Each port is represented by a row entry in the table, with the columns of the table consisting of the following objects for each row entry:

frLportNumPlan: Identifies the network addressing plan for this port. Plans for E.164 and X.121 are specified, although the port may use other plans.

frLportContact: Identifies the contact of this port (e.g., person and address).

Figure 13-1
The Frame Relay MIB tables.

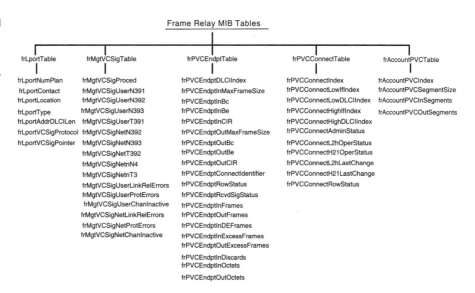

Frame Relay MIB Tables

frLportTable	frMgtVCSigTable	frPVCEndptTable	frPVCConnectTable	frAccountPVCTable
frLportNumPlan	frMgtVCSigProced	frPVCEndptDLCIIndex	frPVCConnectIndex	frAccountPVCIndex
frLportContact	frMgtVCSigUserN391	frPVCEndptInMaxFrameSize	frPVCConnectLowIfIndex	frAccountPVCSegmentSize
frLportLocation	frMgtVCSigUserN392	frPVCEndptInBc	frPVCConnectLowDLCIIndex	frAccountPVCInSegments
frLportType	frMgtVCSigUserN393	frPVCEndptInBe	frPVCConnectHighIfIndex	frAccountPVCOutSegments
frLportAddrDLCILen	frMgtVCSigUserT391	frPVCEndptInCIR	frPVCConnectHighDLCIIndex	
frLportVCSigProtocol	frMgtVCSigNetN392	frPVCEndptOutMaxFrameSize	frPVCConnectAdminStatus	
frLportVCSigPointer	frMgtVCSigNetN393	frPVCEndptOutBc	frPVCConnectL2hOperStatus	
	frMgtVCSigNetT392	frPVCEndptOutBe	frPVCConnectH21OperStatus	
	frMgtVCSigNetnN4	frPVCEndptOutCIR	frPVCConnectL2hLastChange	
	frMgtVCSigNetnT3	frPVCEndptConnectIdentifier	frPVCConnectH21LastChange	
	frMgtVCSigUserLinkRelErrors	frPVCEndptRowStatus	frPVCConnectRowStatus	
	frMgtVCSigUserProtErrors	frPVCEndptRcvdSigStatus		
	frMgtVCSigUserChanInactive	frPVCEndptInFrames		
	frMgtVCSigNetLinkRelErrors	frPVCEndptOutFrames		
	frMgtVCSigNetProtErrors	frPVCEndptInDEFrames		
	frMgtVCSigNetChanInactive	frPVCEndptInExcessFrames		
		frPVCEndptOutExcessFrames		
		frPVCEndptInDiscards		
		frPVCEndptInOctets		
		frPVCEndptOutOctets		

frLportLocation: Identifies the location of this port.

frLportType: Identifies whether the port is a UNI or NNI.

frLportAddrDLCILen: Identifies the length of the address field and the length of the DLCI value for the port. Various combinations allow 2 to 4 octets for the field and 10 to 23 bits for the DLCI.

frLportVCSigProtocol: Identifies the local in-channel signaling protocol that is used at the port. Four protocols are cited: LMI, ANSI T1617D, ANSI T1617B, and ITU-T Q933A.

frLportVCSigPointer: Value of a pointer to the frMgtVCSigTable (see next table).

frMgtVCSigTable. This table contains the objects pertaining to in-channel management. It includes timers, signaling parameters, and statistics on errors detected by the management protocol. Each logical port is represented by a row entry in the table, with the columns of the table consisting of the following objects for each row entry:

frMgtVCSigProced: Indicates whether in-channel signaling procedure is for user-to-network only, or bidirectional between user and network.

frMgtVCSigUserN391: Identifies the user-side N391 full status polling cycle value.

frMgtVCSigUserN392: Identifies the user-side N392 error threshold value.

frMgtVCSigUserN393: Identifies the user-side N393 monitored events count value.

frMgtVCSigUserT391: Identifies the user-side T391 link integrity verification polling timer.

frMgtVCSigNetN392: Identifies the network-side N392 (nN2 for LMI) error threshold value.

frMgtVCSigNetN393: Identifies the network-side N393 (nN3 for LMI) monitored events count value.

frMgtVCSigNetT392: Identifies the network-side T392 (nT2 for LMI) polling verification timer value.

frMgtVCSigNetnN4: Used only for LMI operations, identifies network-side nN4 maximum status enquiries received value.

frMgtVCSigNetnT3: Used only for LMI operations, identifies network-side nT3 timer for the nN4 status enquiries received.

frMgtVCSigUserLinkRelErrors: Contains the number of user-side local in-channel signaling link reliability errors, which includes nonreceipt of status or status enquiry messages, and invalid sequence numbers.

frMgtVCSigUserProtErrors: Contains the number of user-side local in-channel signaling protocol errors pertaining to the header of the message (for example, ambiguous protocol discriminator, call reference, etc.).

frMgtVCSigUserChanInactive: Contains the number of times the user-side channel was declared inactive (N392 errors in N393).

frMgtVCSigNetLinkRelErrors: Contains the number of network-side local in-channel signaling link reliability errors, which includes nonreceipt of status (S) or status enquiry (SE) messages, and invalid sequence numbers.

frMgtVCSigNetProtErrors: Contains the number of network-side local in-channel signaling protocol errors pertaining to the header of the message (for example, ambiguous protocol discriminator, call reference, etc.).

frMgtVCSignetChanInactive: Contains the number of times the network-side channel was declared inactive (N392 errors in N393).

frPVCEndptTable. This table contains objects pertaining to a bidirectional VC segment endpoint. As seen in Fig. 13-2, the endpoint terminates at the logical port at each UNI/NNI machine, and the concatenation of the associated segments form a multinetwork VC.

Each logical port is bidirectional. A DLCI is used to identify the incoming and outgoing frames on each logical port at the endpoint on each Frame Relay node. The associated segments form an end-to-end virtual circuit. The Frame Relay node must map the DLCI from an incoming port to an associated DLCI on the outgoing port. Remember from previous discussions that each connection can have different values for

Figure 13-2
Endpoints.

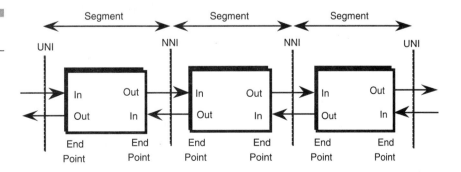

each direction of traffic flow on the VC (asymmetric traffic flow). Each endpoint is represented by a row entry in the table, with the columns of the table consisting of the following objects for each row entry:

frPVCEndptDLCIIndex: This object value is equal to the DLCI value for this endpoint.

frPVCEndptInMaxFrameSize: Indicates the maximum frame size (the I field of the frame) in the ingress (in) direction of the VC. This value cannot exceed the value of ifMtu of the IMIB ifTable.

frPVCEndptInBc: Indicates the committed burst rate (B_c) in the ingress direction of the VC.

frPVCEndptInBe: Indicates the excess burst rate (B_e) in the ingress direction of the VC.

frPVCEndptInCIR: Indicates the committed information rate (CIR) in the ingress direction of the VC.

frPVCEndptOutMaxFrameSize: Indicates the maximum frame size (the I field of the frame) in the egress (out) direction of the VC. This value cannot exceed the value of ifMtu of the IMIB ifTable.

frPVCEndptOutBc: Indicates the committed burst rate (B_c) in the egress direction of the VC.

frPVCEndptOutBe: Indicates the excess burst rate (B_e) in the egress direction of the VC.

frPVCEndptOutCIR: Indicates the committed information rate (CIR) in the egress direction of the VC.

frPVCEndptConnectIdentifier: Associates VC endpoints with one part of the VC segment. Value must be equal to frPVCConnectIndex (in the frPVC ConnectTable). After the associated entries have been created in the frPVCConnectTable, the agent assigns this value.

frPVCEndptRowStatus: Used to create, maintain, and delete rows in this table. Its value is set to *createAndWait*, while the segment is being provisioned, and is changed to *active* after the B_c, B_e, CIR, and frame size objects in this table have been filled in.

frPVCEndptRcvdSigStatus: Indicates the endpoint VC status based on the in-channel signaling procedures. It is set to *deleted, active, inactive,* or *none.*

frPVCEndptInFrames: Indicates number of frames received for this VC endpoint, which includes discarded frames due to excessive frame submission.

frPVCEndptOutFrames: Indicates number of frames sent for this VC endpoint, which includes B_c or B_e frames.

frPVCEndptInDEFrames: Indicates number of DE = 1 frames received for this VC endpoint.

frPVCEndptInExcessFrames: Indicates number of frames received for this VC endpoint that are defined as excess traffic. Discarded traffic is not included in this count.

frPVCEndptOutExcessFrames: Indicates number of frames sent for this VC endpoint that were considered excess traffic.

frPVCEndptInDiscards: Indicates number of frames received at the VC endpoint that were discarded due to traffic enforcement.

frPVCEndptInOctets: Indicates number of octets received at the VC endpoint.

frPVCEndptOutOctets: Indicates number of octets sent for this VC endpoint.

frPVCConnectTable. This table contains objects pertaining to the bidirectional PVC segments, which may be point-to-point, point-to-multipoint, or multipoint-to-multipoint connections. As shown in Fig. 13-3, each row entry in the table models a VC segment, and the columns contain administrative and operational information about the segment. Each PVC segment is identified by a DLCI value and an ifIndex value.

The association between the two endpoints is provided by frPVC-ConnectIndex, which is selected when the entries in the table are created. This value is derived from the management protocol that accesses frPVCConnectIndexValue to obtain the number. This value ranges from 0 to 2,147,483,647, and after a value is selected, the agent changes it for use with the next assigned index value.

The association of the endpoints is also provided by correlating the low port and its associated DLCI with the high port and its associated DLCI. The terms *low* and *high* are based on MIB II's (the Internet MIB) ifIndex value for the logical port for this segment. The terms correspond to the bidirectional VC segment. As Fig. 13-3 illustrates, the flow is from low to high in one direction (low IfIndex to high IfIndex), and high to low in the other direction (high IfIndex to low IfIndex). Each row contains the following columns:

frPVCConnectIndex: Contains a value equal to the frPVCConnectIndexValue, which was described in the previous paragraph.

Figure 13-3
Example of the
Frame Relay PVC
connection table.

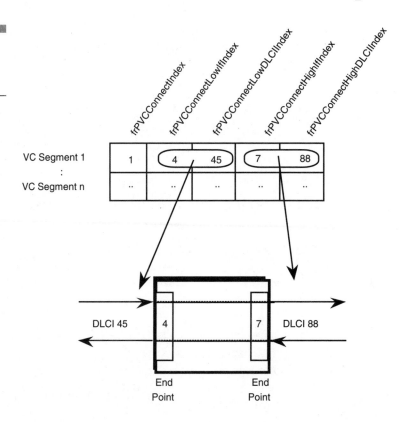

frPVCConnectLowIfIndex: Indicates the low value VC segment endpoint relative to the other endpoint. It is equal to MIB II's ifIndex value of the UNI/NNI logical port.

frPVCConnectLowDLCIIndex: Contains the value of the DLCI for this endpoint.

frPVCConnectHighIfIndex: Indicates the high value VC segment endpoint relative to the other endpoint. It is equal to MIB II's ifIndex value of the UNI/NNI logical port.

frPVCConnectHighDLCIIndex: Contains the value of the DLCI for this endpoint.

frPVCConnectAdminStatus: Indicates the administrative status of the VC segment. The status may be *active, inactive,* or *testing.*

frPVCConnectL2hOperStatus: Indicates the operational status of the VC segment in the low to high direction. The status may be *active, inactive, testing,* or *unknown.*

frPVCConnectH2lOperStatus: Indicates the operational status of the VC segment in the high to low direction. The status may be *active, inactive, testing,* or *unknown.*

frPVCConnectL2hLastChange: Indicates the time the VC segment entered into its current operational state in the low to high direction. It is the sysUpTime object of the IMIB.

frPVCConnectH2lLastChange: Indicates the time the VC segment entered into its current operational state in the high to low direction. It is the sysUpTime object of the IMIB.

frPVCConnectRowStatus: Indicates the status of this entry in the frPVCConnectTable. Takes on values *createAndWait* and *active.*

frAccountPVCTable. This table contains accounting information on a VC segment endpoint. It contains the following row entries:

frAccountPVCDLCIIndex: Takes on the same value as the DLCI value for the segment endpoint.

frAccountPVCSegmentSize: Contains the segment size of the endpoint.

frAccountPVCInSegments: Indicates number of segments received by this VC segment endpoint.

frAccountPVCOutSegments: Indicates number of segments sent by this VC segment endpoint.

Interpretations of the IMIB II Interfaces Group

The interfaces group that is defined in the Internet MIB II (IMIB II) is used by Frame Relay in accordance with the information provided in Table 13-1.

Use of the MIB II Interfaces Group and ifIndex

Table 13-1 describes the relationships between the IMIB interfaces group and Frame Relay. Be aware that the exact use of this group can differ between vendors. The approach described here is one used by Bellcore.

Several objects in this table are relevant to our discussion in this section. The object ifNumber represents a value containing the number of

Table 13-1

Relationship of
Frame Relay and
MIB II Interfaces
Group

- ifIndex: An unambiguous value for each Frame Relay port. Multiple entries may exist for one physical port (e.g., one entry for DS1, and another entry for the Frame Relay DLCIoperating over the DS1). Thus, a physical port may have more than one logical port.

- ifDescr: Textual information describing the interface, typically a product name, a manufacturer name, and a version number of the interface.

- ifType: Identifies the specific type of interface, and is set to 44 for Frame Relay.

- ifMtu: The maximum size of the frame that can be serviced at this port, specified in octets.

- ifSpeed: In bits per second, the value of the port speed capacity, if relevant.

- ifPhysAddress: The port address, which is assigned by the Frame Relay interface provider.

- ifAdminStatus: Describes the administrative state of the port.

- ifOperStatus: Describes the operational state of the port.

- ifLastChange: In sysUpTime, the elapsed time the port entered its current operational state.

- ifInOctets: Total number of octets received at this port since the last reinitialization.

- ifInUcastPkts: The number of unerrored frames received (nonbroadcast frames).

- ifInDiscards: The number of frames discarded at this port because of various problems such as congestion, violation of CIR, and so forth.

- ifInErrors: Number of frames that contained errors, were ill-formed, unintelligible, and so forth (not delivered to the next higher level protocol).

- ifInUnknownProtos: The number of frames discarded because the frame is related to an unsupported or unknown protocol. For Frame Relay, this value is set to zero.

- ifOutOctets: Total number of transmitted octets at this port since the last reinitialization.

- ifOutUcastPkts: Total number of frames sent.

- ifOutDiscards: Total number of outgoing frames (egress direction) that were discarded due to congestion, policing, and so forth.

- ifOutErrors: The total number of outgoing PDUs that contained errors and were discarded.

- ifName: Not used for Frame Relay services.

- ifInMulticastPkts: Total number of unerrored multicast frames received.

- ifInBroadcastPkts: Not used for Frame Relay services.

- ifOutMulticastPkts: Total number of unerrored multicast frames sent.

- ifOutBroadcastPkts: Not used for Frame Relay services.

- ifHCInOctets: Used only for DS3 or higher speed ports. Contains total number of received octets.

- ifHCOutOctets: Used only for DS3 or higher speed ports. Contains total number of transmitted octets.

- ifLinkUpDownTrapEnble: Not defined in the MIB, and is specific to the implementation.

- ifHighSpeed: User data rate across the port. Set to zero if rate is less than 1 Mbps.

- ifPromiscuousMode: Set to false.

- ifConnectorPresent: Set to false.

Note: Received or sent octets refers to the I (information field) in the Frame Relay frame.

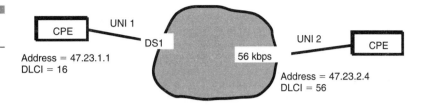

Figure 13-4
UNI configurations.

network interfaces at a system, for example, a router or a switch. The object ifIndex is a value for each interface (or sublayers that operate below layer 3 of the OSI Model). Its value can range from 1 to the value of ifNumber. Since it identifies interfaces below layer 3, multiple instances exist in the interfaces group for a physical port. That is, it can identify a layer 2 interface with one entry in the table, and it can identify a layer 1 interface with another entry.

The object ifType contains a value to identify the type of interface. As examples, ifType = 18 identifies a T1 (DS1) interface, and ifType = 44 identifies a Frame Relay interface, and so forth. Thus, two instances of ifIndex exist for a DS1 physical link, since Frame Relay (as a layer 2/3 protocol) runs on top of DS1, which is a physical layer.

The ifSpeed object describes the access speed of the interface, such as 56 kbps, 1.544 Mbps, and so forth. The ifPhysAddress identifies the address of physical interface, such as an IP, MAC, or ISDN addresses.

Figure 13-4 shows these ideas, and serves as an example for some more thoughts. We assume that UNI 1 is also running fractional T1, with 12 DS0 channels. Its ifType = 0, for *other*. One of the DLCIs at UNI 1 is DLCI = 16; one of the DLCIs at UNI 2 is DLCI = 56. Its ifType is 18.

This arrangement translates into three instances of ifIndex for UNI 1, and two instances for UNI 2. The arrangement is shown in Fig. 13-5. It is

Figure 13-5
Values for ifIndex.

For UNI 1	For UNI 2
Frame relay ifIndex = 1	Frame relay ifIndex = 2
Fractional T1 ifIndex = 3	
DS1 link ifIndex = 5	DS1 link ifIndex = 4

a simple matter to relate the "logical" interface in the interfaces group to a physical address by accessing the interfaces table and reading the ifPhysAddress object that is in the same row as the ifIndex.

Examples of How SNMP and the MIB Are Used for Network Management Operations

As shown in earlier discussions, the ifIndex value is the same as several of the entries in the tables. For example, ifIndex is used to access (index into) a row of the frPVCEndptTable. It is used in conjunction with a DLCI value (for this table the DLCI value is frPVCEndptDLCIIndex).

Figure 13-6 shows one example of how SNMP can use the frPVCEndptTable to obtain network management information. Assume a network manager wishes to know how many frames have been received and discarded (due to excessive frame submission) by DLCI 16 at UNI1 on ifIndex = 1 (the logical Frame Relay interface) since a known initial-

Figure 13-6
Example of a Frame Relay MIB table.

Associated ifindex value	frPVCEndptDLCIIndex	frPVCEndptInMaxSize	frPVCEndptInBc	frPVCEndptInBe	frPVCEndptInCIR	frPVCEndptOutMaxFrameSize	frPVCEndptOutBc	frPVCEndptOutBe	frPVCEndptOutCIR	ifPVCEndptConnectIdentifier	frPVCEndptRowStatus	frPVCEndptRcvdSigStatus	frPVCEndptInFrames	frPVCEndptOutFrames	frPVCEndptInDEFrames	frPVCEndptInExcessFrames	frPVCEndptOutExcessFrames	frPVCEndptInDiscards	frPVCEndptInOctets	frPVCEndptOutOctets
1	16																			
3	16																			
5	16																			
2	56																			
4	56																			

ization time (which is sysUpTime in the Internet MIB—the time since initialization). The SNMP query from the managing system to an agent would appear as (coding has been simplified for readability):

```
GET(sysUptime.0,frPVCEndptIfFrames.1.16, frPVCEndptInDis-
cards.1.16).
```

The .0 following the SysUptime parameter indicates that a single instance of the variable exists (in contrast to a row entry). The .1.16 following the other two variables serve as the indexes into the table (for ifIndex = 1 and DLCI = 16). The response from the agents might appear as:

```
GETRESPONSE(sysUpTime.0 = 12345,frPVCEndptIfFrames.1.16 = 28000,
frPVCEndptInDiscards.1.16 =  1230).
```

The response means that since time 12345, this port received 28,000 frames and discarded 1230 of them.

The Frame Relay MIB Variables.   This part of the MIB contains two variables that are used to describe miscellaneous operations at the user-to-network interface. The following list contains their names and a brief description of their functions:

frTrapState: indicates whether system can generate an SNMP trap message when the status of a DLCI changes.

frDLCIStatusChange: indicates whether the status of a DLCI has changed.

Other Aspects of the Frame Relay Forum MIB

Other information is described in the Frame Relay Forum MIB. For example, the MIB explains which groups and objects are optional, and which are required. It also contains other miscellaneous objects.

Bellcore and ANSI Models for Network Management

Bell Communications Research (Bellcore) has issued specifications on its requirements for Frame Relay network management operations between

Figure 13-7
The Bellcore network
management
configuration.

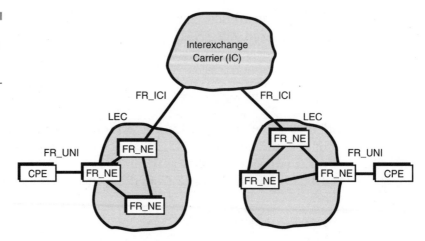

a management system (MS) and a managed system, which is called a
Frame Relay Switching System (FR_SS). Bellcore's GR-1379-CORE specification
describes an information model for use between the MS and FR_SS.
The FR_SS is not the customer premises equipment (CPE), but it must
provide generic interfaces to the CPE, to MSs, and to interexchange carrier (IC) networks. The FR_SS is modeled as one or more Frame Relay network elements (FR_NEs), as shown in Fig. 13-7.

According to Bellcore, these machines can operate at a UNI, between
the FR_NEs through intraswitching system trunks (SS_Trunks), or at the
FR_ICI. Using the Frame Relay Forum's terminology, the FR_ICI and the
NNI can be the same interface. As discussed in Chap. 11, the FR_ICI and
the NNI can complement each other.

Several functions of the model are described by level 1, 2, or 3 functions, and are identified by L1, L2, and L3, respectively. L1 is aligned with
the OSI Model layer 1, and includes physical functions such as modulation, timing, line speeds, and so forth. Level 2 and level 3 are aligned
with the OSI Model layer 2 and some of layer 3. L2 includes functions
such as frame delimited with flags, and frame error checks. L3 functions
pertain to virtual circuit (VC) operations that deal with DLCIs, such as
routing, multiplexing, and congestion and discard operations.

ANSI Definitions of Termination Points

For the Bellcore and ANSI models, a *termination point* (TP) includes a
class of managed objects that delimit transport boundaries and entities

in the network. Each TP contains information on its "direction": whether the TP sends, receives, or does both. Each TP describes associated services such as alarms and operational/administrative states, as well as capacity and usage information. The idea of termination points is shown in Fig. 13-8. The horizontal lines in the figure represent the part of a topology where a termination point is represented.

The span object class originates/terminates at repeaters/regenerators, and bounds the physical portion of the physical medium. The DS3 line and framed path object classes originate/terminate at a multiplexer (for example, DM13). The line object class represents the physical transmission medium, and is an ordered set of spans. The framed path object class is characterized by a specified rate (in bit/s) and a specific frame format.

The information path represents objects that carry information point to point, in this example, between digital terminal equipment. The distinctive aspect of this termination point is that it preserves the contents of information end to end. Also, no frame format is associated with the traffic. In contrast, the DS1 framed path originates and terminates at the DS1 terminal equipment and consists of (in this example) three DS1 channels, but it is associated with a specific frame format.

Finally, the DS1 line object class is the same as the DS3 line object class except it represents DS1 lines. The DS1 channel object class makes up portions of the framed path or information path and represents DS0 signals (2.4–56 kbps). DS1 channels can operate within a DS3 framed path.

Figure 13-8
Termination points.

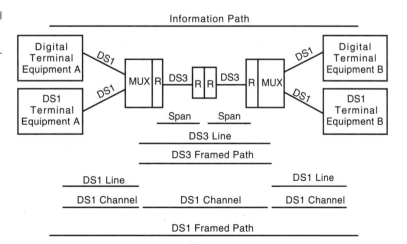

Examples of Inheritance Trees

The Bellcore model uses the OSI recommendations, as well as the network management standards published by the ISO and ITU-T. The uninitiated reader should refer to Chap. 2 before reading this section.

The concepts of inheritance are an integral part of the Bellcore Frame Relay model. To give the reader an idea of the Bellcore approach, this section provides an example of an inheritance tree, and an example of a naming hierarchy. Bellcore GR-1379-CORE should be studied for the other inheritance trees (and naming hierarchies) defined for Frame Relay networks.

Like ANSI, Bellcore defines termination points, but organizes them as shown in Fig. 13-9. This figure also shows the idea of multiple inheritances. The numbers in the figure depict the inheritance idea between the object groupings. The object groupings are "grouped" into circles in the figure. The bold lines that connect the groups (circles) below a given group are subclasses of that group. Inheritance relationships do not exist if bold lines do not connect the groups.

Figure 13-9 also shows the idea of multiple inheritance, and Fig. 13-10 is drawn to aid you in following this discussion. The dashed lines in Fig. 13-10 symbolize an inheritance relationship. DS1 line *trail termination point* (TTP) bidirectional object class is a subclass of three object classes:

- TTP bidirectional object class (inheritance relationship #3)
- DS1 line TTP sink object class (inheritance relationship #4)
- DS1 line TTP source object class (inheritance relationship #5)

Frame Relay Managed Object Classes (MOCs)

The Bellcore model defines 41 managed object classes (MOCs) for Frame Relay operations. This section provides an overview of each of these MOCs, but the reader should study the original specification for more detail on each class and object. User-friendly names are used here in place of the less readable ASN.1 class labels.

This section is intended for readers who need a detailed look at the MOCs. The reader who needs only general information can skip this section. Figure 13-9 is a useful reference when reading this material.

Figure 13-9
Inheritance tree for
termination point
fragment [BELL93a].

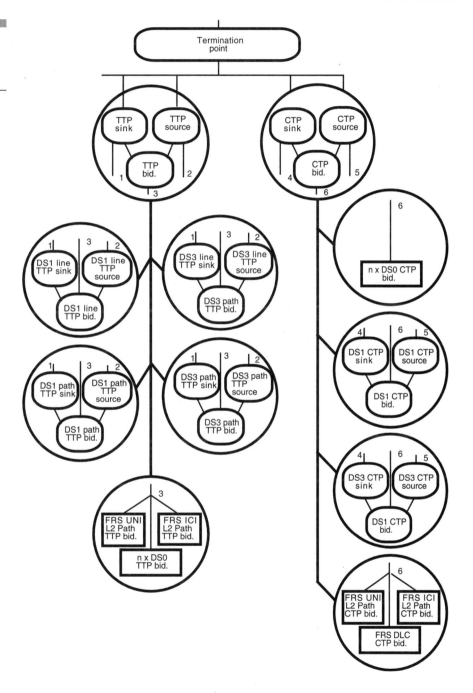

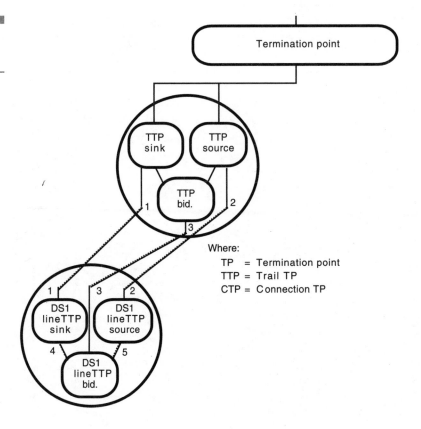

Where:
TP = Termination point
TTP = Trail TP
CTP = Connection TP

Congestion Controls. This class is used to enable and disable supplier-specific traffic controls. By using instances of this MOC, supplier-specific controls such as SMDS and ATM can include their automatic controls.

Carrier Access. This class pertains to operations at the FR_ICI, and is used to represent administrative parameters at this interface. This MOC includes a number of parameters; some notable examples are the number of DLCI octets used at this interface, the maximum permitted size of the I field of the Frame Relay frame, the access speed at the FR_ICI, with DS1 and DS3 rates supported, the information on the virtual circuit termination point (and identifier of the virtual circuit), and the values for the T392, N392, N393, N391, T391, N392, N393 timers and parameters.

Congestion Measurements Current Data. This class represents congestion measurements for a congestable resource, which can be one of three managed objects: an L3 monitoring point, equipment, or common equipment. The measurement of congestion is stored (both maximum and average values), as is the time the report level was entered.

Congestion Measurements History Data. This class is the same as the previous class, but contains information on historical congestion measurements for a congestable resource.

Congestion Level Measurements Current Data. This class contains information on current measurements on a "congestable resource," which means any UNI or ICI connection for each congestion level basis. A level is "entered" when congestion reaches a specified threshold, and is "exited" when congestion falls below a specified threshold. As part of the MOC, counts of discarded frames are collected during a specified measurement interval.

Congestion Level Measurements History Data. This class is the same as the previous class, but contains information on historical congestion measurements for each congestion level.

Cross Connection. This class represents the relationship between a virtual circuit's termination points in a machine. It forms part of a cross connect relationship, and points to instances of the DLC CTP bidirectional class (explained next).

DLC CTP Bidirectional. This class represents a connection termination point (CTP) where each end of a VC is terminated. Each DLCI on a UNI or ICI contains the following information: the DLCI value, the maximum size of the I field that is supported on the VC, the administrative and operational state of the VC, the signaling status of the DLCI (based on messages from LMI or NNI), and information pertaining to alarms and problems. This class also defines ACTIONS for loopback testing between the MS and the managed object.

DLC CTP Bidirectional Current Data. This class maintains a count of the frames lost on each VC for a specified collection interval. The data are collected per PVC segment and identified by a DLCI.

Disagreements Log Record. This class represents log entries for Frame Relay disagreement events, along with the type of disagreement, and the time and date the event was logged. Examples of disagreement types are *unassigned DLCIs have been encountered, I field is too big, disagreement on LMI/NNI signaling type,* and so forth.

Disagreements Current Data. This class contains information on a disagreement collected during a 15-minute interval.

Disagreements History Data. This class is the same as the previous class, but contains information on historical disagreements.

FRS Fabric. This class is used to keep information on the establishment and deestablishment of PVCs. It contains attributes about the administrative, operational, and availability status of a PVC, as well as a set of ACTIONS that manage PVC termination points.

ICI L2 Path CTP Bidirectional. This class represents a termination point of an L2 Frame Relay link connection. Two pointers are used to identify a connection: an upstream connectivity pointer and a downstream connectivity pointer. These pointers point to the ICI L2 Path TTP bidirectional object (discussed next).

ICI L2 Path TTP Bidirectional. This class represents an L2 FR_ICI termination point.

ICI L3 Congestion Current Data. This class contains information on the congestion measurements for each DLCI. It includes information on FECN and BECN bit set counts, as well as the number of DE bit set counts.

ICI L3 Congestion History Data. This class is the same as the previous class, but contains information on historical congestion data.

L2 Congestable Resource Current Data. This class contains information on measurements for each congestable resource (switch, etc.). The following information is provided: frames with FECN/BECN bits set at both ingress and egress points; frames with DE = 1 that are blocked from entering the congested object; frames with DE = 1 that are discarded by the congested object; frames with DE = 0 that are blocked from entering the congested object; and the number of frames and octets processed by the resource at both ingress and egress points.

L2 Congestable Resource History Data This class is the same as the previous class, but contains information on historical L2 congestable resource data.

L2 Path TTP Bidirectional Current Data. This class represents performance monitoring data on level 2 errors for a trail termination point (TTP), which include frame check sequence (FCS) errors, and errors in which the bits between the Frame Relay flags do not form an integral number of octets.

L3 Current Data. This class contains information on level 3 problems, including invalid DLCIs, invalid extended address (EA) field in the frame, and I field in frame too small or too large.

L3 Monitoring Point. This class represents the monitoring of level 3 activities for level 3 at both FR_UNIs and FR_ICIs.

L3 Protocol Abnormality Log Record. This class contains information on level 3 problems (abnormalities), or problems in status signaling (LMI, for example).

Performance Scheduled Event Record. This class stores historical performance counts on notifications that were emitted from several objects of other classes.

SS Trunks. This class pertains to the administration of Frame Relay SS trunks. It contains the following objects: a trunk ID and trunk group name; maximum bandwidth provisioned for the trunk; level 2 protocol supported; current value of bandwidth allocated for the PVCs on the trunk; the transport instance (termination point); access speed of the trunk; and other information such as state of the trunk.

Status Signaling Network Side Current Data. This class represents managed objects for each UNI and ICI. It supports the monitoring of invalid and incorrect events captured by the status signaling protocol on the network side of the interface. Events are captured for the following types of conditions (this is not an exhaustive list): invalid Frame Relay field (UI frame not allowed, but received, for example); neither an SE nor an S message received; length is not valid; an invalid status signaling protocol message was received; incorrect sequence number; various timers and polling counts exceeded, and so forth.

Status Signaling User Side Current Data. This class contains the same type of information as the preceding class, except for the user side of the interface.

Subscriber Access.   This class pertains only to the UNI, and represents the configuration and administration parameters needed to support the end user at the UNI. Information is available for these types of objects (not an exhaustive list): UNI identifier; interface identifier; DE bit-setting rules; administrative and operational states of the UNI; maximum size of I field of the frame; use of a status signaling protocol; access speed of interface, and so forth.

Switch Parameters.   This class contains objects that are administered for the FR_SS, and have the following information: maximum size of the I field of the frame; object to handle buffer (memory) overrun in machines; and counters to store billing information.

Traffic Load Current Data.   This class contains objects that have information on the current traffic load for a UNI, ICI, or each DLCI for these interfaces. The following information is available: number of frames and octets at egress and ingress, and a count of aborted frames at ingress (not available for each DLCI).

Traffic Load History Data.   This class is the same as the previous class, but contains information on historical traffic load, collected during the previous two 15-minute collection intervals.

Trunk Current Data.   This class represents scheduled measurements, on a current basis, on the trunk activity between two FR_NEs, and at the ICI. Information is available on average and peak trunk utilization at ingress and egress, and variance of trunk utilization at ingress and egress.

Trunk History Data.   This class is the same as the previous class, but contains information on historical trunk data.

Trunk Special Study Current Data.   This class represents data collected on trunk utilization and the peak value of trunk utilization over a specified collection interval, which can range from 1 second to 1 minute for DS1 and DS3 rates, with a default value of 10 seconds for DS1 and 1 second for DS3.

Trunk Special Study History Data. This class is the same as the previous class, but contains information on special study history data.

UNI L2 Path CTP Bidirectional. This class represents a level 2 connection termination point (CTP) for a Frame Relay link. It contains attributes such as operational state, alarm status, current problem list, channel number, cross-connection pointer, and so forth.

UNI L2 Path TTP Bidirectional. This class represents a trail termination point (TTP) for an FR_UNI signal. It contains attributes such as administrative and operational states, alarm status, current problem list, and so forth.

UNI L3 Congestion Current Data. This class contains objects that represent congestion measurements for each DLCI at level 3, and at an FR_UNI. It contains information such as the number of times the DE bit was set by the FR_SS, frames discarded due to excessive burst, frames in the egress direction whose DE bits are set to 1, and so forth.

UNI L3 Congestion History Data. This class is the same as the previous class, but contains information on UNI L3 congestion history data.

nxDS0 CTP Bidirectional. This class represents the connection termination point of an nxDS0 link.

nxDS0 TTP Bidirectional. This class represents the trail termination point of an nxDS0 link.

SUMMARY

Frame Relay networks are now mature enough to have extensive management operations embedded in them. The use of the Simple Network Management Protocol (SNMP) and the Frame Relay MIB is prevalent, especially at the Frame Relay UNI. The Common Management Information Protocol (CMIP) is used to a more limited extent in performing network management operations, especially between Frame Relay switches. Object libraries and management information bases (MIBs) are widely used, and the Bellcore management model and the Frame Relay MIB published by the Frame Relay Forum have served as the main standards for these services.

New Features
of Frame Relay

During the years of 1996 to 1998, the Frame Relay Forum added three new features to Frame Relay. One of them deals with fragmenting longer frames into smaller frames. Another deals with running voice over Frame Relay (VoFR), which encompasses the fragmentation operations. The third feature deals with procedures to establish and manage multiple links between Frame Relay nodes. This chapter provides a synopsis of these operations, and describes the three functions: (1) PVC fragmentation, (2) voice over Frame Relay (VoFR), and (3) multilink Frame Relay (MFR). We begin this discussion with an analysis of PVC fragmentation.

PVC Fragmentation

The Frame Relay Forum publishes FRF.12 titled, *Frame Relay PVC Fragmentation Implementation Agreement.* This specification defines how Frame Relay machines fragment long frames into a sequence of short frames at the sender and reassemble these short frames into the original frame at the receiver. The fragmentation operation was developed by the Frame Relay Forum to support delay-sensitive traffic such as voice applications.

The approach is to multiplex the shorter frames onto the same physical interface that support longer frames. In other words, it is possible to interleave delay-sensitive traffic and non-delay-sensitive traffic. Obviously, this feature allows the sharing of the link by both real-time and non-real-time traffic. The size of the fragments is implementation-specific and the fragment size can be configured based on the attributes of the line and interface as well as local clocking mechanisms, such as a channelized or an unchannelized interface. The idea is to allow each local interface to be responsible for fragmentation.

Fragmentation Models

Fragmentation functions (FF) can be implemented at (1) a UNI (DTE-DCE configuration), (2) an NNI, or (3) an end-to-end (DTE-to-DTE con-

Figure 14-1
UNI fragmentation and reassembly.

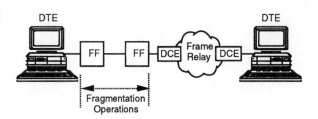

Figure 14-2
NNI fragmentation
and reassembly.

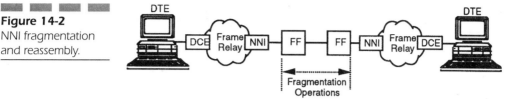

figuration). Figures 14-1, 14-2, and 14-3 show these three models. The UNI fragmentation operation is local to an interface and can take advantage of transporting larger frames over the backbone network at the high bandwidths of the backbone links. The transmission of these longer frames is more efficient than the transport of a larger number of smaller fragments. In addition, in case a DTE does not implement fragmentation, this model allows the network to act as a proxy for this DTE.

Some DTE-DCE interfaces operate in a *channelized mode,* which means that the speed (in bps) that is made available to the user is not as high as the physical speed of the interface. For example, a DS1 interface operates at a physical speed of 1.544 Mbps, yet a user may be given a DS0 64 kbps speed. Fragmentation can be used to optimize the operation based on the speed of the interface.

Also, fragmentation is quite useful if a UNI must support real-time and non-real-time traffic, since the fragments can be tailored to meet the delay and throughput requirements of the application.

One rule that is important to remember is that UNI fragmentation applies to all DLCIs on an interface, including DLCI 0.

As shown in Fig. 14-2, the NNI fragmentation operation, as the name implies, is performed between the Frame Relay networks at the NNI. There is little to be said about this model since it is straightforward, and adheres to the same rules as UNI fragmentation.

For the third case (Fig. 14-3), the end-to-end fragmentation occurs between peer DTEs. This model can be useful if the intervening network does not support fragmentation or if the NNI does not support fragmentation. End-to-end fragmentation is performed on a PVC-by-PVC basis, and not on an interface basis.

Figure 14-3
End-to-end frag-
mentation and
reassembly.

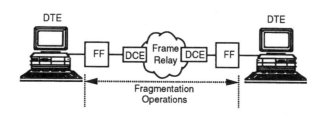

Fragmentation Headers

Figure 14-4 shows the format for the fragmentation header for interface (UNI, NNI) fragmentation. The header is two octets in length and precedes the conventional Frame Relay header. The contents of the header are as follows.

■ The beginning (B) bit is set to 1 for the first data fragment of the original frame. It is set to 0 for all other fragments of the frame. The ending (E) fragment bit is set to 1 for the last data fragment of the original data frame and it is set to 0 for all other data fragments. A data fragment can be both a beginning and ending fragment; therefore, it can have both the B and E bits set to 1.

■ The control bit is set to 0 and is not used in the current implementation agreement. It is reserved for future operations.

■ The sequence number is incremented for each data fragment transmitted on the link. A separate sequence number is maintained for each DLCI at the interfaces.

The low-order bit of the first octet of the fragmentation header is set to 1 and the low-order bit of the Frame Relay header is set to 0. These bit settings are used to distinguish the headers from each other and for the receiver to be aware if it is receiving the proper header, and thus acts as a checkpoint that the fragmentation peers are configured properly.

Figure 14-4
UNI and NNI formats
for fragments.

Bit 8	Bit 7	Bit 6	Bit 5	Bit 4	Bit 3	Bit 2	Bit 1	Octet
B	E	C	Sequence number of high order 4 bits				1	1
Sequence number of low order 8 bits								2
DLCI high six bits						C/R	0	3
DLCI low four bits				F	B	DE	1	4
Payload								5 – n
Frame Check Sequence (FCS)								5 – n + 2

Notes: Octets 1 and 2: Fragmentation header
Octets 3 and 4: Frame Relay header

End-to-End Fragmentation

The end-to-end fragmentation also uses the multiprotocol encapsulation operation in accordance with Frame Relay Forum's specification FRF.3.1, titled *Multiprotocol Encapsulation Agreement*. The unnumbered information (UI) octet (octet 3 in Fig. 14-5) is used for this process (0x03), and the network layer protocol ID (NLPID) value of 0xB1 (octet 4 in Fig. 14-5) has been assigned to identify the fragmentation header format. The format for the DTE-to-DTE operation is shown in Fig. 14-5 and the rules for encoding these headers have been explained in other parts of this book.

Fragmentation Procedure

The fragmentation procedures are based on RFC 1990, titled "The Point-to-Point Protocol (PPP) Multilink Protocol (MP)," August 1996. An example of fragmentation and reassembly operations is shown in Fig. 14-6. The Q.922, optional PAD, and the NLPID fields are removed by the transmitter and placed in the first fragment. Each fragment must be transmitted in the same order of its relative position in its original frame, although fragments from multiple PVCs may be interleaved with each other across one interface. The receiving machine must keep track of the incoming sequence numbers and use the beginning and ending bits for proper reassembly of traffic. If lost fragments are detected and/or sequence numbers skipped, the receiver must discard all current-

Figure 14-5
End-to-end formats
for fragments.

Bit 8	Bit 7	Bit 6	Bit 5	Bit 4	Bit 3	Bit 2	Bit 1	Octet
DLCI high six bits						C/R	0	1
DLCI low four bits				F	B	DE	1	2
0	0	0	0	0	0	1	1	3
1	0	1	1	0	0	0	1	4
B	E	C	Sequence number of high order 4 bits				R	5
Sequence number of low order 8 bits								6
Payload								5 − n
Frame Check Sequence (FCS)								5 − n + 2

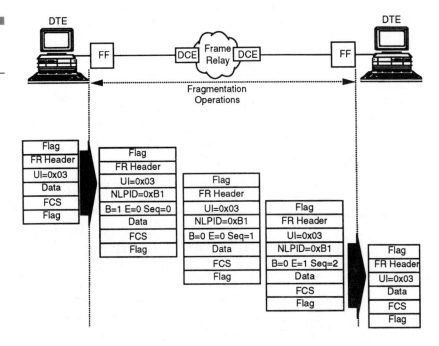

Figure 14-6
Example of end-to-end fragmentation.

ly assembled fragments and fragments subsequently received for that PVC until it receives the first fragment of a new frame (that is to say, a new beginning bit).

Voice over Frame Relay (VoFR)

Due to the widescale use of Frame Relay, there has been considerable interest in expanding Frame Relay networks to support voice traffic (as well as data traffic, for which Frame Relay was designed). The Frame Relay Forum has published a specification for this process, titled *Voice over Frame Relay Implementation Agreement—FRF.11.*

The major components of this specification deal with analog-to-digital, digital-to-analog, voice compression operations, and the transmission of the digitized images in the Frame Relay frame. In addition to the transfer of the voice traffic, the frames can also convey data and fax images, as well as the signaling needed to set up, manage, and tear down the voice or fax connection. Support is provided for dialed digits, line seizures, and other signals and operations used in telephony.

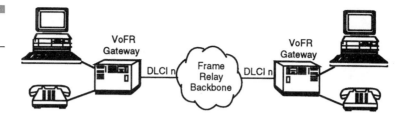

Figure 14-7
Service multiplexing.

Service Multiplexing

One of the key components of voice over Frame Relay (VoFR) is called *service multiplexing*, which supports multiple voice and data channels on a single Frame Relay connection. This concept is shown in Fig. 14-7. Multiple streams of user traffic (called *subchannels*) consisting of different voice and data transmission flows are multiplexed across one DLCI (DLCI n in this example). VoFR is responsible for delivering the frames to the receiving user in the order in which they were sent from the transmitting user.

Figure 14-8 shows the relationships of the subchannels to the DLCIs. The user applications at A and B are multiplexed into one virtual circuit, identified with DLCI 5. The user application at C is multiplexed into another virtual circuit, identified with DLCI 9. It is the job of the VoFR gateway to assemble the subchannels into the Frame Relay frame. Users B and A may be sending traffic that pertains to one overall traffic flow (for example, a conversation on the telephone that discusses the data

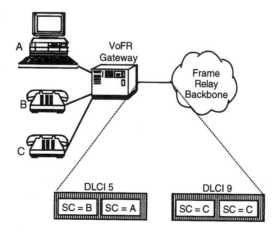

Figure 14-8
Subchannel (SC) concept.

Figure 14-9
The payload sub-
channel header.

Bit 8	Bit 7	Bit 6	Bit 5	Bit 4	Bit 3	Bit 2	Bit 1	Octet
EI	LI	Subchannel ID (CID) (least)						1
CID (most)		0	0	Payload Type				2a
Payload Length								2b
Payload (voice, data, fax, dialed digits, or signaling)								2c

Where:
CID   Subchannel ID
EI   Extension indication
LI   Length indication

exchanged and exhibited on a workstation screen). Frame Relay does not define how these two images are played out at the receiver's machines. This aspect of multiservice multiplexing is left to specific vendor implementations.

Each subframe is uniquely identified with a header, which contains a *subchannel identifier* (CID). Figure 14-9 shows the fields (information elements) of the subframe header. The *extension indication* (EI) bit is set to indicate the presence of octet 2a. It must be set when a subchannel identification value is greater than 63 or when a payload type is indicated. This restriction is a result of the subchannel identification code being limited to six bits. If a larger number is needed, the CID is extended to octet 2a. A CID consisting of values 0–63 is called a *low-numbered subchannel*, and values greater than 63 are called *high-numbered* subchannels.

The *length indication* (LI) bit is set to indicate the presence of octet 2b. This bit of the last subframe is not set which indicates that the payload length field and the payload is not present. The subchannel identification bits contain the identifier of the specific subchannel. The payload type bits indicate the type of payload encapsulated in the subframe. The four bits are coded as follows:

Bit 4	Bit 3	Bit 2	Bit 1	
0	0	0	0	Primary payload transfer syntax
0	0	0	1	Dialed digit transfer syntax
0	0	1	0	Signaling bit transfer syntax
0	0	1	1	Fax relay transfer syntax
0	1	0	0	Primary payload silence indication

Overview of Payload Types

Five payload types are carried inside the VoFR frame. The *primary* payload contains the voice traffic. The *dialed digit* payload contains the called party number, as well as information that indicates the pace at which the calling party is entering the called number digits into the telephone keypad.

The *signaling bits* payload contains the signaling bits needed to manage certain aspects of the call, based on the ABCD signaling bits in T1 systems.

The *fax* payload contains fax images, which are transmitted in accordance with ITU-T fax standards, with some additional VoFR features, discussed later.

The *primary payload silence indication* traffic is used to indicate periods of time when the conversing party is not talking. This payload is coded in accordance with the standards specified in the primary payload. As examples, ITU-T G.729 and ITU-T G.723.1, Annex A define the procedures to invoke silence compression operations.

For the transfer of data, there is no VoFR subframe header. Rather, the data are encapsulated into the Frame Relay frame in accordance with the encapsulation operations described in other parts of this book.

Examples of Subframe Contents

Figures 14-10 through 14-13 show examples of how the subframe may be coded. These examples are derived from FRF.11 and more detailed information is available in Section 3.3 of this specification. We will use DLCI 16 for all of these examples and note the two octet Frame Relay header contains the value of 16 for the DLCI. Keep in mind the header also contains other fields such as BECN, FECN, DE, and so on.

Figure 14-10 shows a frame that contains a single voice sample for one subchannel. In this example, octets 2a and 2b are not coded and the pay-

Figure 14-10
One subframe of
voice traffic.

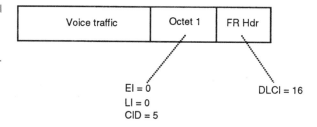

Figure 14-11
One subframe with a
high-numbered
channel.

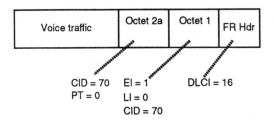

Figure 14-11
One subframe with a
high-numbered
channel.

load sample follows immediately after octet 1 of the subframe header.

Figure 14-11 is an example of a frame containing a single voice sample in which octet 2a is included. The payload type is set to 0 which indicates that primary payload is contained in the frame. The transfer syntax is the single voice sample. Notice that the CID has a value greater than 63, so octet 2a is used to extend the CID value. The EI bit in the first octet indicates the extension of octet 2a.

Figure 14-12 shows a frame that contains multiple subchannels and therefore is coded with multiple subframes. The channels are identified with CIDs 5 and 6. For this example, the payload type indicates dialed digits, which implies the existence of octet 2b. Also notice the use of the LI bit, set to 1 and 0, respectively, in the two subfield headers. The LI bit of the last subframe within a frame is always set to 0, and the payload length field is not present.

The last example (Fig. 14-13), is a variation of the previous example showing multiple subframes carrying voice traffic. This syntax does not carry octet 2a, but does carry octet 2b. Octet 2a is not present if EI is set to 0, because a payload of 0 is assumed.

Figure 14-12
Multiple subframes.

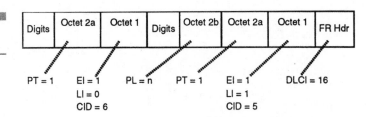

Figure 14-13
Multiple subframe of
voice traffic.

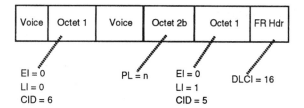

Contents of the VoFR Frame

The principal purpose of VoFR is to carry voice traffic. But as stated earlier, some of the frames in a stream carry dialing information, signaling information, data traffic, and fax traffic. This section of the chapter describes each of these traffic types. Before discussing these types of traffic, we examine the specifications for the coding and decoding of voice traffic.

Voice Traffic

VoFR supports several specifications that define the coding and decoding of the voice traffic. The reader can refer to the Annexes in FRF.11 for more detail. For your convenience, the technologies that are supported are listed in Table 14-1. I have added to Table 14-1 another vocoder (ITU-T G.723 and Annexes) that will surely be used, but is not part of FRF.11 at this time. All organizations that belong to the International Media Teleconferencing Consortium (IMTC) have selected G.723.1 for their basic vocoder.

Dialing Information

The dialed digit payload contains the dialed digits entered by the calling party as well as several control parameters. The transmission occurs over an all-digital network and the telephone signals are *dual tone multifrequency* (DTMF) signals. DTMF is not permitted, so binary representations are substituted for the analog signals.

Table 14-1

Voice Support in
VoFR

Reference Document	Description
ITU G.729/ITU G.729 Annex A	Coding of Speech at 8 kbps using Conjugate Structure-Algebraic code Excited Linear Predictive (CS-ACEP) Coding, March 1996
ITU G.711	Pulse Code Modulation of Voice Frequencies, 1988
ITU G.726	40, 32, 24, 16 kbps Adaptive Differential Pulse Code Modulation (ADPCM), March 1996
ITU G.727	5-, 4-, 3-, and 2 bits Sample Embedded Adaptive Differential Pulse Code Modulation, November 1994
ITU G.764	Voice packetization—Packetized voice protocols, December 1990
ITU G.728	Coding of Speech at 16 kbps Using Low-Delay Code Excited Linear Prediction, November 1994
ITU G.723.1	Dual Rate Speech Coder for Multimedia Communications Transmitting at 5.3 & 6.3 kbps, March 1996
ITU G.723.1, Annex A	Silence Compression Scheme, March 1996
ITU G.723.1, Annex B	Alternative Specification Based on Floating Point Arithmetic, March 1996
ITU G.723.1, Annex C	Scaleable Channel Coding Scheme for Wireless Applications, March 1996

Dialing Procedures

Figure 14-14 shows an example of how the dialed digits are placed into
the dialed digit payload. When the VoFR transmitter detects a dialed
digit from the calling party, it starts sending a dialed digit payload,
repeated every 20 ms. As shown in Table 14-2, each dialing payload covers 60 ms of digit on/off edge information, and there is redundancy of
edge information. Upon the VoFR receiver receiving the dialed digit
payload, it generates the dialed digits according to the location of the on

Figure 14-14
Procedure for the
dialed digits.

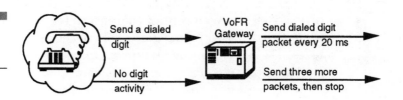

Table 14-2

Dialed Digit
Payload Format

Bit 8	Bit 7	Bit 6	Bit 5	Bit 4	Bit 3	Bit 2	Bit 1	Octet
Sequence number								6
Reserved 000			Signal Level					7
Digit Type [0]			Edge Location [0]					8
Reserved 000			Digit Code [0]					9
Digit Type [-1]			Edge Location [-1]					8
Reserved 000			Digit Code [-1]					9
Digit Type [-2]			Edge Location [-2]					8
Reserved 000			Digit Code [-2]					9

and off edges. After an off edge and before an on edge, silence is applied to the duration and digits are applied after an on edge and before an off edge.

For the dialing procedures, the receiver maintains a *record* (a repetition) of the two last time intervals, known as "recent" for the last set of bits, and "previous" for the set of bits that followed the recent set of bits. By using the sequence number in the packet, the receiver knows if it is receiving contiguous or noncontiguous frames, and react accordingly. To handle lost frames, if the sequence number in the payload is one greater than the last received sequence number, the receiver appends the current edge values to the previously received information. If the sequence number is two greater than the last received sequence number, the receiver appends the recent and current edge information to the previously received information. If the sequence number is three greater than the last received sequence number, the receiver appends the previous, recent, and current edge information to the previously received information. If the sequence number is three more than the last received sequence number, the receiver appends the previous, recent, and current edge information to the previously received information, and fills the missing frames (a gap) based on the previously received payload.

Dialing Values and Payloads

The binary representations are called *digit codes* and their values in relation to DTMF digits are shown in Table 14-3. In addition, Table 14-4 shows the coding for the digit type field.

Table 14-3

Dual Tone Multi-frequency Codes

Digit Code	DTMF Digit
00000	0
00001	1
00010	2
00011	3
00100	4
00101	5
00110	6
00111	7
01000	8
01001	9
01010	.
01011	#
01100	A
01101	B
01110	C
01111	D
1000–1111	Reserved

Each dialed digit contains three "windows" of digit transition, with each window a 20-ms period. This approach creates 60 ms worth of dialed digit information. As shown in Table 14-2 the first window represents the current 20-ms period, the second window is the window previous to the current period, and the third window is the window previous to the current period.

The contents of the payload are as follows (see Table 14-2):

■ *Sequence number:* A sequence number appended to each VoFR fragment and each increment of the sequence number equals a period of 20 ms. The 20-ms period (even multiples of 5 and 10 ms) is used to stay in sync with the various timing rates of voice vocoders. For example, ITU-T G.729 codes the speech images in 10-ms frames, and ITU-T G.711 (and others) use 5-ms samples. It is easier to construct subframes of the same time duration than to use different formats and different time periods.

Table 14-4

Digit Types
(See Table 14-2)

Code	Digit Type
000	Digit Off
001	Digit On
010–111	Reserved

■ *Signal level:* A value to represent a range between 0 to −31 in dBm0. This value represents the power level of each DTMF frequency.

■ *Digit type:* A description of the presence or absence of a digit. A value of 000 indicates "digit off," and a value of 001 indicates "DTMF on."

■ *Edge location:* A 20-ms window is used to encode an edge when a digit is turned on or off, which represents the delta time 0 to 19 ms from the beginning of the current frame. If there is no transition, the edge location is set to 0 and the digit type of the previous windows is repeated. For example, if the calling party presses a number on the keypad for a long period, the edge location is set to 0, and the digit is repeated. This approach allows the service provider to adjust to the speed in which the calling party enters the dialed numbers into the telephone keypad, and provide "filler" in between. It also allows lost frames to be handled by placing repeating information in the payload.

Signaling Information

VoFR uses the ABCD signaling bits defined in the T1 systems, and local access signaling. These bits convey a variety of information, and Frame Relay does not act on these bits, nor is it aware of their functions. They are passed transparently through the Frame Relay system to-and-from the calling and called parties. However, Frame Relay does provide options on how the bits are coded in the subframe, because telephony signaling also provides options. So, we need to digress a moment and discuss these signaling bits.

As the T1 family of digitized voice systems evolved, the need for more elaborate signaling mechanism became important. But, at the same time, the evolution had to take into account the "older" T1 systems, and therefore a T1 system had to support different signaling schemes. Most of these operations take place in T1 multiplexers and channel banks.

The bits are encoded into the frame of a T1 frame. The process is called "bit robbing" because the user traffic bits are periodically replaced (robbed) by the insertion of the signaling bits. The D4 and D5 T1 channel banks use the 8th bit with a 4-state and 16-state scheme, respectively. For the D4 bank, the A bit is sent in the 6th frame and the B bit is sent in the 12th frame. For the D5 channel bank, the A and B bits are sent as in the D4 scheme, then the C bit is transmitted in the 18th frame and

Table 14-5

Use of the 8th Bit

	Superframe	
Frame	**2-State**	**4-State**
6	A	A
12	A	B

	Extended Superframe		
Frame	**2-State**	**4-State**	**16-State**
6	A	A	A
12	A	B	B
18	A	A	C
24	A	B	D

the D bit is transmitted in the 24th frame. In summary, Table 14-5 shows these operations. These conventions are known as the *superframe* and the *extended superframe.*

The meaning of the bits depends upon the specific local loop access signaling method, such as loop start, ground start, and loop battery reversal configuration. It is beyond the scope of a Frame Relay book to describe in detail the functions of user-network access signaling, but Fig. 14-15 should be of use to the reader.

The telephone system was designed to perform signaling by onhook and offhook operations. The *onhook* operation means the telephone set is not being used, a term derived in the old days when the telephone handset has placed on a hook (later a cradle) when it was not being used. The *offhook* is just the opposite; the handset is being used—it is lifted from the telephone.

The offhook and onhook operations change the electrical state of the line between the user terminal and the telephone central office (or PBX). The signals listed in Fig. 14-15 are onhook or offhook signals of various durations to convey different meanings, as summarized in the far right-hand column of the table.

These signals are variations of the onhook and offhook operations. The telephone system maps some of these signals into the ABCD bits of a T1 frame.[1] Since Frame Relay is not using T1, it still must support ABCD signaling.

[1]The ABCD bits are carried inside the T1 frame and are used to denote alarms, active/inactive user lines, loop closure, and so forth. More information on ABCD signaling is available from Bellcore document TR-NWT-000303, "Integrated Digital Loop Carrier System Generic Requirements, Objectives and Interfaces."

Figure 14-15
Signaling summary.

Name	Type	Direction Originating	Terminating	Meaning
Connect	Offhook	──────────>		Request service and hold connection
Disconnect	Onhook	──────────>		Release connection
Answer	Offhook	──────────>		Terminating end has answered
Hangup	Onhook	<──────────		Message complete
Delay start	Offhook	<──────────		Terminating end not ready for digits
Wink start	Offhook	<──────────		Terminating end ready to receive digits
Start dialing	Onhook	<──────────		Terminating end ready for digits
Stop	Offhook	<──────────		Terminating end not ready for further digits
Go	Onhook	<──────────		Terminating end ready for further digits
Idle trunk	Onhook	<──────────>		
Busy trunk	Offhook	<──────────>		

Tables 14-6 and 14-7 show some examples (not all inclusive) of operations that pertain to loop start, ground start, and loop reverse battery in the local loop GR-303 specification (published by Bellcore).

Table 14-6

ABCD Codes for Locally Switched Circuits from Network to User (Not All-inclusive)

ABCD Code	Loop Start	Ground Start	Loop Reverse Battery
0000	-R ringing	-R ringing	
0010	DS0 AIS	DS0 AIS	DS0 AIS
0100	RLCF	RLCF	
0101	LCF	LCF	LO
0111	DS0 Yellow	DS0 Yellow	DS0 Yellow
1111	LCFO	LCFO	LC

Table 14-7

ABCD Codes for
Locally Switched
Circuits from User
to Network (Not
All-inclusive)

ABCD Code	Loop Start	Ground Start	Loop Reverse Battery
0000		Ring Ground	
0010	DS0 AIS	DS0 AIS	DS0 AIS
0100			RLCF
0101	LO	LO	LCF
0111	DS0 Yellow	DS0 Yellow	DS0 Yellow
1111	LC	LC	

The legend for these tables are:

AIS	Alarm Indication Signal
CF	Current Feed
DTF	Dial-Tone First
LC	Loop Closure
LO	Loop Open
LCF	Loop Current Feed
RLCF	Reverse Loop Current Feed
LCFO	Loop Current Feed Open
Reserved	for superframe–to–extended superframe translation

VoFR supports the ABCD signaling with a transfer syntax of 15 octets, as shown in Fig. 14-16. Up to four signaling bits can be coded, which contain 60 ms of samples. The time for each sample is 2.0 ms. Each packet in the subframe contains 10 new samples for the current 20-ms time interval. The packet also contains a repetition of the two last time intervals, known as "recent" for the last set of bits, and "previous" for the set of bits that followed the recent set of bits. The reason for coding redundant signaling bits is to accommodate to the possibility of losing frames (and to the fact that Frame Relay does not resend lost or errored frames). By using the sequence number in the packet, the receiver knows if it is receiving contiguous or noncontiguous frames, and react accordingly.

For 16-state signaling, all four bits are used (ABCD). With 4-state signaling, the AB bits are repeated in the C and D fields respectively. For 2-state signaling, the A bit is repeated in all the other bit positions.

Signaling Procedures

It is not efficient to send signaling information when the user terminals are not signaling. As shown in Fig. 14-17, VoFR handles this situation by sending a signaling packet every 20 ms as long as there are transitions in

Figure 14-16
VoFR signaling bits.

Bit 8	Bit 7	Bit 6	Bit 5	Bit 4	Bit 3	Bit 2	Bit 1	Octet
AIS	Sequence number							1
D	C	B	A	D	C	B	A	2
D	C	B	A	D	C	B	A	3
D	C	B	A	D	C	B	A	4
D	C	B	A	D	C	B	A	5
D	C	B	A	D	C	B	A	6
D	C	B	A	D	C	B	A	7
D	C	B	A	D	C	B	A	8
D	C	B	A	D	C	B	A	9
D	C	B	A	D	C	B	A	10
D	C	B	A	D	C	B	A	11
D	C	B	A	D	C	B	A	12
D	C	B	A	D	C	B	A	13
D	C	B	A	D	C	B	A	14
D	C	B	A	D	C	B	A	15
D	C	B	A	D	C	B	A	16

Notes: Rows 2–6 are previous samples.
Rows 7–11 are recent samples.
Rows 12–16 are current samples.

the signaling bits. As discussed earlier, each packet is 60 ms in duration, and contains redundant signaling information.

If the signaling bits do not change for 500 ms, the VoFR transmitter alters the frequency that it sends the signaling packets to one every 5 seconds. During this period of signaling inactivity, the sequence number is not incremented, which allows the receiver to discard this packet (or use the first value to set its current values).

Figure 14-17
Procedures for
processing the
signaling bits.

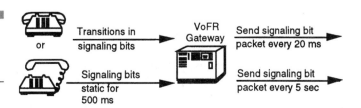

At the receiver, the sequence number is used to determine if the traffic is arriving in the proper order, and processes the traffic in the following manner:

- Sequence number is 1 greater than last received sequence number: Append current signal bits to previously received values

- Sequence number is 2 greater than last received sequence number: Append recent and current signal bits to previously received values

- Sequence number is 3 greater than last received sequence number: Append previous, recent, and current signal bits to previously received values

- Sequence number is more than 3 or the last received sequence number: Append previous, recent, and current signal bits to previously received values, and fills in any gaps with the values in the previously received packet

Data Traffic

Data traffic can be transmitted between two VoFR users and remain transparent to the telephone connection. The data traffic is coded as fragments according to the Frame Relay Forum's Standard FRF.12, discussed in other parts of this chapter. Since this subject is covered elsewhere, we do not repeat it here.

Fax Traffic

Fax traffic is transported by VoFR using the same concepts employed for data, dial digits, and signaling traffic. The fax traffic is encapsulated into the Frame Relay subframe, and remains transparent to the Frame Relay network. The VoFR gateway is responsible for handling the fax-specific operations.

VoFR supports the worldwide standard for Group 3 facsimile systems, which is defined in ITU-T T.4 (1993). In addition to T.4, VoFR supports several ITU-T V Series modems, as well as the V.17 fax specification for 7.2; 9.6; 12.0; and 14.4 kbps transmission rates. The modems supported by VoFR are summarized in Table 14-8.

Table 14-8

VoFR Support of V
Series Rates (in
addition to V.17)

Series Number	Line Speed	Modulation Rate	Carrier Frequency	FDX or HDX	Modulation Technique	Bits Encoded
V.21	300	300	1080 and 1750	FDX	FS	1:1
V.27	4800	1600	1800	Either	PS	3:1
V.27 *ter*	4800	1600	1800	HDX	PS	3:1
V.27 *ter*	2400	1200	1800	HDX	PS	2:1
V.29	9600	2400	1700	Either	QAM	4:1
V.29	7200	2400	1700	Either	PS	3:1
V.29	4800	2400	1700	Either	PS	2:1
V.33	14400	2400	1800	FDX	QAM	7:1

The entries in the rows and columns of the Table 14-8 mean:

Entries	*Explanation*
Line Speed	Speed in bits per second (bps).
Modulation Rate	The rate of the signal change of the carrier on the channel, in baud.
Full Duplex	FDX: Full Duplex
Half Duplex	HDX: Half Duplex
Modulation Technique	The description of the modulation technique where:
	FS: Frequency Shift
	PS: Phase Shift
	QAM: Quadrature Amplitude Modulation
	FM: Frequency Modulation
	TCM: Trellis Coded Modulation
HDX or FDX	Specifies if modem operates at half duplex (HDX) or full duplex (FDX)
Carrier Frequency	Describes the frequency at which the modem operates
Bits Encoded	Describes the number of bits encoded per signal change (baud). For example, 2:1 means two bits encoded per baud.

Since Frame Relay must convey fax and modem control signals between the user machines, the VoFR subframe for fax traffic is coded to identify operating parameters that are needed between the sending and receiving fax/modems. As examples, the subframe contains informa-

Figure 14-18

Example of VoFR
fax/modem payload.

Bit 8	Bit 7	Bit 6	Bit 5	Bit 4	Bit 3	Bit 2	Bit 1	Octet
EI1 = 1	Sequence number				Relay Command = 001			1
Time Stamp Least Significant Byte								2
EI2 = 0	Time Stamp Most Significant Byte							3
HDLC	Reserved			Modulation Type				4
Frequency Least Significant Byte								5
Frequency Most Significant Byte								6

tion on the modulation type used by the sending modem, the type of modem (V.17, V.33, etc.), and the bps rate (14.4 kbps, etc.). The subframe for fax support contains several different formats to convey this information. We will take one example to illustrate how VoFR supports fax applications, the V.17 14.4 kbps fax/modem, a common machine in businesses and homes today.

Figure 14-18 shows the fax payload format, and Fig. 14-19 shows an example of VoFR fax/modem operations. The fax/modem information elements are placed in octet 2c (the payload element) of the subframe (see Fig. 14-9). This payload packet is called the *modulation turn-on packet*. This packet is sent when the VoFR gateway detects a frequency tone, at which time the VoFR sends at least 3 of these packets. The EI1 and EI2 bits are set to 1 and 0, respectively (they are header extension bits), and

Figure 14-19

Example of VoFR
support for fax
transmissions.

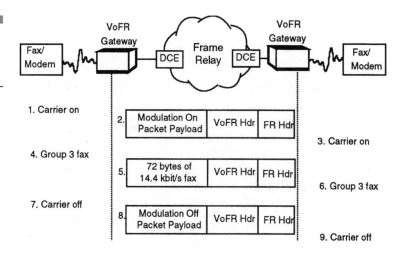

the sequence number remains at 0 during this handshake phase. The Relay Command field is set to 011 (modulation-on) to indicate that a carrier has been detected. The time stamp is used to provide timing to the demodulator, and is coded in 1 ms units (and must be accurate to ±5 ms). The timing assumes free-running clocks with no synchronization between them. The HDLC bit is used if an HDLC frame is used between the modems (bit = 1, HDLC is applied).

The modulation type is set to identify the type of modem that is sending this information. The receiving modem uses this information to adjust its operations to this modem type. This information is conveyed in analog signals to the VoFR gateway, which converts the signals to four-bit codes. For our example, the modulation type code for a 14.4-kbps V.17 fax/modem is 1011. The last field in this example is the frequency information element, and it is coded to indicate the sending modem's frequency tone in Hertz units. This field is important because some modems operate with more than one frequency.

The VoFR gateway continues to interpret the fax/modems analog signals and maps them into the Frame Relay subframes. After the handshake, it places the fax images into the subframes and sends them to the receiving VoFR gateway. At this machine, the data fields in the subframe are mapped back to analog signals for interpretation and processing at the receiving fax/modem.

The VoFR gateway sends Group 3 T.4 fax payload every 40 ms. Therefore, the number of bits in the packet vary, depending on the bit rate of the fax machines. Table 14-9 shows the bit rate of the V Series machines and the corresponding bytes carried in each packet that is placed in the subframe.[2]

Table 14-9

V Series Bit Rates and Corresponding Bytes Per Packet

Bps	Bytes/packet
14000	72
12000	60
9600	48
7200	48
4800	24
2400	12

[2]A small point here, but FRF.11 uses the term "modulation rate" erroneously. This term in the document should be transfer rate in "bits per second." The modulation rate is defined in *baud,* or with a more recent term, *symbol rate.*

Voice Traffic

Table 14-1 in the first part of this chapter lists the vocoder specifications that are supported by VoFR. It is beyond the scope of the book to describe the detailed operations of vocoders. However, this section provides an overview of how VoFR handles ITU-T G.723.1 traffic. I have selected this specification because of its use in the industry and the fact that is it being supported as the preferred vocoder specification by the International Media Teleconferencing Consortium (IMTC).

The G.723 vocoder is designed to perform conventional telephone bandwidth filtering (based on G.712) of the voice signal, sample the signal at the conventional 8000 Hz rate (based on G.711), convert the 16-bit linear PCM code for input to the encoder. The decoder part of the vocoder performs a complementary operation on the output to reconstruct the voice signal.

The vocoder encodes the voice signal into frames based on linear predictive analysis-by-synthesis coding. A coder is capable of producing two rates of voice traffic: (1) 6.3 kbps for the high rate, and (2) 5.3 kbps for the low rate. The high rate coder is based on Multipulse Maximum Likelihood Quantization (MP-MLQ), and the low-rate coder is based on Algebraic-Code-Excited Linear-Prediction (ACELP).

The encoder operates on frames of 240 samples each to support the 8000 sample per second input speech stream. Further operations (a high pass filter to remove the DC component) result in four subframes of 60 ms each. A variety of other operations occur, such as the computation of an LPC filter, unquantized LCP filter coefficients, and so on, resulting in a packetization time of 30 ms.

After the digitized frames are created by the coder, they are encapsulated into the VoFR voice information field (see Fig. 14-20). For MP-MLQ, the information field is 24 octets, and for ACELP, the information field is 20 octets. The voice packets are transported through the Frame Relay network and passed to the decoder. The decoder converts the digital images to the output voice signal, which is played out to the receiver.

Multilink Frame Relay (MFR)

Multilink Frame Relay (MFR) is used to group or aggregate bandwidth on a set of Frame Relay links between two machines, as depicted in

Figure 14-20
Transport of voice
traffic.

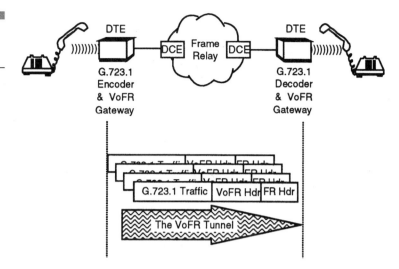

Fig. 14-21. MFR is useful for Frame Relay customers who need to use bandwidths greater than T1 but less than T3. In addition, some customers need to aggregate multiple DS0s and MFR provides for these features. The approach is to use software to support the service in contrast to a similar solution called inverse multiplexing, which uses hardware. The software solution is less expensive than its hardware counterpart.

Currently, MFR supports only PVCs, while implementation of SVCs is for further study. MFR operations can exist at both the UNI and NNI. MFR relies on fragmentation operations, discussed earlier in this chapter.

Figure 14-21
Multilink Frame Relay
(MFR).

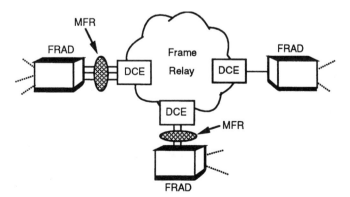

MFR uses the concept of a bundle, which other technologies call connection sets or link sets. The *bundle* is a group of one or more links that are aggregated together. Each link in the bundle is called a *member* of the bundle. The MFR users (upper layer protocols such as IP) are not aware of the bundling process, which appears as one single, larger bandwidth logical link.

The basic concept behind MFR is to aggregate T1/E1 links, but other link types can be supported. As a general rule, one-to-twelve links are optimum for the aggregation value and for the sake of simplicity, each member of the bundle should have the same bandwidth. This approach simplifies the receiver's job of combining fragments from the constituent links.

The software reassembly and aggregation process at the receiver will create latency. However, the Frame Relay Forum states that the latency is acceptable if fragmentation of voice–over–Frame Relay frames occurs before queuing the frames over the multilink interface.

The frame format for MFR is shown in Fig. 14-22. The MFR header consists of two octets that precede the single link Frame Relay header. The header is the same format as the header established in the Frame Relay PVC fragmentation specification (FRF.12, discussed earlier in this chapter). For this explanation, the MFR operation uses two types of frames that are differentiated by the C-bit in the fragmentation header. If the C-bit is set to 0, the fragment payload contains either user data or conventional link management data. If the C-bit is set to 1, the fragment contains MFR control data. The B, E, and sequence bits are coded in accordance with the FRF.12 specification.

The payload format with the C-bit = 1 is coded as shown in Fig. 14-23. The purpose of this frame is to verify that the constituent link member within the bundle is operational.

Figure 14-22
Multilink frame format.

Bit 8	Bit 7	Bit 6	Bit 5	Bit 4	Bit 3	Bit 2	Bit 1	Octet
B	E	C	Sequence number of high-order 4 bits				1	1
Sequence number of low-order 8 bits								2
DLCI high six bits						C/R	0	3
DLCI low four bits				F	B	DE	1	4
Payload								5 – n
Frame Check Sequence (FCS)								5 – n + 2

Notes: Octets 1 and 2: Fragmentation header
Octets 3 and 4: Frame Relay header

Figure 14-23

Multilink frame
format with C = 1.

Bit 8	Bit 7	Bit 6	Bit 5	Bit 4	Bit 3	Bit 2	Bit 1	Octet
B	E	C = 1	Sequence number of high-order 4 bits				1	1
Type = 01 (keep-alive) or 02 (keep-alive replay)								2
Length								3
Arg 1								n
Arg 2								n
Type = 0 (no additional payload)								n
FCS								n

Notes: Octets 1 and 2: Fragmentation header
Octets 3 and 4: Frame Relay header

The type field is coded as follows:

- *Type field = 01:* Identifies a keep-alive request. The argument with the keep-alive request is a timestamp that is represented in ms.

- *Type field = 02:* Identifies a keep-alive reply. The argument in this protocol call data unit must include the timestamp that was received in the keep-alive request.

- *Arg fields:* Provides additional information, if needed. For a keep-alive request the arg field is a two-octet timestamp (in ms).

The operations of these two protocol data units is largely self-descriptive. When a sender sends a keep-alive request message the receiver must respond with a keep-alive reply. This "ping" indicates if the link is operational. The manner in which the ping occurs (timers and retries) is implementation-specific.

SUMMARY

The recent additions to Frame Relay capabilities translate into a more diverse technology. The most significant part of these changes is the voice over Frame Relay (VoFR) operations. The fragmentation procedure is an important component of VoFR. Multilink Frame Relay (MFR) provides a tool for aggregating bandwidth, and provides alternate physical links for backup purposes. It also offers an alternative to hardware-based inverse multiplexing.

VoFR is new to the industry, and it has competitors, namely voice over IP (VoIP) and voice over ATM. It remains to be seen how VoFR will fare in the marketplace, but the widespread use of Frame Relay is a positive sign for the technology.

The Frame
Relay Market

This chapter reviews the progress Frame Relay has made in the marketplace. It also summarizes several surveys of the customers of Frame Relay networks that explain how and why Frame Relay is being used.

Descriptions of Services

Table 15-1 summarizes some of the service offerings that are provided by a number of Frame Relay service providers.

Fixed-based CIR is based on a fixed price per month. It is similar to private line pricing, and the customer can transmit as much data as the port speed allows. In contrast, the cost of usage-based CIR is based on the actual usage of the network.

Some network providers offer zero CIR. With this service, there is no guarantee of sustained bandwidth. If the network must shed traffic, this type of traffic is the first to be discarded.

Most Frame Relay network providers offer incremental CIR, in which CIR can be purchased in kbps increments, such as 16 kbps, 4 kbps, and the like. Providers vary on how a user can burst traffic into the network. The duration of bursting can either be less than some time limit or any amount of time subject to network congestion.

Some providers offer a service called *over subscription*. Each PVC on a given port is given the port speed (T1, fractional T1, etc.). If only one PVC is active, it can operate at the full rate of the physical port. If multiple PVCs are active, they must compete for port bandwidth.

Asymmetric PVCs are another offering provided by some networks. As its name implies, it allows different CIRs to be provided in each direc-

Table 15-1		
	■ Fixed-based CIR:	Fixed price per month; similar to private line price
Frame Relay	■ Usage-based CIR:	Price based on actual usage
Service Offerings	■ Zero CIR:	No guarantee of sustained bandwidth; first to be discarded
	■ Incremental CIR:	CIR in kbps increments
	■ Duration of bursting:	(a) a time limit, or (b) any amount of time subject to network congestion
	■ Over subscription:	Each PVC on port given port speed, and PVC contend for bandwidth
	■ Asymmetrical PVCs:	Different CIR in each direction on the virtual circuit

tion on the virtual connection. It is useful for applications such as file transfer that have more traffic going in one direction than another.

Use of the Services at UNI

Although Frame Relay provides a very flexible and useful mechanism for policing traffic and charging for network usage, not all users care about how all this is factored into the decision to adopt Frame Relay. Figure 15-1 shows how the users of Frame Relay view these operations (both in terms of what is being offered and what is anticipated).

The initial offerings of Frame Relay did not offer much beyond a fixed-rate CIR, with the pricing targeted around 25 to 30 percent of a comparable leased line. More recent offerings provide usage-based or zero CIR.

Most public Frame Relay offerings in North America charge a monthly rate, based on the circuit speed, with options typically ranging from 56–64 kbps to DS1 rates. Network usage incurs a monthly charge based on megabytes transported through the network. Additionally, most networks charge based on the CIR provided to the user.

Most of the Frame Relay service providers offer integrated access. This enables a user site to multiplex different types of applications (voice, video, data) across the Frame Relay UNI to the central office. At the central office, the traffic is demultiplexed and sent to the appropriate switches to handle the specific type of traffic.

Figure 15-1
Type of service at the UNI (now offered, and anticipated).

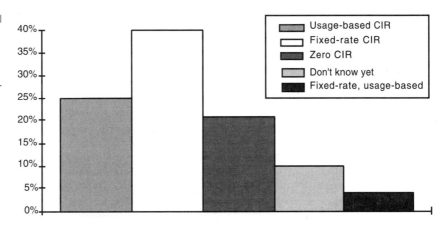

Major Applications Using Frame Relay

It comes as no surprise that the applications that benefit from Frame Relay are those in need of high bandwidth bursty services (see Fig. 15-2). Thus, file transfer applications rate high as a major reason for using Frame Relay. So do applications performing database inquiries that might entail a large transfer of information from a database, with bandwidth and response requirements quite similar to those of file transfer.

The various surveys reporting on the use of Frame Relay also report that email is a primary user. At first glance, this might seem surprising, because this type of application does not require much bandwidth. Nevertheless, email is so prevalent in many organizations that any (effective) new carrier service such as Frame Relay will find applications migrating to its services.

What Frame Relay Is Augmenting or Replacing

It appears that Frame Relay is on target. It was envisioned a few years ago to offer an alternative to leased lines, and to provide an easy way to augment existing services. Additionally, the potential ability to connect

Figure 15-2
Key applications using Frame Relay.

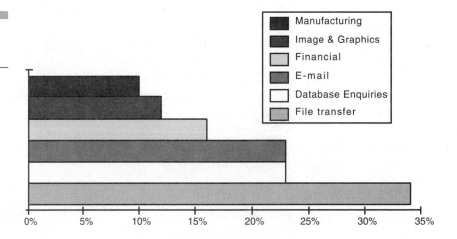

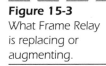

Figure 15-3
What Frame Relay
is replacing or
augmenting.

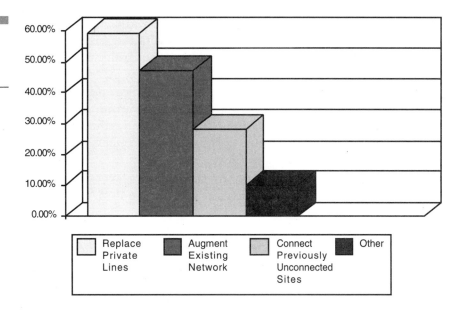

previously unconnected sites was viewed as a positive aspect of the
Frame Relay approach. As Fig. 15-3 shows, current users of Frame Relay
are finding its original promise to be true.

SUMMARY AND SOME FINAL THOUGHTS

As I have stated several times in this book, Frame Relay is a big success
story, primarily because of its attractive price/performance features. In
the second edition, I made these statements: "...some of my associates and
clients believe Frame Relay will not be in the industry for an extended
period. They claim ATM will erode some of the Frame Relay market
(1996–1997), and eventually Frame Relay vendors will replace Frame
Relay switches in the wide area network with cell-based ATM switches
(1997–1998)." Well, it did not happen, but ATM is now being deployed in
backbone, high-capacity networks.

In the meantime, Frame Relay has continued to grow and expand
into many network products. Any technology that becomes embedded
into products assures itself of a long life, if for no other reason than it is
difficult and expensive to remove the technology. In addition, Frame
Relay is not a complex technology, and it is assimilated easily into current architectures.

My view is that Frame Relay and ATM will coexist for a number of years. If Frame Relay products that support voice and video become widespread, they will certainly retard the progress of ATM.

Nonetheless, unlike Frame Relay, ATM is designed for voice, video, and data traffic. With Frame Relay, voice and video are add-ons. Additionally, Frame Relay is not designed to run on LANs, while ATM is. This latter point is quite important because many companies are looking to ATM to increase the LAN's capacity. Frame Relay is not designed to provide this kind of service.

We should not overlook the Internet protocols—IPv4, IPv6, and related protocols, such as the Resource Reservation Protocol (RSVP), the Real Time Protocol (RTP), and the Real Time Control Protocol (RTCP). Nor should we overlook the Fast LANs, such as Fast Ethernet, and Gigabit Ethernet. The enhanced IP Protocol suite and the Fast LANs are positioned to compete with Frame Relay in some markets.

Frame Relay is designed to support WANs. Fast and Gigabit Ethernet support LANs. IP and ATM are positioned for both LANs and WANs, but they may compete for the same market. They are increasingly expanding their support of multiservice applications.

The question of which of these technologies serve the application best and will ultimately prevail is far from resolved, and is the subject of another story (and maybe another book).

For the present, thank you for reading this book. I hope it has been a useful experience for you.

APPENDIX A

A TUTORIAL ON
NETWORK MANAGEMENT
PROTOCOLS, MIBS,
AND OBJECT LIBRARIES

The International Standards Organization (ISO) has been working on the development of several Open Systems Interconnection (OSI) network management standards for a number of years. Another major thrust into network management standards has been through the Internet activities. These initial efforts were organized through the ARPANET research project that originated in the United States. In 1971, the Defense Advanced Research Projects Agency (DARPA) assumed the work of this earlier organization. DARPA's work in the early 1970s led to the development of the *Transmission Control Protocol and the Internet Protocol* (TCP/IP).

In the last few years, the Internet task forces have assumed the lead in setting standards for the Internet, and have fostered two network management standards. One protocol is the *Simple Network Management Protocol* (SNMP).

Terms and Definitions

The OSI and Internet network management standards define several terms (summarized in Table A-1). This section examines them in more detail—the responsibility for a *managing process* (called a *network management system* in some vendors' products) and a *managing agent* (also known as an *agent process*). In the strictest sense, a network management system really contains nothing more than protocols that convey information about network elements back and forth among various agents in the system and the managing process.

One other component is vital to a network management system. It is called the *management information base* or library (hereafter called an MIB). This conceptual object is actually a database that is shared between managers and agents to provide information about the managed network elements.

Table A-1

Key Terms in
Standardized
Network
Management

- Agent
  Reports to the managing process on the status of managed network elements.
  Receives directives from the managing process on actions it is to perform on these elements.

- Managing process
  Directs the operations of the agent.

- MIB (Internet)
  Used by the agent and managing process to determine the structure and content of management information—describes the managed objects.

- Managed Object (OSI)
  A representation of the managed resource—defines how resource can be managed by a management protocol.

- Managed Object Definition (OSI)
  How resources can be managed; operations performed on them, and information they can generate.

The OSI network management standards use many of the concepts of object-oriented design (OOD). The concept of OOD originated in the early 1970s. The notion of an object as a construct for manipulation (in effect, a programming construct) first appeared in Simula, a language used to program computer simulations.

The resources that are supervised and controlled by network management are called *managed objects* (see Fig. A-1). A managed object can be anything deemed important by organizations using the OSI network management standards. As examples, hardware such as switches, workstations, PBXs, PBX port cards, and multiplexers can be identified as managed objects. Software, such as queuing programs, routing algorithms, and buffer management routines, can also be treated as managed objects.

Figure A-1
Object-oriented
design (OOD)
concepts.

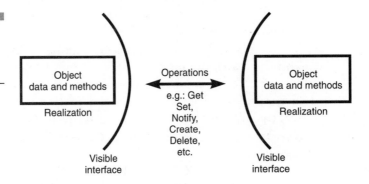

The OSI Network Management Model

Figure A-2 provides a general view of the OSI network management model. The managing system is responsible for directing the actions of the managed system. The managed system consists of a remote manager in addition to the managed objects. This remote manager is comprised of a local representative for the agent called an agent—hence its name. It is the agent for the remote manager. The agent is responsible for receiving network management messages from the managing process and ensuring that proper access control measures are taken regarding the managed objects. It is also responsible for providing and controlling local logging operations and, through the use of an *event forwarding discriminator* (EFD), it makes decisions whether messages are to be returned to the managing process.

Although this picture shows a one-to-one relationship between a managing process and a managed system, the managing process can also act as an agent (managed) process. No restriction exists on the roles that these two entities play. Indeed, the roles may be exchanged.

It is also useful to note that while the OSI model in this figure has the managed object as part of the managed system, this need not be the case in the real world, because the managed system need not control the managed objects. Once again, it is important to understand that OSI merely represents how messages are emitted between the systems and how the managed objects are viewed. It is quite permissible for other

Figure A-2
The OSI management model.

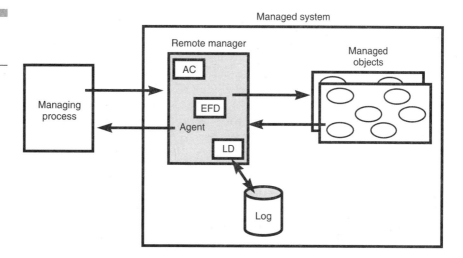

systems to have a view of the same resource, and that view might be different. As an example, one router among others in an internet might be viewed as being present or absent, depending on the particular state of the router at a given time. Therefore, this managed object might be viewed differently by other systems, and its attribute values would then also be viewed differently.

OSI Information Modeling

Bellcore models information on Frame Relay interfaces using the OSI model. This section provides a review of the concepts of information modeling. As explained in the section "Terms and Definitions," the resources that are supervised and controlled by OSI network management are called *managed objects* (MO). Note that an MO is a representation of how a resource can be managed by a management protocol; it is not a thing in itself. It is an abstraction of a physical or logical entity (which is how Bellcore views an MO).

A managed object is completely described and defined by four aspects of OSI network management:

- Its *attributes* (characteristics or properties) at its interface (visible boundary)
- The *operations* that can be performed on it
- The *notifications* (reports) it is allowed to make
- Its *behavior* in response to operations performed on it

Managed objects have certain properties that distinguish them from one another. These properties are called *attributes*. The purpose of an attribute is to describe the characteristics, current state, and conditions of the operation of the managed objects. Associated with the attributes are attribute *values*. For example, an object (such as a PBX line card) might have an attribute called *status* and a value of *operational*.

Each attribute consists of one type and one or more values. For example, a type might be labeled the operational state of a packet switch. The values for this type might be *disabled, enabled, active,* or *busy.*

The OSI Network Management Layers

The OSI network management model is consistent with the overall OSI application layer architecture.

The *systems management application service element* (SMASE) creates and uses the *protocol data units* (PDUs) transferred between the management processes of the two machines. These data units are called *management application data units* (MAPDUs).

The SMASE can use the communications services of *application services elements* (ASEs) or the *common management information service element* (CMISE). As depicted in the Fig. A-3, the use of CMISE implies the use of ROSE and ACSE.

Figure A-3
The OSI management layers.

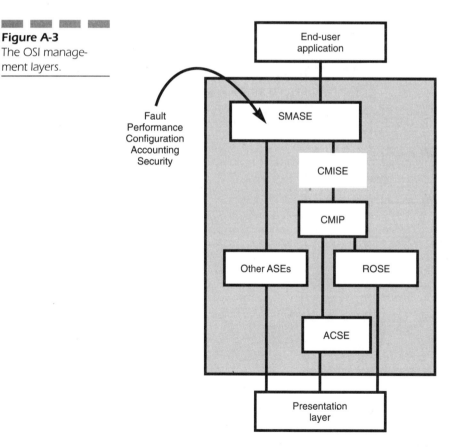

In accordance with OSI conventions, two management applications in two open systems exchange management information after they have established an application context. The application context uses a name that identifies the service elements needed to support the association. ISO 10040 states that the application context for OSI management associations implies the use of ACSE, ROSE, CMISE, and SMASE.

The Internet Network Management Layers

As shown in Fig. A-4, the layering for the Internet suite is simpler than the OSI suite. The simple network management protocol (SNMP) forms the foundation for the Internet architecture. The network management applications are not defined in the Internet specifications. These appli-

Figure A-4
The Internet network management layers.

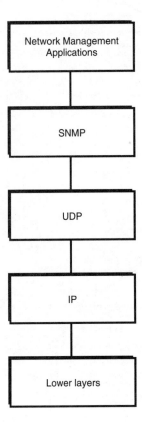

Network Management Applications

SNMP

UDP

IP

Lower layers

cations consist of vendor-specific network management modules, such as fault management, log control, security and audit trails, and so on. As illustrated in the figure, SNMP rests over the *User Datagram Protocol* (UDP). UDP in turn rests on top of IP, which then rests upon the lower layers (the data link layer and the physical layer).

Naming and Name Registration

The ISO and ITU-T have jointly developed a scheme for naming and uniquely identifying objects, such as standards, member bodies, organizations, protocols—anything that needs an unambiguous identifier. As depicted in Fig. A-5, the scheme is a hierarchical tree structure wherein the lower leaves of the tree are subordinate to the leaves above. The

Figure A-5
The registration
hierarchy.

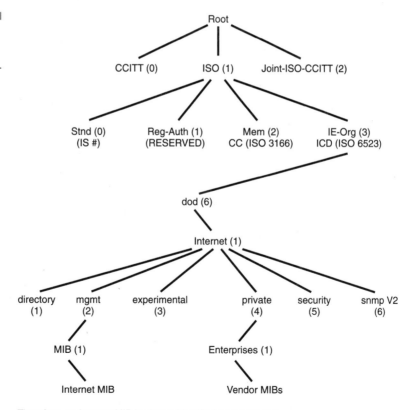

Therefore, an Internet MIB is always identified as 1.3.6.1.2.1.xxxx
Where xxxx is the remainder of the OBJECT IDENTIFIER

upper branches identify the authorities as ITU-T (0), ISO (1), or an object that is developed jointly by these organizations (2).

The ISO uses four arcs below the root to identify standards, registration authorities, member bodies, and organizations. Below these four arcs are other subordinate definitions that are chosen to further identify some type of object.

The Management Information Base (MIB)

The management information base (MIB) is one of the most important parts of a network management system. The MIB identifies the network elements (managed objects) that are to be managed. It also contains the unambiguous names that are to be associated with each managed object.

From a conceptual viewpoint, MIBs are really quite simple. Yet if they are not implemented properly, the network management protocols (such as CMIP and SNMP) are of little use. These network management protocols rely on the MIB to define the managed objects in the network.

It should be emphasized that the MIB represents the managed objects. After all, the MIB is a database that contains information about the managed objects. For example, an MIB can contain information about the number of packets sent and received across an X.25 interface, it can contain statistics on the number of connections that exist on a TCP port, and so forth.

The MIB defines the contents of the information carried with the network management protocols. It also contains information that describes each network management user's ability to access elements of the MIB. For example, one user might have read-only privileges in an MIB, while another might have read/write privileges.

Network management protocols (with few exceptions) do not operate directly on the managed object—they operate on the MIB. In turn, the MIB is a reflection of the managed object. In effect, it is the conceptual, abstract representation of the managed objects. How this reflection is conveyed is a proprietary decision. A managing or managed system need not know about the database organization of a network element, because it operates on the MIB, which represents the managed objects. The important aspects of the MIB are that it defines the elements that

Table A-2

What Is a Management Information Base (MIB) (from the Internet Point of View)?

- A network management database

- Describes the managed objects that are implemented at network components

- Provides a unique id of each managed object
  Examples: "ifType" for type of interface
  ("6" = Ethernet, 19 = E1)

- Defines how users may access network management data.
  Examples: READ ONLY, WRITE ONLY, etc.

- Stores statistical information pertaining to managed objects
  Examples: "ipInReceives = 4000" = IP router has received 4000 datagrams

- snmpInTooBigs = 32" = 32 SNMP messages have been received with an error status that message is too big

- Describes contents/structure of TLV fields of the network management message
  Type (T)   Always defined (e.g., INTEGER)i
  Length (L) Sometimes defined (e.g., one byte for Ethernet ifType, but variable for ipInReceives)
  Value (V)   Sometimes defined (e.g., 6 for Ethernet ifType, but variable for ipInReceives)

- Network management components must have compatible MIBs for full internetworking to occur

---

are managed, how the user accesses them, and how they can be reported. Table A-2 summarizes these thoughts.

CMIP and CMISE

The common management information service element (CMISE) is defined in ISO 9595. As the title suggests, it identifies the service elements used in management operations, as well as their arguments (parameters). It also provides a framework for common management procedures that can be invoked from remote locations.

The reader should remember that the OSI service element standards contain the rules for the creation and use of primitives between adjacent layers in the same machine. These primitives and their parameters are mapped into a PDU, which is transmitted across the communications link(s) to another machine. The network management messages (PDUs) are described in the common management information protocol (CMIP). Table A-3 provides a summary of the CMIP/CMISE operations.

Table A-3

CMIP/CMISE
Operations

- *M-EVENT-REPORT:* This service is used to report an event to a service user. Since the operations of network entities are a function of the specifications of the managed objects, this event is not defined by the standard but can be any event about a managed object that the user chooses to report. The service provides the time of the occurrence of the event as well as the current time.

- *M-GET:* This service is used to retrieve information from its peer. The service uses information about the managed object to obtain and return a set of attribute identifiers and values of the managed object or a selection of managed objects. It can only be used in a confirmed mode and a reply is expected.

- *M-CANCEL-GET:* This service is invoked by the user to request a peer to cancel a previously requested M-GET service. It can only be used in a confirmed mode and a reply is expected.

- *M-SET:* A CMISE user can use this service to request the modification of attribute values (the properties) of a managed object. It can be requested in a confirmed or nonconfirmed mode. If confirmed, a reply is expected.

- *M-ACTION:* This service is used by the user to request that another user perform some type of action on a management object, other than those associated with attribute values (state changes, etc.). It can be requested in a confirmed or nonconfirmed mode. If confirmed, a reply is expected.

- *M-CREATE:* This service is used to create a representation of another instance of a managed object, along with its associated management information values. It can only be used in a confirmed mode and a reply is expected.

- *M-DELETE:* This service performs the reverse operation of the M-CREATE. It deletes an instance of a managed object. It can only be used in a confirmed mode and a reply is expected.

SNMP

The simple network management protocol (SNMP) uses relatively simple operations and a limited number of PDUs to perform its functions (see Table A-4). Like most management protocols, SNMP uses *Gets* to retrieve information and *Sets* to modify information. The Get Response is used with a Get, Get-Next, and a Set. The trap is an unsolicited notification. SNMP does not have OOD foundations. Thus, it has no inheritance PDUs such as Create and Delete.

Two PDUs were added to SNMPv2. The Get Bulk is used to access multiple instances of objects, and the Inform Request is used between managers to inform each other about various activities.

Table A-4

SNMPv2 PDUs

- *Get Request:* Used to access the agent and obtain values from a list. Contains identifiers to distinguish it from multiple requests as well as values to provide information about the status of the network element.

- *Get-Next Request:* Permits the retrieving of the next logical identifier in an MIBtree.

- *Get Response:* Responds to the Get Request, Get-Next Request, and the Set Request data units. Contains an identifier that associates it with the previous PDU. Also contains identifiers to provide information about the status of the response (error codes, error status, and a list of additional information).

- *Set Request:* Used to describe an action to be performed on an element. Typically, used to change the values in a variable list.

- *Trap:* Allows the network management module to report on an event at a network element or to change the status of the network element.

- *Get Bulk:* Added to SNMPv2, retrieves multiple instances of an object.

- *Inform Request:* Added to SNMPv2, exchanged between management applications.

APPENDIX B

The purpose of this appendix is to provide the reader with an overview of the asynchronous transfer mode (ATM). This information is especially useful when reading Chap. 12, which contains descriptions of internetworking Frame Relay and ATM networks.

Characteristics of ATM

The *asynchronous transfer mode* (ATM) forms the basis for some of the emerging broadband, multimedia networks. This technology provides bandwidth-on-demand access to a network by multiplexing user information into fixed-length slots called *cells*. The main difference between Frame Relay and ATM is that Frame Relay permits the use of variable-length PDUs. ATM PDUs (cells) are always fixed at 53 bytes.

The traffic is identified and managed through virtual connection identifiers, much like the Frame Relay DLCI. In ATM, the identifiers are called *virtual path identifiers* (VPIs) and *virtual channel identifiers* (VCIs). Even though two numbers may be used to identify traffic, their use is quite similar to the Frame Relay DLCI.

ATM has attracted considerable attention in the telecommunications industry. Other than the fact that new technologies invite articles in trade magazines, why has ATM drawn so much attention?

First, ATM is one of the few technologies that supports the transport of voice, video, and data applications over one medium and one platform. Second, ATM is one of the few technologies to support LAN, WAN, and MAN traffic with one platform. Frame Relay's inherent design is not set up for voice or video, although it is technically feasible to run these types of applications across a Frame Relay network. Additionally, Frame Relay is not designed to run on a LAN.

ATM is also designed to facilitate the implementation of many of these services in hardware, which translates into fast processing of all traffic and low delay through switches and networks.

Like Frame Relay, ATM enables a user to obtain scalable bandwidth and bandwidth on demand. A user need not be allocated fixed bandwidth, as in a time division multiplexed system. Since ATM does not define a specific port speed at the ATM and user devices, an ATM device can support different link speeds, and the switching fabric can be upgraded (made faster) as more devices (and/or more traffic) are added to the system.

ATM Layers

As depicted in Fig. B-1, the ATM layers are similar to the layers of other technologies (the Metropolitan Area Network [MAN] and the switched multimegabit data service [SMDS]). ATM provides convergence functions for connection-oriented variable bit rate (VBR) applications, and connectionless services with variable bit rates. In addition, provision is made for isochronous services, such as voice, video, and music, with convergence functions to provide support for constant bit rate (CBR) services.

Figure B-1
ATM layers.

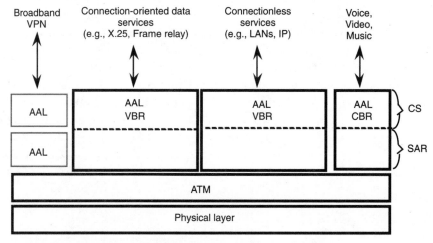

Note: Dashed box means AAl services may not be required
Where:

AAL	ATM adaptation layer
CBR	Constant bit rate
CS	Convergence sublayer
IP	Internet protocol
LANs	Local area networks
SAR	Segmentation and reassembly
VBR	Variable bit rate
VPN	Virtual private network

Broadband virtual private networks (VPN) may or may not use the services of the ATM adaptation (AA) layer. The decision to use this service depends on the nature of the VPN traffic as it enters the ATM device.

Segmentation and reassembly operations are provided for all services that might use PDUs different from those of an ATM cell.

These convergence services provide standardized interfaces to the ATM layer. This layer is then responsible for relaying and routing traffic (as well as multiplexing) through the ATM network.

The physical layer is made up of SONET, SDH, DS1, DS3, and so forth. As far as possible, ATM operations are kept transparent to the physical layer.

The ATM UNI

Figure B-2 highlights some of the major aspects of the ATM user-to-network interface (UNI). First, like Frame Relay, it is connection-orient-

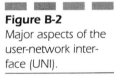

Figure B-2
Major aspects of the user-network interface (UNI).

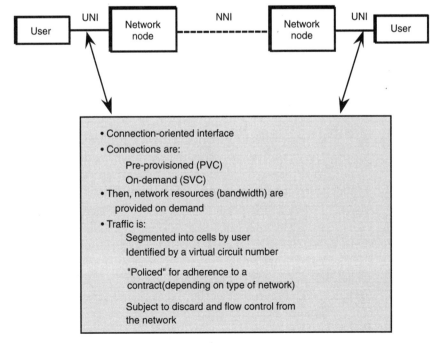

ed, and cells are associated with preestablished virtual connections, or set up on demand with switched virtual calls. Traffic must be segmented into cells before the ATM node can process it. The switch uses a virtual circuit number to identify the connection with which the cell is associated.

Like the DLCI of Frame Relay, the virtual circuit number has local significance; therefore, it is a local matter as to how mapping occurs between the two UNIs. However, the ATM network must preserve cell sequencing for each virtual connection in order to facilitate the reconstruction of individual cells into the form of the original traffic at the receiving node.

As of this writing, two interfaces are defined in ATM: the *user-to-network interface* (UNI) and the *network node interface* (or network-to-network) (NNI). Figure B-2 summarizes some of the major operations at the UNI. The UNI interface defines procedures for transmission and reception of data between the user and the ATM node.

The ATM NNI

Presently, two network-to-network interfaces (NNI) are under development for ATM (see Fig. B-3). A public NNI is being developed by the ITU-T, and a private NNI is being developed by the ATM Forum.

The private NNI was due for completion some time in 1995. It will allow different vendors' ATM machines to communicate with one another. The communications will utilize the standard UNI switched virtual call (SVC) procedures, with additional information added in the SVC messages. The major aspects of the private UNI will focus on route discovery, building routing tables, and maintaining an awareness of the "reachability" of other ATM nodes. It is based on hierarchical routing and hierarchical addresses. Advertisements are part of this specification, with information on link state metrics and bandwidth availability.

Since the private NNI is under development, the ATM Forum has published an interim specification, called the *interim interswitch signaling protocol* (IISP). It is a low-function protocol, with no dynamic route discovery. Tables are preconfigured, although SVC operations enable switches to request connections with each other.

The so-called public NNI is being developed by the ITU-T. Signaling System No. 7 (SS7) has been adapted for use with this specification. As a general description, SS7's ISDN user part (ISUP) and message transfer

███ ███ ███ ███

Figure B-3
Major aspects of the
network-to-network
interface (NNI).

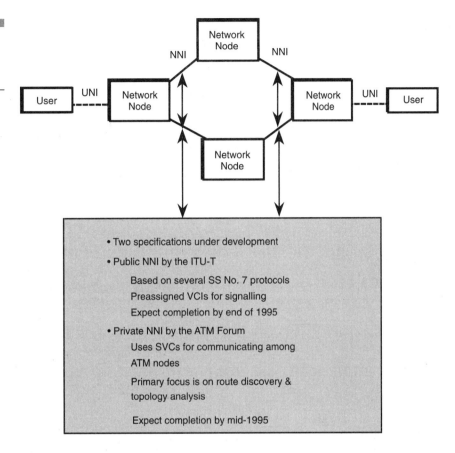

- Two specifications under development
- Public NNI by the ITU-T

    Based on several SS No. 7 protocols

    Preassigned VCIs for signalling

    Expect completion by end of 1995

- Private NNI by the ATM Forum

    Uses SVCs for communicating among

    ATM nodes

    Primary focus is on route discovery &

    topology analysis

    Expect completion by mid-1995

part 3 (MTP 3) have been modified for the public NNI. These protocols run on top of ATM and some type of physical layer. A special AAL called the *signaling ATM adaptation layer* (SAAL) rests between the ATM layer and the SS7 layers. It was anticipated that most of the public NNI standards would be in place by the end of 1995.

The ATM ICI

An ATM internetworking specification is published as a *network node interface* (NNI) by the ITU-T in recommendation G.708. Its counterpart, published by the ATM Forum, is called the *broadband intercarrier interface* (B-ICI) Version 1.0. The principal difference between these two specifications lies at the physical layer. The NNI specifies SDH. The B-ICI specifies SONET or DS3. Of course, other physical layers are technically feasible. Figure B-4 shows an example of the B-ICI as published by the ATM Forum in its June 1993 Version 1.0 specification.

Figure B-4 shows the relationship of the B-ICI to other interfaces and protocols, notably Frame Relay, circuit emulation service (CBR traffic), cell relay traffic, and SMDS. All these technologies, as well as ATM, pro-

Figure B-4
Major aspects of the intercarrier interface (ICI).

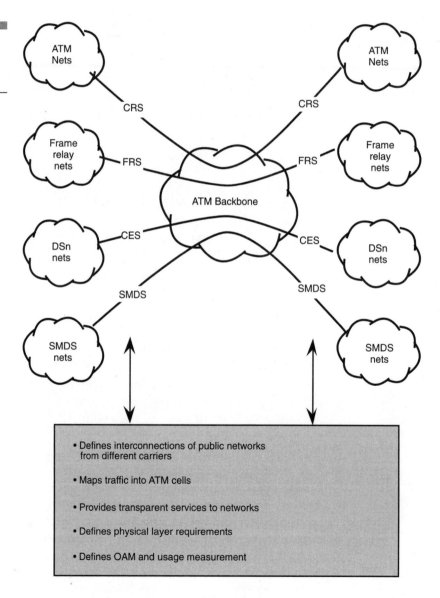

- Defines interconnections of public networks from different carriers

- Maps traffic into ATM cells

- Provides transparent services to networks

- Defines physical layer requirements

- Defines OAM and usage measurement

vide for the *user-to-network interface* (UNI), which is sometimes called the *subscriber-to-network interface* (SNI).

ATM Switching

Switching is performed in an ATM-based network through the use of the VPI/VCI contained in the header of the ATM cell. The VPI/VCI is not an explicit address like a 32-bit IP address or a 14-digit X.121 address. Rather, it is a label. The label is used at the ATM switch to determine how to relay traffic to the next node.

Explicit addresses are not feasible in cell technology due to the very short size of the protocol control information (PCI). Five bytes of header precludes using lengthy explicit addresses.

The ATM machine receives an incoming cell on a port, and reads the VPI/VCI value. This value has been reserved to identify a specific end user for a virtual circuit. It also identifies the next node that is to receive the traffic. The ATM switch then examines a routing table in order to match the incoming number and incoming port to an outgoing number and outgoing port. In this manner, relaying can be performed quite quickly at the switch.

The header in the outgoing cell is changed, with the new VPI/VCI value placed in the field of the cell header. The new value is used by the next ATM switch to perform subsequent routing operations.

The ATM Adaptation Layer (AAL)

The AAL is organized to support different types of service classes. The classes are defined with regard to

- timing needed between source and destination
- bit rate (variable or constant)
- connectionless or connection-oriented operation

Classes A and B require timing relationships between the source and destination. Classes C and D do not require timing relationships. A constant bit rate is required for class A; variable bit rates are permitted for classes B, C, and D. Classes A, B, and C are connection-oriented; class D is connectionless.

These classes are used to support different types of user applications. For example, class A is designed to support a constant bit rate requirement for, say, voice or video coding. On the other hand, class B, while connection-oriented, supports a variable bit rate. Class B supports applications such as variable bit rate video coding. For example, variable bit rate coding could be supported by information retrieval services, in which large amounts of video traffic are sent to the user and then long delays ensue as the user examines the information. As a result of this type of exchange, a variable bit rate is needed.

Class C services are the connection-oriented data transfer services such as X.25-type connections.

Conventional connectionless services such as datagram networks are supported with class D services.

AAL PDUs

As depicted in Fig. B-5, the ATM adaptation layer (AAL) uses type 1 protocol data units (PDUs) to support applications requiring a constant bit rate transfer to and from the layer above AAL. It is also responsible for the following tasks: segmentation and reassembly of user information; handling of variable cell delay; detection of lost and missequenced cells;

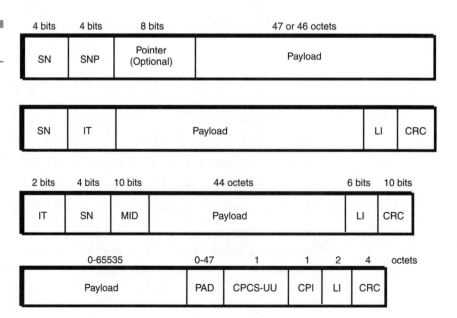

Figure B-5
The AAL PDUs.

source clock frequency recovery at the receiver; correction of all one-bit errors in the PDU and detection of all two-bit errors.

The AAL type 1 PDU consists of 48 octets, with 47 octets available for the user's payload. The first header field is a *sequence number* (SN), and is used for detection of mistakenly inserted cells or lost cells. The other header field is the *sequence number protection* (SNP), and is used to provide for error detection and correction operations.

The AAL type 1 conversion sublayer is responsible for clock recovery for both audio and video services.

AAL type 2 is employed for variable bit rate (VBR) services in which a timing relationship is required between the source and destination sites. For example, class B traffic, such as variable bit rate audio or video, falls into this category. This category of service requires that timing information be maintained between the transmitting and receiving site. It is responsible for handling variable cell delay, and for detecting and handling lost and missequenced cells.

The PDU for AAL type 2 consists of both a *header* and a *trailer.* The header consists of a *sequence number* (SN) and an *information type* (IT) field. The length of these fields and their exact functions have not been determined as of this writing. Obviously, the SN will be used for detection of lost and mistakenly inserted cells. The IT field can contain the indication of *beginning of message* (BOM), *continuation of message* (COM), or *end of message* (EOM). It might also contain timing information for audio or video signals.

The AAL type 2 trailer consists of a *length indicator* (LI), which will be used to determine the number of octets in the payload field. Finally, the *cyclic redundancy check* (CRC) will be used for error detection.

The original ATM standards established AAL3 for VBR connection-oriented operations, and AAL4 for VBR connectionless operations. These two types have been combined, and are treated as a single type. As the AAL standard has matured, it has become evident that the original types were inappropriate. Therefore, AAL3 and AAL4 were combined due to their similarities.

The AAL 3/4 PDU carries 44 octets in the payload, and 5 fields in the header and trailer. The 2-bit segment type (ST) is used to indicate the beginning of message (BOM), continuation of message (COM), end of message (EOM), or single segment message (SSM). The sequence number is used for sequencing the traffic. It is incremented by one for each PDU sent, and a state variable at the receiver indicates the next expected PDU. If the received SN is different from the state variable, the PDU is discarded. The *message identification* (MID) subfield is used to reassemble traffic on a given connection. The *length indicator* (LI) defines the size of the payload. Finally, the *cyclic redundancy check* (CRC) field is a 10-bit field used to determine whether an error has occurred in any part of the cell.

AAL 5 was conceived because AAL 3/4 was considered to contain unnecessary overhead. It was judged that multiplexing could be pushed up to any upper layer, and that the BAsize operations to preallocate buffers at the receiver were not needed.

Figure B-5 shows the format of the type 5 PDU. It consists of an 8-octet trailer. The PAD field fills out the PDU to 48 octets. The CPCS-UU field is used to identify the user payload. The *common part indicator* (CPI) has not been fully defined in ITU-T I.363. The length field (L) defines the payload length, and the CRC field is used to detect errors in the SSCS PDU (user data).

Type 5 is a convenient service for Frame Relay because it supports connection-oriented services. In essence, the Frame Relay user traffic is given to an ATM backbone network for transport to another Frame Relay user.

INDEX

M

N

ABOUT THE AUTHOR

Uyless Black is a world-renowned authority on computer communications who lectures in the United States and abroad on a wide range of communication topics. The president of Information Engineering, Inc., a Virginia-based telecommunications consulting firm, he has advised many companies, including Bell Labs, AT&T, Bell Northern Research, Noretl, and Bellcore, on the effective use of computer communications technology. He is also the author of 20 critically acclaimed books, including four from McGraw-Hill: *The V Series Recommendations, The X Series Recommendations, TCP/IP and Related Protocols,* and *Network Management Standards.*